IN QUEST OF JINNAH
Diary, Notes, and Correspondence of
Hector Bolitho

Mohammad Ali Jinnah

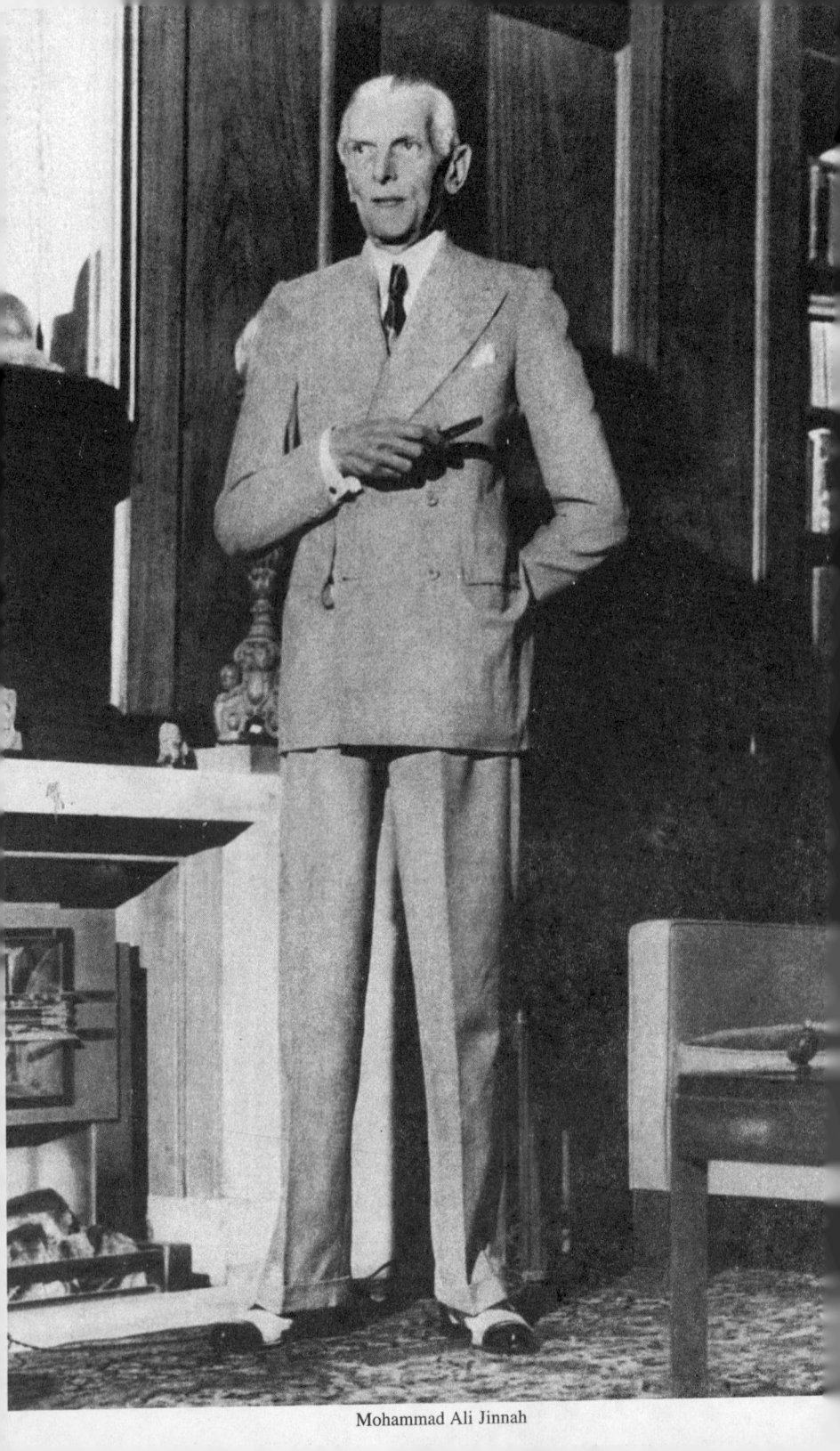

IN QUEST OF JINNAH
Diary, Notes, and Correspondence of Hector Bolitho

Edited by
Sharif al Mujahid

OXFORD
UNIVERSITY PRESS

OXFORD
UNIVERSITY PRESS

Great Clarendon Street, Oxford OX2 6DP

Oxford University Press is a department of the University of Oxford.
It furthers the University's objective of excellence in research, scholarship,
and education by publishing worldwide in

Oxford New York

Auckland Cape Town Dar es Salaam Hong Kong Karachi
Kuala Lumpur Madrid Melbourne Mexico City Nairobi
New Delhi Shanghai Taipei Toronto

with offices in

Argentina Austria Brazil Chile Czech Republic France Greece
Guatemala Hungary Italy Japan Poland Portugal Singapore
South Korea Switzerland Turkey Ukraine Vietnam

Oxford is a registered trade mark of Oxford University Press
in the UK and in certain other countries

© Oxford University Press 2007

The moral rights of the author have been asserted

First published 2007

All rights reserved. No part of this publication may be reproduced, translated,
stored in a retrieval system, or transmitted, in any form or by any means,
without the prior permission in writing of Oxford University Press.
Enquiries concerning reproduction should be sent to
Oxford University Press at the address below.

This book is sold subject to the condition that it shall not, by way
of trade or otherwise, be lent, re-sold, hired out or otherwise circulated
without the publisher's prior consent in any form of binding or cover
other than that in which it is published and without a similar condition
including this condition being imposed on the subsequent purchaser.

ISBN 978-0-19-597901-5

Typeset in Times
Printed in Pakistan by
Kagzi Printers, Karachi.
Published by
Ameena Saiyid, Oxford University Press
No. 38, Sector 15, Korangi Industrial Area, PO Box 8214
Karachi-74900, Pakistan.

Contents

Preface	vii
Introduction	xi

Part One
Diary and Notes: November 1951–May 1953 — 1

Part Two
Hector Bolitho and Majeed Malik Correspondence — 93

Part Three
Hector Bolitho Miscellaneous Correspondence — 140

Part Four
Contemporary Reviews — 160

Part Five
Expunged Passages from *Jinnah: Creator of Pakistan* — 187

Afterword
My 'Pakistan Day Complaint'
by Hector Bolitho — 215

Index — 219

Preface

A long, protracted search, several detours, and considerable investment in terms of time, travel, and expenses finally landed me at the repository where Hector Bolitho's papers concerning his study of Jinnah were lodged. That study, which Bolitho had undertaken at the request of the Pakistan government, was first published under the title, *Jinnah: Creator of Pakistan*, by John Murray (London) in late 1954.

Bolitho gave away his Jinnah papers for a consideration to Charles Leslie Ames, a St. Paul (Minnesota, USA) businessman, sometime during 1959–60; Bolitho's last letter in this collection is dated 17 October 1960. Later, Ames donated his collection on South Asia (including Bolitho's papers) to the University of Minnesota, St. Paul, where the Ames Library on South Asia was set up.

Among Bolitho's papers, the more important items are the original, unabridged and unexpurgated manuscript of *Jinnah: Creator of Pakistan*, his 'Diary and Notes: December 1951–May 1953', and some letters to and from him concerning his study.

His 'confidential' 'Diary and Notes' is invaluable as a source book on Jinnah. During his visit to Pakistan and India during late 1951/early 1952, Bolitho spoke to some two hundred people who knew Jinnah, some of them intimately, besides a sizeable number of people in England. The most striking thing is that all the interviewees—some of them uncharacteristically, especially Pakistanis who regard him as an icon—were frank, incredibly so, dilating at length on both Jinnah's strengths and weaknesses without reserve, and highlighting in some detail *both* his triumphs and discomfitures.

These interviews, conducted over a period of a little over eighteen months from November 1951 to May 1953, form the bulk of the manuscript, which itself runs to some 43,000 words. 'These notes, the greater part of which could not be used in my biography...', Bolitho feels, 'will be invaluable to anyone writing about Jinnah, or Pakistan, in the future.'

Bolitho had originally copyrighted his notes and made them 'confidential until 1 January 1963', but later to 'until... I die'. He died on 12 September 1974. The present volume *In Quest of Jinnah,* is an edited version of his 'Diary and Notes'.

Bolitho was a novelist, historian and biographer. Born in Auckland, New Zealand, in 1897, he was a reporter on a newspaper at 17, toured the Antipodes with the Prince of Wales (later Edward VIII) at 21, moved to England at 24, and published his first novel at 25. By the time he took up the Jinnah assignment in June 1951, he had produced some 46 books of history, biography, travelogues and fiction, besides three edited volumes of letters. Thus he approached the task of writing the Jinnah story with a rich and versatile background, both in research and writing. And *Jinnah* is his only work to survive, as yet, fifty-two years down the road.

Of all the biographies of Jinnah, including the much acclaimed *Jinnah of Pakistan* (1984) by the American ace historian on South Asia, Professor Stanley Wolpert, Bolitho's *Jinnah* makes the most extensive and adroit use of oral history. This he did, in part, to offset the numerous handicaps that hedged him, especially Fatima Jinnah's rather inexplicable hostility to his writing the biography, in part to overcome his own deficiency in terms of the historical background of India, especially under British imperial rule (1858–1947), an area where Wolpert commanded an enormous edge, and, above all, to get behind the mask and unravel the intricacies of thought behind his subject's policies and postures, moves and counter-moves, decisions and predilections. The anecdotes that Bolitho records straight from Jinnah's colleagues, lieutenants, followers and political opponents within four years of his death, when memory does not normally perform its inscrutable mischief, constitute, as it were, the major strength of Bolitho, and his 'Diary and Notes' records the basics of the most authentic oral history of Jinnah and of what H.V. Hodson calls 'the last struggle... of three... well balanced adversaries'—the British, the Congress and the Muslim League,[1] perhaps the most authoritative British account of the last decade of the British Raj. Hence whether Bolitho's *Jinnah* continues to be read and/or consulted or not, his 'Diary and Notes' will, hopefully, command a source book status on the founder of Pakistan.

Besides interviews, Bolitho's notes include his impressions of places he visited during his travels in Pakistan; some description, historical or otherwise, of these places; his impressions and opinions of people he met or encountered during his travels, and his own feelings about Pakistan and Pakistanis, and their idiosyncrasies. The major problem with Bolitho, that he is much too opinionated, is discussed in some detail in the Introduction. For now, suffice it to say that some of his opinions are much too controversial and explosive, even insufferable—such as those on Fatima Jinnah, Jinnah's youngest sister, and companion for twenty years (1929–48). Perhaps he was trying to get even with her for refusing to help with the book, and allow access to the Jinnah Papers, to which, in any case, she had no right, because, in principle, they belonged to the nation, rather than to her personally.

Yet, Bolitho's opinions are extremely interesting and revealing, extending a helping hand in fathoming his complex personality, his preferences and prejudices, his strengths and weaknesses. These, in turn, help explain the sort of biography he had produced, and the roles he had assigned to various characters therein. For these reasons, his remarks and comments, however harsh and stinging, have been retained in the present edited work. The current environment in Pakistan, in terms of examining the roles, politics and postures of past leaders, considered icons and sacred cows till the late 1980s, has enabled me to retain the remarks and comments, however unfair and injudicious at times, of those whom Bolitho interviewed. However, some of the material, such as historical description or some letters not materially relevant to an unravelling of Jinnah's politics and personality have been deleted, if only to preclude an unwarranted deflection from the central focus of the work. Notes have been added in square brackets, wherever necessary, in order to pinpoint errors of facts or dates.

I had retrieved Bolitho's diary way back in October 1984, but decided to postpone its publication till the arrival of fair weather. Only a short while before, my *Jinnah: Studies in Interpretation* (1981) had provoked Z.A. Suleri, editor of the *Pakistan Times,* to mount a campaign against it, for whatever reasons. This comprised a series of articles in his daily paper (18 and 21 August and 11 September 1981), and scores of telegrams sent to the authorities concerned, calling for a ban on the book, and my dismissal as the Quaid-i-Azam Academy's Director. To cut a long story short, the authorities did step in, but I was able to weather the engulfing storm, thanks to Syed Sharifuddin Pirzada, who, as Chairman of the Quaid-i-Azam Biography Committee, had written the foreword to the work.[2] This episode, however, produced one positive result: the lingering suspicion that the study was government-sponsored was scotched forever. Bolitho is, in part, explosive stuff, and I was not prepared to undergo another excruciating dose of trauma. Now that the environment is more open, the nation having become mature to a point that it takes even criticism of Jinnah, in its stride, I feel emboldened enough to get on with the job. I am sure, this book will represent a notable contribution to both Jinnah studies and Pakistani historiography.

I am grateful to my long-time friend, Dr Saleem M.M. Qureshi (Professor Emeritus, University of Alberta, Canada), and David Lelyveld (Columbia University) for providing me some clues to the Bolitho Papers, and to Dr Syed Jaffar Ahmed for reading/reviewing the Introduction. I am also beholden to Dr Muhammad Reza Kazimi whose persistence and patience, besides editorial assistance, saw this publication through the press; but I alone am responsible for errors, lapses or inadequacies, if any. Above all, I would like to record my gratitude to Ms Ameena Saiyid, the moving spirit behind substantially and significantly helping Pakistan become a 'reading' nation.

Sharif al Mujahid
Karachi
1 July 2006

NOTES

1. H.V. Hodson, *The Great Divide: Britain–India–Pakistan* (London: Hutchinson, 1969), p. 38.
2. See Akbar S. Ahmad, *Jinnah, Pakistan and Islamic Identity* (Karachi: OUP, 1997), p. 28.

Introduction

Bolitho's 'Diary and Notes' is invaluable, not only for the sort of first-hand data it yields on Jinnah, his politics and personality, but also about the clues it provides for the author, his orientation and temperament, his preferences and prejudices. These, in turn, provide an explanation of the sort of biography he has written, since his likes and dislikes are writ large throughout his work, despite the hundreds of enforced amendments and deletions suggested by Majeed Malik.

The present Introduction seeks to focus on two major aspects: first, it seeks to reconstruct the portrait of Jinnah as it emerges from the series of interviews conducted by Bolitho, while simultaneously pinpointing the inaccuracies and lack of accurate information on the interviewees' parts, on the basis of solid evidence available in the present study itself or elsewhere. After all, internal evidence itself does not become historical fact unless validated externally. Second, it attempts to pinpoint Bolitho's personal bias and prejudices in comprehending and interpreting the places he had visited, the sights he had occasion to see, the people he had met, and the stories he had heard during his six-month sojourn on the subcontinent. Documentation is provided only for citations other than those included in the present work.

* * * *

The portrait of Jinnah that emerges from Bolitho's interviews is a rather a mixed one, with several interviewees contradicting each other. However, the bare bones of the Jinnah story, backed by solid evidence, are as follows:

Jinnah was born into a reasonably affluent family for the time, his father being engaged in profitable business. The story about his studying school texts under the light of a street lamp, current for a long while, is utter nonsense. Nanji Jafar, six years his junior, tells us that he 'went to school in a carriage while other boys walked'. Jinnah's father gave him a cricket set while he was in school, which Jinnah gifted away to Jafar on the eve of his departure for England in 1892. Not only did Jinnah shun playing marbles, then in vogue throughout the subcontinent, but he also urged other boys in the neighbourhood to 'stand-up out of the dust and play cricket'. So passionately was he possessed of this idea that he even taught other boys to play cricket, but without being a bully. His father had the foresight and the resources to send him to England to study law, recalls Dina Wadia, Jinnah's only child. Actually, he was sent to study business management, but he developed a penchant for politics after listening to the great British Liberal stalwarts in the House of Commons during the initial months of his four-year stay (1892–96) in London, and got himself bathed in the Liberalism of Lord Morley which was then in full sway. The Liberals had come into power under Gladstone in August 1892, and as Jinnah told Dr Ashraf, 'I grasped that Liberalism, which became part of my life and thrilled me very much'.[1] That penchant, which stayed with him till the end, led him to opt for law, abandoning his initial business-training plans. This, *inter alia,* highlights his independence and decision-making power, even at this initial stage.

When Jinnah began his professional life in Bombay, he had three or four years of struggle without briefs, but would not give up on his predetermined ambition. By about 1900, he was, however, a success, and a member of the prestigious Orient Club in Bombay where Sir Cowasjee Jehangir met him in 1901. 'He was even more pompous and independent during those lean years', recalls Sir Cowasjee. A good many of his friends and acquaintances thought that Jinnah was 'no lawyer [but] a brilliant advocate', but Major Haji, Secretary to the Aga Khan III, dismissed this assertion, arguing that:

> ... he was the only Mohammedan lawyer of consequence in his time. There were one or two other Muslims practicing [law] but they were insignificant. It is not fair to say that Jinnah was merely a good advocate. This opinion is held by Hindus, who will not credit a Muslim with the facility to 'know' law, and how to interpret law. As an advocate, Jinnah outshone his fellows. His appeal to the judge and jury was dynamic, but he certainly also knew the law.

Others have also testified that Jinnah outshone everyone else as an advocate, and they usually attribute this to his remarkable clear headedness.

One of his prime ambitions was to become the highest paid lawyer in India, and this he achieved[2]: his daily fee in 1936 was Rs 1,500, computed from the day he left Bombay to the day he returned. His stockbroker, Shantilal L. Thar, puts his fortune at Rs 6–7 million in 1947 (equivalent to Rs 120 million today), a fabulous sum he had earned mostly through his practice, with his investments yielding but a fraction of it.

Jinnah was a political animal from the very beginning. He talked of nothing but politics, all the time, but 'with all the differences and bitterness of political life, he was never malicious. Hard may be, but never malicious', says Sir Cowasjee. Jinnah talked of politics even with his stockbroker, but there was no bitterness in his tone and tenor. Thar recalls that 'he propounded his faith in Pakistan, but without ever being bitter against the Hindus. By nature, he was not anti-Hindu...' This aspect of his politics is confirmed by Jamshed Nusserwanjee, former Mayor of Karachi. Nor was there any 'ill-feeling' between Jinnah and Gandhi, or any dislike for each other. Thar also recalls Jinnah's estimate of the Indian princes in 1946: he extolled the late ruler of Baroda as being 'head and shoulders above all the other rulers', the late Maharaja of Mysore as a 'great gentleman' the late ruler of Gondal as 'all head and no heart' and the Nawab of Bhopal as having 'both head and heart'. It is rather interesting (and surprising) that the Nizam, the nawabs of Rampur and Bahawalpur, the major Muslim princes, or even the Khan of Kalat, with whom he had personal relations, do not figure in his list, and that when it comes to evaluation, Jinnah's choice cuts across the Hindu–Muslim divide. This is because, in raising the Pakistan banner, he was not launching a crusade against the Hindus as such, but proclaiming Hindus and Muslims as separate nations, so that they could acquire power in their respective demographically dominant regions. To claim substantial or absolute power for Muslims in their regions by no means entailed antagonism or enmity towards Hindus. Unfortunately, however, this was precisely what the Congress protagonists, propagandists and publicists harped upon, *ad nauseum,* damning and decrying Jinnah as the arch villain in the Indian political drama.

Inter alia, this also highlights his overriding sense of impartiality, attested to by Major Haji, on the basis of his personal experience. His father took him to Jinnah, in Bombay, in 1920, and said, 'Make him as brilliant as you are'. Jinnah replied, 'He can come and work in my chambers, but he must shine with his own brilliance'. Jinnah never used his influence to gain him a favourable position. He 'was impartial, and did not give favours', recalls Haji.

Jinnah has often been accused of being vain, arrogant, and cold. He was hard, but not harsh. What some people considered arrogance was essentially his aggressive self-confidence, since he believed in himself all the way. Also, as a politician he kept his distance especially with his equals, lest he should be obliged to give in on some point or another. Yet incredibly perhaps, he talked freely with his stockbroker, his physician (Dr D.K. Mehta), and even with Sir Cowasjee. Actually, one had to come close to Jinnah, both to gain his confidence and to discover his virtues, as Sir Francis Mudie, former Governor of Sindh and the Punjab—who 'probably knew Jinnah better than any other British Officer in India' and who was 'certainly the only British civilian who knew him at all well'—found out after August 1947. 'I always found him very pleasant socially ... Officially until near the end ... I found him open to reason or at least to argument. In the end I got to know that I could trust him completely', recalls Mudie.

Nor was Jinnah cold to all. He 'loved talking to people who were not Muslims', says Thar. Mazhar Ahmad, his naval ADC, adds a new dimension: as he 'grew old, he liked to have young men about [around] him. His secretaries and ADCs were all young. He came to enjoy the stimulus of young people and seldom refused to speak to them in audiences, no matter how busy he was.' Hashimi found that he 'relaxed with younger people who were not directly related to him and who had no political axes to grind'; he also loved them. That is precisely what a fourteen-year old Tahira Hayat Khan (later Tahira Mazhar Ali Khan), though not a Muslim Leaguer, discovered when she cycled her way to Mamdot Villa, where Jinnah was staying, in 1940(?) and asked the *chowkidar* to inform Jinnah that she was there. 'He was very nice to me and told me that he knew the stance of the Communist Party. I showed him a pamphlet I was carrying in which the Communist Party had declared its support for an independent country. He said we did not need to fear because he would be able to see our friends just as he was going to visit Bombay regularly...'[3]

According to Mudie, Jinnah was not really cold, and he gives a capital instance of the great emotional strain under which he had been living under the cold exterior:

> In judging Jinnah, we must remember what he was up against. He had against him, not only the wealth and brains of the Hindus, but also nearly

the whole of British officialdom and most of the Home politicians, who made the great mistake of refusing to take Pakistan seriously. Never was his position really examined.... No man who had not the iron control of himself that Jinnah had could have done what he did. But it does not follow that he was really cold. In fact no one who did not feel as Jinnah did, could have done what he did.

To this may be added Nusserwanjee's remark: 'He was emotional and affectionate, but he was unable to demonstrate it. All was control, control!.' 'He kept his thoughts, his emotions, to himself', recalls Rabbani, his Air ADC, but his gardener testified that he was always kind to servants.

Jinnah also cared for those who worked for him. When he was staying at Sir Cowasjee's country house, K.H. Khurshid (Secretary to Jinnah, 1944–47) recalls:

> Jinnah [was] worried lest I was bored. He asked, 'Do you read Shakespeare?' I confessed, 'Not since school'. He went into town and brought back a whole set of Shakespeare, Shelley and Keats, for me to read.

He was also loyal and faithful to friends and colleagues who stood by him through thick and thin, despite what Habibullah says. Jinnah told Ahsan, his naval ADC, in Fatima Jinnah's presence at the Amir of Bahawalpur's palace, in Malir:

> 'Nobody had faith in me, everyone thought I was mad—except Miss Jinnah'. He then paused and added, 'But, of course, if she hadn't believed in me all along she would not be sitting here now'.

Mudie confirms, 'He was thoroughly loyal to those who had supported him in the past. That was the real reason why he did not dismiss Mandot, the Punjab Premier.' This was also the reason why he was so soft towards Liaquat Ali Khan on the Liaquat–Desai Pact (1945), which was contracted behind his back as he lay seriously ill at Matheron, while the Congress mercilessly denied Bhulabhai Desai, the hero of the INA trials (1945–46), the Congress ticket for a Central Assembly seat in the 1945–46 general elections. Yet, as Nurse Dunham and Habibullah Ibrahim found out and Admiral Jefford discovered when he stood up to Jinnah and earned his respect, that Jinnah always liked people with views of their own—people of independent thought.

Jinnah was 'never a demonstrative person. He always controlled and held back any kind of emotion. He was reserved, dignified and lonely', recalls Nusserwanjee. He had high walls built around his person, within which he cloistered himself unassailably. Only twice did he let down his guard: the first time was at Ruttie's funeral rites in the Khoja Cemetery, at Mazagoan, Bombay, on 22 February 1929. He sat beside Kanji Dwarkadas 'for all the five hours' and 'put up a brave face after a tense silence', reports Dwarkadas. 'When Ruttie's body was being lowered down the grave, Jinnah was not able to control his emotions. He broke down and wept like a child.'[4] The second time was when he visited the Hindu refugee camp in Karachi on 7 January 1948, after the unpremeditated Karachi riot, the only one to occur in Pakistan's capital.

Not only did he severely abstain from working on the emotions of the people, whatever the temptation, and whatever the provocation, as during the emotively charged Khilafat agitation (1920–22), or during the traumatic days following Bihar's ghastly anti-Muslim pogrom (1946); he also never succumbed to displaying any showmanship or penchant for public relations in his entire political career. Nevertheless, he worked for the poor all the time, as his strong advocacy of Gopal Krishna Gokhale's Elementary Education Bill (1911) in the Imperial Legislative Council indicates. What else had this advocacy stemmed from except his overriding concern to improve the lot of the poor, open for them the doors of opportunity, and give them access to new vistas of progress and self development? This had also inspired his unending striving for the Indianisation of the services and adoption of social welfare-oriented measures during his long parliamentary career (1910–47). Some thirty-five years after his Council speech, he showed the same concern, this time in his address to Muslim League workers in Calcutta on 27 February 1946:

> I am an old man. God has given me enough to live comfortably at this age. Why would I turn my blood into water, run about and take so much trouble? Not for the capitalists surely, but for you, the poor people ... in Pakistan, we will do all in our power to see that everybody can get a decent living.[5]

Despite all of this, however, in contrast with Gandhi he would never touch the poor, if only because he was the least demonstrative, if not for his rigid sense of cleanliness and fastidiousness. Indeed, his dislike of touching and being touched was phenomenal. 'He would devote his mind and even his life to helping the poor, but he did not wish to shake hands with them', says Mazhar Ahmad. To S.N. Baqar, Director General, Civil Defence, his attitude was: 'You must be saved. But I do not want you to come and thank me.' The emotion of gratitude was repulsive to him, in part because, to quote his physician, Jinnah was essentially 'a thinker, not a feeler'.

His fastidiousness and penchant for cleanliness were remarkable. Remember, while still a young boy, he told other boys in the neighbourhood, 'Don't play marbles. It dirties your clothes.' He always lived in style: he spent his huge earnings lavishly on a lifestyle described as upper class English. Once out of his lean years, he lived in big, spacious houses, well furnished, with his garden tidy and impressively landscaped, and with a retinue of servants. He was always fond of good clothes, good food, and good living. When in 1901, while still recovering from his lean professional years, he met Sir Cowasjee at Bombay's Orient Club, 'his clothes already had distinction'. Every one who had met him, throughout his life, has confirmed that he was always impeccably dressed. He was choosy in the choice of his clothes to a point that he was known as the best-dressed politician in India as revealed by his photograph when being received by Lord Wavell at the Viceroy's House in Simla on 25 June 1945, before the start of the first Simla Conference. He usually dressed in Saville Row suits, silk shirts, Parisian ties and two-tone shoes, while for the Muslim League annual sessions and other League gatherings, from 1937, he appeared dressed in tight *achkan, sherwani*, black shoes and an expensive Karakuli cap which immediately became not only known as Jinnah cap but also as a symbol of one's allegiance to the Muslim League and, later, Pakistan. From 1943 onwards he substituted his tight *achkan* for the Punjabi and north-western region's *shalwar*, if only to establish some sort of sartorial rapport with the larger of the two regions he claimed for Pakistan. In an age when *swadeshi* or hand-spun clothes were a passport to political success, Jinnah, except when at Muslim League moots and rallies, appeared in western dress, quite often with a solar hat (as at the Simla Conference in 1945). Of cufflinks alone, he reportedly had some sixty pairs. Indeed, Jinnah's refined taste was proverbial.

In food too, Jinnah was always choosy. During his Delhi-Karachi flight, Ahsan, his naval ADC, tells us, 'Jinnah complained bitterly—about the quality of the food, the inferior china and cutlery—and the thermos which had been provided [The picnic lunch had been prepared by the Viceroy's servants].'

For most of his life Jinnah had lived in fabulous houses—the huge bungalows in Little Gibbs Road, in Hampstead Heath, on the outskirts of London, in Mount Pleasant Road in Malabar Hills, Bombay, and at 10, Aurangzeb Road in New Delhi. So imposing and well known was his Little Gibbs Road residence that the Parsi ladies whom Bolitho happened to accost in its vicinity on 18 May 1952, twelve years after it had been vacated by Jinnah and torn down to build new apartments, knew its exact location. Likewise, his Mount Pleasant Road residence was known as the 'Jinnah Residence', even to ordinary taxi drivers, long after Jinnah had left. He liked spacious, high-walled houses, and the garden had to be very tidy. He was even selective in his choice of flowers, and instinctively abhorred a huge garden overcrowded with many plants, lest it should look like a jungle. Indeed, 'Jinnah loved [and liked to savour] beautiful things and surrounded himself with them', says Majeed Malik. Perhaps this was the prime reason that he, whom even Dina Wadia calls a 'celibate', fell for Ruttie, the *crème de la crème* of the Bombay debutantes.

Everything in his legal chambers—which were well furnished and grand—was spotless. Not only was his house amongst the most tastefully decorated, but he was also one of the foremost connoisseurs of carpets in the country, with carpets and Mughal paintings being his weaknesses. Although a good many of his carpets were pilfered or cavalierly given away in the late 1960s and 1970s, when Shireen Bai, Jinnah's younger sister, occupied the Mohatta Palace, in Karachi, after Fatima Jinnah's death in 1967, some of the precious ones can still be seen at the Quaid-i-Azam Mausoleum Museum, Flagstaff House, and at Jinnah's birthplace on Newnham Road, Kharadar, Karachi. The impression, given by some of the interviewees, that he had no taste for architecture, furniture, etc., seems to be out of tune with the reality. The idea that Ruttie opened up a new world of taste for him may be valid up to a point, but given the sort of person Jinnah was, Ruttie's catalytic role alone could not, and would not, have worked unless Jinnah had an intrinsic tendency within himself for this world of taste. After all, given his extremely demanding professional life, his hectic public life and his core characteristic of singleness of purpose in respect of these two watertight compartments, Jinnah could not possibly have had the time and the requisite frame of mind to pursue all his tastes, or even go in for recreation. 'My profession is such that it never allows me time for recreation', he told Sir Evelyn Wrench in Bombay, in 1942.[6]

Several of the interviewees including Noman, Bakar, and Claude Batley, the architect of his Mount Pleasant Road residence, spoke of Jinnah's parsimony and thriftiness. 'House keeping was strictly parsimonious.... nobody was ever asked to dine at the last moment', one of Jinnah's acquaintances in Bombay told Bolitho. This was confirmed by his secretary, Usman Ahmad Ansari, during 1939–40, in an interview with the present editor, in London, in 1985. 'Jinnah', said Ansari, 'would not ask anyone to join him if he barged in while he was dining—even if he be the Nawab of Bhopal', which did happen once or twice when Ansari was serving Jinnah. Jinnah's concern for details is usually seen as fussiness. He would routinely put down on paper all that he had earned and all that he had spent, and demand of others, even Fatima Jinnah, an account of the money they had spent. When Jinnah moved into Government House in Karachi, he called for the inventory and checked it himself. He was the one to note that the croquet set and books from the library were missing—the one taken away by Governor Mudie's military secretary to Lahore, and the other by Governor of Sindh, Ghulam Husain Hidayatullah, who had occupied the Government House for a short while before Jinnah moved in. But instead of being branded as fussiness, such meticulous attention to detail should be put down to his being methodical and to his business management sense, as compared with most Indians, especially Muslims, who have traditionally been given to ostentatious living and extravagance, even to the point of mortgaging their ancestral properties and pawning off or selling the family silver for a mere song. Thus attention to detail is usually cited as evidence of parsimony: He would never pay for any work that he considered substandard. When there was a leak in his Malabar Hills residence, 'he was furious.... He haggled with the contractors and insisted on reductions', recalls Batley. Moreover, his penchant for detail gave him an enormous edge over both his political colleagues and opponents in discussions and negotiations.

And if he was so parsimonious, how does one account for his renting, purchasing or building such fabulous houses, in Bombay, Delhi and London? He bought South Court, in Bombay, from Sir Victor Sassoon, as early as 1912, for Rs 125,000, a stupendous sum at the time, and gave it to Ruttie when he married her on 19 April 1918.[7] Also, his palatial residence in Mount Pleasant Road took a whole year to build! How does one explain the enormous amount of jewellery he gave to Ruttie in just eleven years of their married life? It is indeed mind bobbling—listed in over seven handwritten pages, now a part of the Quaid-i-Azam Papers in Islamabad. How does one rationalize his giving away some half a million pounds sterling for charitable purposes in his will executed on 30 May 1939 in Bombay? This allocates only paltry sums to his relatives, apart from Fatima Jinnah and Dina Wadia, while bequeathing enormous sums to the University of Bombay, the Anjuman-i-Islam School, Bombay, and the Anglo-Arabic College, Delhi, with all his residuary estate, including the corpus that may fall after the lapse of life interests or otherwise, to be divided equally between the Aligarh Muslim University, the Islamia College, Peshawar, and the Sindh Madrasatul Islam, Karachi.[8] Again, how does one account for Jinnah himself paying all the expenses connected with his political work throughout his life, or his footing, in part, the hefty Cecil Hotel bill for the Muslim League Working Committee members' stay during the Simla Conference in June–July 1945? Thar, who dealt with Jinnah's investments for some eleven years, and who should know better than most about Jinnah's money matters, says, 'Once he had made the investments he would not bother to ask the price thereafter... If any of my suggestions did not yield a good result, he never referred to it, even casually.' Hence his conclusion: 'Although he was thrifty, he never pursued money in a cheap way'. In support of his contention, Thar cites an instance of Jinnah refusing to take a fee from a client when he succeeded on an appeal, because he had originally offered to pursue the case further for free. Bakar also talks of Jinnah returning extra money in a case he had conducted, with a note, 'This is the amount you paid me. This was my fee. Here is the balance.' Others have also cited such instances which underscore, not only Jinnah's honesty and integrity, but also his aversion to the accumulation of wealth *per se*.

Because of his iron control Jinnah is usually regarded as being bereft of all emotions. 'He was by nature celibate', says Khurshid. This is confirmed by his daughter. Hence Jinnah's romance with, and marriage to, Ruttie, the beautiful daughter of the multimillionaire Sir Dinshaw Petit, when she was still in her teens, caused everyone to speculate. It has seldom been mentioned that it was Ruttie who had chased him.

It so happened that in a case concerning the Tata Iron and Steel Works, Jinnah appeared before the Privy Council in London, in late

1913, and was able to secure a favourable verdict. His client, Jamshed Tata, the young, dashing scion of the Tata family, was engaged to Sir Dinshaw Petit's eldest daughter, Homie. Both she and her younger sister, Ruttie, were then studying for their baccalaureate in Nice, southern France. Jamshed Tata asked Jinnah if he would look up his fiancée, in Antibes before taking the ship from Marseille to Bombay. Sir Dinshaw asked Ruttie to receive their guest at Nice railway station, late in October 1913: this was probably their first meeting. Ruttie was then 13, and Jinnah 36 years old. Another story, related by a family friend, Haji Mohammad Dossa, would have us believe that Jinnah was entrusted with the task of teaching English to Ruttie, and that they read John Galsworthy's *Forsythe Saga* together.

At any rate, in the summer of 1916, Jinnah was a houseguest of Sir Dinshaw, the Parsi baronet and business magnate of Bombay, at the summer resort of Darjeeling, nestled in the Himalayas. Ruttie, then 16, was on hand to provide company to the much sought after barrister and the rising politician. Ruttie was entranced by Jinnah's singular success in crafting the Congress–League Lucknow Pact of December 1916. She was at Lucknow, along with her mother, when Sarojini Naidu, popularly known as the 'nightingale of India', dedicated her poem on India to Jinnah.[9] Jinnah was then edging towards 40, but was straight, brisk, tall, urbane, polished and handsome, immaculately clad, courtesy personified, courtly mannered, and impressive—as ever. If Lady Wavell found Jinnah 'one of the handsomest men I have ever seen; he combined the clear cut, almost Grecian features of the West, with Oriental grace and movement'[10] in the middle 1940s, when he was in his late 60s, how would Ruttie have found him some three decades earlier? He excited her young imagination as no one else had, and she hero-worshipped him. As noted earlier, the emotion of gratitude was repulsive to him. Not inexplicably, therefore, it was she who asked him to marry her. Reportedly Jinnah answered, 'It seems to be an interesting proposition!' says Noman. Not only Ruttie's family but the entire Parsi community of Bombay was up in arms. Determined to abort the union, Petit moved the courts and got an injunction, restraining Jinnah from seeing Ruttie. Jinnah, committed to upholding the law and the courts' honour throughout his life, abided by the courts' ruling, despite his unswerving attachment. On her part, Ruttie cared little and bided her time. Two months after she turned 18, when she found her parents still adamantly against the match, 'she took her umbrella and went straight to Jinnah's house'. They were married a day later, according to Muslim rites. The fruit of their happy wedlock was the birth of a daughter, in London, some sixteen months later. Despite the Petits' boycott of the Jinnah–Ruttie union and their estrangement, Jinnah joyously went along with the suggestion that the child be named Dina after Ruttie's mother.

'He loved my mother', insists Dina Wadia. 'He never loved anyone else.... My father loved nobody but my mother', she emphasizes, time and again. 'I loved my wife and she loved me, but we could not get along together', Jinnah told Majeed Malik. 'Jinnah needed understanding and patience', but 'his wife had neither. She was gay and impressionable and liked to shock him', says Begum Shah Nawaz. Uncharacteristically, Jinnah patiently and gallantly put up in silence with her capricious and Bohemian pranks and postures for a long while if only to keep their marriage together.[11] But it was bound to fail given their respective temperaments. His break with Ruttie, reportedly caused by Sarojini Naidu, who was in love with 'this beautiful boy', as she described him once, and Kanji Dawarkadas, who was interested in Ruttie himself, and, later, her death, caused Jinnah immense grief and left a permanent void. Jinnah did not meet anyone for a fortnight and smoked hundreds of cigars and wore a block band on his arm, says Hashimi. His marriage, says Khurshid, 'opened, for the first time, and closed thereafter for ever, the door of his emotions. Never again did he trust all his heart to a human being. From then on, even his warmth was calculated.'

Thus, the death of his wife, compounded by the loss in marriage of his only daughter to a non-Muslim, Neville Wadia,[12] meant for Jinnah the end of family life. According to Peer Tajuddin, 'When domestic happiness was lost and family felicity disappeared, it left a scar on Jinnah's mind and the sadness was reflected in his character. But Jinnah was not inclined to be soft, and to admit defeat in love and domestic affairs was not in his nature'. But, contrary to the general impression, throughout the rest of his life he continued to yearn for family life and domestic happiness: he told Begum Shah Nawaz in 1946, 'I have my grandchildren to play with', and barely a few months before he died, he asked Dina Wadia to bring her children and stay with him for a while. He was very fond of his grandson, Nusli,[13] who took a fancy to his cap, during their last meeting in Bombay in mid-1946, following the long drawn-out critical negotiations with the Cabinet Mission.

The Aga Khan, himself an aristocrat, considered Jinnah 'instinctively and essentially an aristocrat'. A good many of Bolitho's respondents considered him arrogant, proud and aloof, but not really rude. When he was really rude, it seems, he meant to send out a message, at once loud and clear, that he would never be cowed.[14] An unnamed private secretary to the Viceroy told Professor Khalid B. Sayeed, 'Jinnah was deliberately rude to gain a point or gain a better consideration of his views from the Viceroy'.[15] This means not inherent rudeness, but *intentional* rudeness and *deliberate* bad manners employed to gain a political point here and an edge there. H.V. Hodson, former Reforms Commissioner, cites a series of incidents and events from Jinnah's last years to drive home this vital Jinnah characteristic.[16] He was much too selective in putting on a pleasant demeanour or a rude posture, depending upon the circumstances, and *not* necessarily the person, by whom he was confronted. Otherwise, given his political feud with Nehru, running and snowballing for almost a decade, how could he permit himself to be photographed with him in such a jovial mood, at the London airport on 2 December 1946, before the abortive London Conference?

If he was rude at all it was only to his 'equals'. In contrast: 'He was always so gracious to ladies', recalls his mother-in-law, Lady Petit, adding, 'He would compliment us on our saris. The other politicians were grand and swept one aside.' This unsuspected aspect of his personality was confirmed by one of the Parsi ladies Bolitho accosted on Little Gibbs Road who said, 'I knew him quite well. I used to see him—almost everyday. So erect and so charming. He always took off his hat and said, "Good Morning".' Is it not rather strange that a person described by all and sundry as being utterly devoid of emotion, should be so courteous to ladies? Does it, by any chance, betray a deep yearning for female company in the deepest recesses of his heart, a yearning which his inherent pride and aversion to favours, compounded by his penchant for an 'iron control of himself', precluded from finding a crystalline expression throughout his life—except when he, per chance, stayed under the same roof with Ruttie for a week or two in Darjeeling's idyllic surroundings?

All whom Bolitho spoke to have spoken of Jinnah's honesty, integrity and incorruptibility, while Sir Cowasjee especially emphasised his sense of justice and lack of bitterness and malice, despite all the political differences between them. He 'would not accept [any] office', says Feroz Khan Noon, while Tajuddin asserts that, he 'couldn't be purchased by anybody'. 'His great hold on the Muslims of India', says Mudie, 'was due to his reputation for absolute strength and integrity and any compromise might have been interpreted as a sign of weakness. It might even have been suggested that he had been bought.'

Almost everyone Bolitho interviewed and almost every commentator on Pakistan since 1947, has alluded to Jinnah's 'singleness of purpose', and 'single mindedness', but none has attempted to explain why this characteristic should stand out so conspicuously in his public life and overshadow all of his other traits. Is it because Jinnah himself more than anyone else was painfully aware of his limited resources? '... outside the twin spheres of law and politics he has few resources and few accomplishments', wrote Sarojini Naidu in 1917,[17] thirty years before Jinnah became the architect of Pakistan. 'He was what God made him, not what he made himself', but 'he could see around corners, with a sixth sense', says Sir Cowasjee. This comment does not precisely conform to the hard facts of his life, for an in-depth study of Jinnah indicates his instinctive and inherent aversion to becoming involved in, and frittering away his energies on, too many things; to spreading himself thinly. To quote Naidu, again, the '... true criterion of his greatness lies [among other things] not in a diversity of aims... but rather in a lofty singleness and sincerity of purpose'.[18] That, also, in part explains his impassioned concentration on one issue at a time. First, it was to shine as a barrister and ensure a comfortable lifestyle for himself. He refused to dart out into public life, despite urging from his colleagues, till he had made his pile. After this, he joined the Congress, and made his place secure in the echelons of nationalist leadership. By 1913, when he had led a deputation of 'Congress wallas' to Lord Crewe, Secretary of State, on the reform of the India Council, this goal was accomplished more or less.[19] Then he stepped on to the Muslim League platform, whose leadership had been courting him since 1911, without, however, snapping his umbilical chord with the Congress. He was elected President for the League's Lucknow session in 1916, where he crafted the Congress–League Lucknow Pact and ensured that the League's separate electorates demand was finally conceded by the Congress, for the first (and last) time. Elected as the League's Permanent President in 1919, he stayed with the League to the end, however fitful and adverse were its fortunes. For some twenty-seven years he concentrated consistently on Hindu–Muslim unity and an ironclad Hindu–Muslim settlement, guaranteed constitutionally.

From 1937 onwards, he concentrated solely and untiringly on organising the disparate Muslim community, fragmented both horizontally and vertically, under the Muslim League's banner—to confront the entrenched Congress both at the polling booth and in the streets. In 1940, he launched the demand for Pakistan, goaded and galvanised Muslims in its support, and wrested Pakistan from unwilling hands within seven years. This he did through a three-tiered complex of skilful negotiations, tactical moves, and mobilizing Muslims for revolt and sacrifices, whatever the odds and whatever the circumstances. Finally, during 1947–48, he worked himself to death to secure Pakistan's sheer survival in the most treacherous circumstances which no other nation in the modern world was born into has confronted.[20] In the words of historian, Percival Spear,

> ...Jinnah stands alone among the nation-builders of Pakistan in a way that no Indian, not even Mahatma Gandhi, stands among Indian patriots. Of him it can be said with some truth, that "alone he did it".[21]

Of course, as Sir Cowasjee says, Jinnah was, in the first place, 'what God made him', as we all are but he was *also* what he had made of himself. If as Karl Marx says, 'men make their own history',[22] the activities of individuals, such as Jinnah, cannot help being important in history. Nor can such individuals be dismissed as 'of no account'. It was not merely the Muslim crisis in 1937, the nadir in Muslim India's chequered history since 1858, that really made Jinnah what he came to be during the epochal 1937–47 decade, but something more that was equally important. For, in terms of a visionary approach, personal talent, political and intellectual leadership, organisational skills, resolute action, and concrete achievements, Jinnah had given at least as much to the formulation, conceptualization and realization of the concept of Pakistan as he had received influences, legacies and 'support' from the historic realm—in terms of traditional values, political forces, ideological orientation, institutional entities, communication networks, and mass response. Indeed, in a substantial and significant sense, his individual genius served as the creative force in Indo-Muslim history at this critical juncture.

Such is the general composite portrait of Jinnah that emerges out of Bolitho's interviews and the reviews of his work, supplemented by hard evidence from elsewhere. It is not the usual stereotyped cardboard portrait that has been fed to Pakistanis over the years; after the sketching in of this composite portrait, the earlier one is bound to be consigned to oblivion. Jinnah's repertoire of strengths and weakness delineated in the present study will help researchers and scholars, not only to analyse Jinnah as a person but also to explain some crucial but enigmatic segments of his politics and postures. It is rather interesting that the Indian and British respondents are far more fair and nearer to the truth about him than their Pakistani counterparts. Is it perhaps because, having unduly adulated Jinnah to the high skies in public, they had a chance, indeed the chance of a life time, to go to the other extreme in private—not only to focus specifically on his weaknesses, but also to make a mountain of them? It would indeed be rewarding to juxtapose the Pakistani version with those of the others, including those offered in the reviews of Bolitho's work published at the time. Hopefully, such an exercise would yield a more accurately balanced estimate of Jinnah as a person, as a lawyer and advocate, as a politician and as the architect of Pakistan.

Jinnah is, of course, the founding father, and the most revered icon in Pakistan's national pantheon. But he was *still* a human being—a human being with both strengths and weaknesses. His enormous strengths overshadow and overwhelm his weaknesses, but Jinnah himself frowned upon his deification: 'I am an ordinary man, full of sin', he told Ispahani. And deification is no substitute for the upholding of the principles which he so fervently cherished. What Jinnah himself would have considered his greatest tribute was for Pakistanis to translate his ideals into social action, rather than merely recall his efforts and pay lip service to his incredible achievements, ritually and routinely. He wished for Pakistan to be modern, progressive, forward-looking, social welfare-oriented, egalitarian, democratic and Islamic.

* * * *

The major problem with Bolitho is that he is imperious and self-righteous. His opinions, always candid and mostly terse, are far from dispassionate and discrete: in fact, for the most part they border on intemperance. His predilections are much too striking and obvious. Indeed, his boorish attitude and prejudices, not only deep-seated, but also smacking of rank racism and a brazen colonial hangover, coruscate out of his caustic remarks throughout his 'Diary and Notes'.

Bolitho was not fully committed to his task, and it took eleven months before he warmed to it. 'There is a touch of affection coming to my task', he writes in his Diary on 18 May 1952: 'I went towards his house [in Little Gibbs Road] with a deeper sense of dedication than I had when I began my trip, almost a year ago'.

Despite this, however, he never misses a chance to criticise Jinnah: when he visited the Jinnah House in Mount Pleasant on 19 May 1952, and saw 'a grand portico, a marble terrace, balconies and then, within, high rooms', he remarks, 'I suppose ambitious men, born in little houses, require these assurances. It is very natural.... The idea of Jinnah expressing his ambitions in a big house, with big rooms come back when I saw what was his library. Vow! Yet he was no reader, except for his smattering of Dickens.' Elsewhere, he remarks, 'This was the house, built on the ruins of his marriage, in the first years of his unbridled worldly success'.[23]

Incredibly, Bolitho does not seem to have even bothered to read Jinnah's 11 August address, *carefully*. Although Jinnah, early in his speech, says, 'Dealing with our first function in the Assembly, *I cannot make any well-considered pronouncement at this moment, I shall say a few things as they occur to me*',[24] the novelist in Bolitho makes Jinnah 'leave this fault-finding expeditions to return to his desk, where he worked, for many hours, on the Presidential Address he was to give to the Constituent Assembly of Pakistan, on August 11' (emphasis added).[25]

Towards Pakistan Bolitho was brazenly unsympathetic: he was not in the least interested in her problems and difficulties. When, during the course of a discussion at Governor Din Mohammed's lunch, on 30 April 1952, Pir Ali Mohammad Rashidi asked him, 'But you are interested in Pakistan. Mr Bolitho', he replied, 'I am interested in my task, which is to write a biography of Mohammad Ali Jinnah'.

For everything Pakistani—furnishing, cuisine, English, manners, attitudes, stories, and numerous other things—he had nothing but utter contempt. To him, Pakistanis 'need the discipline of people from colder countries... You might have an official class, trained in a colder climate and flown to Pakistan for spells of three months, for administrative duties. Then flown back again.' How remarkable! Does this require any comment? Equally revealing are some of the comments by Bolitho on people and places he had met or visited:

1. On Pakistanis and Jinnah: 'I am at a loss in dealing with them [Pakistanis], because I am impatient with compromise. I deal in black and white and I have no subtlety. I am shocked one moment and delighted the next, and don't seem able to steer between the rocks. I am drawn to Jinnah because of this. He was completely un-oriental in his ethics. Odd, I dislike his rudeness, but must relate

it to his honesty. I dislike his class-consciousness, but understand it. Sometimes, when I am harassed by the incompetence I endure, I look at the photograph of Jinnah on my desk and almost pray to it for help.'
2. On stories told by Pakistanis and Indians: 'I wonder how true these stories are how much they have been embroidered. They sound too slick. I have come to the conclusion that I must suspect all these anecdotes until I have heard them confirmed by a Briton. And what a monstrous admission this is! And yet, I wonder. I think that Englishmen tell the truth—all things being comparative. At least, they are seldom malicious.'
3. On Fatima Jinnah: 'She has definitely refused to help with the biography.... I believe she is dominated by resentments. Not one kind word about anybody, or anything.... My opinion is unfair because I began disliking her for refusing to help over the book. She wore native dress and my prejudice being what it is, I saw her as a cross between a vulture and a camel.... What nice woman ever really wished to be dentist!'
4. On Khwaja Nazimuddin: 'He told me nothing of value—whether because he is too clever to commit himself, or because he is not interested in remembering Jinnah, or because he is an amiable ass, without the depth, that might retain an impression, I do not know. I thought him quite incapable. He could not even cut his melon properly....'
5. On Pir Pagaro: 'That strange and savage inheritance—and the villa at Pinner [England], where the English tried to refine him.'
6. On Pakistani cuisine, furniture, décor, etc.: 'After being entertained to curry struggles in Pakistani houses, without one object worth looking at, it was a delight to eat at a table [at the British High Commission, in Karachi] with good silver and see pictures and furniture that brought some of the beauty of England into this parched, ugly city—all camel dung and sand'.

A major clue to Bolitho's general attitude and temperament is that he incessantly pined for recognition. '*At last*, I was invited to lunch by the British High Commission' (emphasis added), he notes with glee. When the news of the death of King George VI came, he could not resist noting down: 'I feel strongly isolated—thinking of the day I first met him at Glamis—when he was still Duke of York. I drove out with Lord and Lady Kinnaird, to tea with them. Afterwards, when we were leaving, he came down, and opened the door of the car. And the little girl, who handed the bread and butter, is now my *sovereign*' (italics added). And his Diary mentions a good many names of the rich and the famous and anecdotes concerning them, which have been excised in the edited version since they are not germane to the Jinnah story.

Bolitho felt at home with but few Pakistanis, only those with a complete western orientation. He admired Begum Liaquat for her serenity, for making every possible gesture to make him comfortable, for her being very generous and touching. But all his admiration and enthusiasm evaporated when she meets him twice, after his return to England: 'She was kind and helpful to me in Karachi, and going to her home was pleasant. But here, in London, I do not like having to sit in silence while she talked of "that Mountbatten woman". It was insulting and I am angry.'

Nothing, perhaps, brings out his colonial hangover as much as his remarks about the removal of the British rulers' statues in India and Pakistan. During his Lahore visit, it saddened him to see Queen Victoria's statue removed from under its ornate canopy near the Punjab Assembly, and consigned to a cellar in the museum. His feelings on this score are, of course, understandable, but what is simply inexplicable is that he contrasts this act of 'ingratitude' with the British 'generosity' in putting up plaques on the buildings where Jinnah and Gandhi had resided in London, during their student days. Bolitho is not so blind that he cannot see the cardinal difference between the removal of the statues and the putting up of plaques. The statues were meant to proclaim and celebrate the British victory over Indians and the glory of the Raj. At the same time, they served to remind Pakistanis and Indians, after 1947, of their erstwhile servitude to the British. In contrast, the plaques commemorating the years Jinnah and Gandhi had spent in London are meant to glorify the 'blessings' of the Raj: how it has contributed significantly during their formative years, to their becoming the architects of independent Pakistan and India. And in putting up those plaques the British were, and are, basically glorifying not Jinnah and Gandhi, nor Pakistan and India, but their own role and contribution in making them what they came to be several decades later.

During his stay in Pakistan, wherever and whoever he visited, from the Prime Minister downwards, Bolitho was courted, feted and feasted as a most honoured guest. Some thirty dishes of rich food were served at a luncheon for him by the chieftains at Jamrud, with a servant standing behind him 'with a fan, three feet high, with which he kept the flies away'. He was indeed given VVIP treatment. He and his associate had three rooms at Hotel Metropole for over five months, and all his expenses were paid, besides an undisclosed but enormous sum for the biography. Yet he had not an iota of sympathy for, nor interest in, Pakistan! Not one good word for Pakistan and Pakistanis. On the contrary, he was rude, extremely so. He asked (read order) Qudratullah Shahab,[26] then an officer in the Information Ministry, not to ring for the bearer of his hotel room to have his shoes polished but to take them to the bearer himself and bring them back duly polished.

It was fortunate that the Pakistan government's contract with him included 'enforced amendments and deletions', otherwise, given his ignorance of Indian history and politics, and his contempt for Pakistani society, culture, customs and behaviour patterns, one can only imagine what he would have actually produced.

Hector Bolitho's contribution must, however, be acknowledged on two counts. First, he floated the idea of purchasing Jinnah's birthplace, Wazir Mansion, and converting it into a museum and a library. This he suggested to G. Allana, who invited him to lunch at his bungalow on Karachi beach where Bolitho had gone to swim. His Highness the Mir of Hunza was also present. 'It is a great honour that you have come to Pakistan to write the biography of Quaid-i-Azam', said Allana in all sincerity, and offered to do 'anything' for him. And on Bolitho's suggestion at that time, the Wazir Mansion was purchased by the government within a week. 'A great many people claimed that it was their idea', says Bolitho, adding, 'but I'd had my way and I don't mind two hoots who enjoys the credit'.

More important is Bolitho's contribution to preserving for posterity a treasure trove of oral history concerning Pakistan's founding father. But for his interviews with people who had known Jinnah personally in various capacities, and at various stages of his life, recorded within four to five years of his death, a good deal of oral history would have been lost for ever. This is a contribution, at once more important and more significant than the biography he has written. For these reasons, whether his *Jinnah* lives or not, his 'Diary and Notes' will as long as Pakistan lives. And therein lies the prime significance of the present work—*In Quest of Jinnah*.

Sharif al Mujahid

INTRODUCTION

NOTES

1. Hector Bolitho, *Jinnah: Creator of Pakistan* (London: John Murray, 1954), p. 9.
2. Dr G.M. Mehkri, who, as a doctoral candidate in sociology, spent some five years in Bombay, told the editor the following story: once Jinnah and Bhulabhai Desai, the leader of the Congress Party in the Indian Legislative Assembly (1936–45), who successfully defended the Indian National Army (INA) officers, enlisted by Subhash Chandra Bose in 1943–45, were sipping tea in the Bombay High Court cafeteria. An agent came and asked Desai about the fee he would charge for a certain case and Desai named a sizeable amount. Then he asked Jinnah what he would charge. With his eyes fixed on the table and without turning to the agent, Jinnah simply said, 'Twice the amount my friend has named'!
3. Shehar Bano Khan, 'Tahira Mazhar Ali: An Activist to the Core', 'The Review', *Dawn* (Karachi), 28 July–3 August 2005, pp. 21–22. It is, however, not clear from her account whether she had an appointment or not.
4. Kanji Dwarkadas, *Ruttie Jinnah: The Story of a Great Friendship* (Bombay: Kanji Dwarkadas, 1963), p. 57.
5. Khurshid Ahmad Khan Yusufi (ed.), *Speeches, Statements and Messages of the Quaid-i-Azam* (Lahore: Bazm-i-Iqbal, 1996), IV: 211–12.
6. Bolitho, op. cit., p. 142.
7. Mohammad Aziz Haji Dossa, 'South Court in Mumbai', *Dawn*, 11 October 2004, p. 6 (letter).
8. Part of this payment was made during Fatima Jinnah's lifetime, and the final payment, in 1998, by the Quaid-i-Azam estate administrators. Since the Aligarh University in India refused to name any project after Jinnah, the Quaid-i-Azam Aligarh Education Trust was created with the Sindh High Court's permission in the 1980s. Each of these three institutions received Rs 10,800,600 bequeathed by him from his residual estate including the corpus. *Dawn*, 4 July 1998 and 30 July 2005, p. 18. The present Administrator of the Quaid-i-Azam Estate is Liaquat Merchant, the grandson of Mariam Bai, Jinnah's sister, and his grandnephew. The bungalow currently occupied by the Corps Commander, Lahore, also belonged to Jinnah, and displays a plaque, 'Jinnah House'.
9. She would later [1918] edit a volume of his speeches and writings, with her 'biographical appreciation', entitled, *Mohamed Ali Jinnah: An Ambassador of Unity*.
10. Bolitho, op. cit., p. 213.
11. For instance, while driving to dine with the Governor, stopping the carriage, buying a roasted corn-cob from a man beside the road and eating it as they approached Government House, or buying a banana from a barrow and eating it as they walked along the street, almost at the entrance of the Savoy Hotel.
12. A Parsi-born Christian businessman in Mumbai, India and son of Mr Nowrosjee Wadia who had founded the reputed Bombay Dyeing & Manufacturing Company in 1879.
13. He is the chairman and majority owner of Bombay Dyeing, a major textile company in India.
14. Into this genre of rudeness as a political tactic fall his storming out on Governor Willingdon's dinner in Bombay in 1918, and walking out on Lord Linlithgow, the Viceroy, again in Bombay, in 1941; or telling the Viceroy in mid-September 1939,

after the outbreak of the war, that 'he was too busy to come until 1st October' for political parleys with him and Gandhi (Lord Glendon, *The Viceroy at Bay* [London: Collins, 1971], p. 142). He told Wavell he could not come to Simla till 3 May 1946 for the second Simla Conference (Penderal Moon (ed.), *Wavell: The Viceroy's Journal* [London: Oxford, 1973]), and kept others waiting.

15. Khalid B. Sayeed, 'The Personality of Jinnah and his Political Strategy', in C.H. Philips and Mary Dooreen Wainwright (eds.), *The Partition of India: Polices and Perspectives* (London: George Allen and Union, 1970), p. 277.
16. H.V. Hodson, 'Quaid-i-Azam and the British', in Ahmad Hasan Dani (ed.), *World Scholars on Quaid-i-Azam Mohammad Ali Jinnah* (Islamabad: Quaid-i-Azam University, 1979), pp. 241–54
17. Sarojini Naidu (ed.), *Mohamed Ali Jinnah: An Ambassador of Unity* (Madras: Ganesh, 1917), p. 18.
18. Ibid., p. 19.
19. On Jinnah's association with the Congress, see Sharif al Mujahid, 'Jinnah and the Congress Party', in D.A. Low (ed.), *The Indian National Congress: Centenary Hindsight* (Delhi: OUP, 1988).
20. Ralph Braibanti, former Professor Emeritus and Director, Islamic and Arabic Development Studies, Duke University, South Carolina, USA, in the *Journal of South Asian and Middle Eastern Studies*, Fall, 1996.
21. See Percival Spear's review titled *Jinnah, The Creator of Pakistan* reproduced in 'Part 4: Contemporary Reviews' of this volume. Some of Jinnah's personal attributes which determined his politics and posture, have been succinctly delineated by Spear in this review.
22. Karl Marx and Frederick Engels, *Selected Works* (Moscow: Progress Publishers, 1970), I:398.
23. His marriage belonged to the pre-February 1929 period and the construction of 'the house' was not begun till sometime in 1939.
24. Quaid-i-Azam Mohammad Ali Jinnah, *Speeches and Statements 1947–48* (Islamabad: Directorate of Films & Publications, 1989), p. 43.
25. Bolitho, op. cit., p. 197.
26. Qudratullah Shahab, *Shahabnama* (Lahore: Sang-e-Meel Publications, 1987), pp. 426–27.

PART ONE

Diary and Notes
November 1951–May 1953

"These notes, the greater part of which could not be used in my biography of Mohammed Ali Jinnah, will be invaluable to anyone writing about Jinnah, or Pakistan, in the future."

– Hector Bolitho

These are confidential diary and notes written by Hector Bolitho, from November 1951 to May 1953. It includes interviews with the following, in England, Pakistan and India.

– Sharif al Mujahid

– INTERVIEWS –

In Pakistan

Salman Ali	Press Attaché, Pakistan High Commissioner's Office, London. Later ambassador to Russia.
K.H. Khurshid (1924–1988)	Private Secretary to Jinnah (1944–1947). Later President of Azad Kashmir
Habib Ibrahim Rahimtoola (1912–1991)	Pakistan High Commissioner, London.
Mazhar Ahmed	Naval ADC to Jinnah. Died in a helicopter crash in the early sixties, with his newly wedded wife, Salma, near Bandung, Indonesia.
Members of Jinnah's family	
S.N. Baqar	Director General, Civil Defence.
Col. Majeed Malik (1902–1976)	Principal Information Officer, Government of Pakistan. Col. Majeed Malik was the first Indian to be appointed a full colonel in the British

	Army. He was the first accredited correspondent of Reuters in India before he joined the army.
Mohammed Noman (1914–1972)	Former Secretary to Jinnah; General Secretary, All India Muslim Students Federation, 1937–1938; Vice President, 1938–1944.
Ghulam Ali Allana (1906–1985)	Former Mayor of Karachi Chairman of the Press Commission of Pakistan in 1948. Founded the Islamic Chambers of Commerce & Industry in 1949 and was its President for five years, the longest term held by any individual.
Sheikh Abdul Qadir	Chief Inspector of Police, Karachi.
M. Ashir (d. 1964)	[News] Editor of *Dawn*, Karachi.
Miss Fatima Jinnah (1893–1967)	Sister of Mohammed Ali Jinnah.
Begum Ra'ana Liaquat Ali Khan (1905–1990)	Wife of Nawabzada Liaquat Ali Khan, the first Prime Minister of Pakistan.
Wing Commander Ata Rabbani	First air ADC to Jinnah for over seven months—from 14 August 1947 to 29 March 1948.
His Highness the Mir of Hunza	
Sir (Robert) Francis Mudie (1890–1976)	Governor of Sindh 1946–7; Governor of West Punjab from 15 Aug. 1947.
Pir Ali Mohammad Rashidi (1905–1987)	Editor, *Sind Observer*, Karachi; Minister, Government of Pakistan, Aug. 1955–Sept. 1956, 1957.
Admiral J.W. Jefford (1901–1980)	Pakistan's first Naval Chief.
Jamshed Nusserwanjee (1886–1952)	A friend of Jinnah. First and longest serving Mayor of Karachi.
Abdul Wahid	*Dawn* representative in Lahore.
Begum Jahan Ara Shah Nawaz (1896–1979)	Delegate to Third Round Table Conference, London, 1932; Member, Viceroy's Executive Council, 1943–1945; Member, Pakistan Constituent Assembly, 1947–1954.

DIARY AND NOTES

Prof. B.A. Hashmi (d. 1966)	Principal of Central Training College, Lahore; Vice Chancellor, University of Karachi, 1957–1961.
Farruk Amin	Former Secretary to Jinnah.
His Highness The Aga Khan (1877–1957)	Head of the Ismaili community; Leader of the Simla Deputation that waited on the Viceroy, 1906; President, All India Muslim League, 1910–1913; Leader of the Muslim delegation to the Round Table Conference, London, 1930–30; First Pro Chancellor, Aligarh Muslim University, 1920–32; President, Assembly of the League of Nations, 1937.
'Sonny' Habibullah	Once Secretary to Jinnah. Later Textile Commissioner of Pakistan.
Owain-Jones	Senior British Council Representative in Pakistan.
Peer Tajuddin	Barrister in Lahore.
Lt.-Gen. Sir Ross McCoy	Chief Military Adviser, Pakistan Army.
James Hardy	Asst. Dist. Commissioner of Police, who was present when Liaquat Ali Khan was assassinated.
Brig. Sir Hissamud Din Khan	
Khan Abdul Qayyum Khan (1901–1981)	Chief Minister, NWFP, 1947–1953 President, Pakistan Muslim League, 1957–58.
Major Mumtaz Ahmed Khan	Officer in Khyber Pass.
Lt. Comm. S.M. Ahsan	Naval ADC to Jinnah. Later Chief of Naval Staff, Pakistan and Governor, East Pakistan.
Letters from Miss Jinnah and Begum Liaquat Ali Khan	
Atiya Begum	
Din Mohammed (1886–1965)	Governor of Sindh, 1948–1952.
Pir Pigaro	Spiritual head of the Hurs (Sindh).
Sir Shah Nawaz Bhutto	Diwan of Junagadh.
Khawaja Nazimuddin	Premier, East Bengal, 1947–48

(1984–1964)   Governor General, 1948–1951;
                               Prime Minister of Pakistan,
                               1951–1953.

In Bombay

Sir Cowasjee Jehangir   Philanthropist.
(1879–1962)

Kanji Dwarkadas   Labour lawyer, animal rights activist,
                               author.

C.N. Joshi   Lawyer.

Motilal Setalvad   Attorney General.

Morarji Desai (1896–1980s)   Chief Minister in Bombay, 1946–1950;
                               Prime Minister of India, 1977–1979.

Raja Sir Maharaj Singh   Former Governor of Bombay.
(1878–1959)

Lady Petit   Mother-in-law of M.A. Jinnah.

Neville Wadia   Son-in-law of Jinnah.

Claude Batley   Architect who built Jinnah's house.

Shantilal L. Thar   Jinnah's stockbroker.

In England

Sir Feroz Khan Noon   Prime Minister of Pakistan (1957–8).
(1893–1970)

Nasim Ahmed (d. 1990)   London Correspondent *Dawn*.

Major Haji   Secretary to Aga Khan.

Gen. Sir Frank Messervy   First Commander-in-Chief,
                               (1893–1974) Pakistan Army.

Letter from Bombay
Corporation confirming
facts about early life of
Fatima Jinnah

Dina Wadia (b. 1919)   Jinnah's daughter

Lady Eugenie Wavell   Wife of Viceroy of India (1943–7).

Lord Wavell (1883–1950)   C-in-C, India (1942–3) then Viceroy of
                               India (1943–7).

– 20 November 1951 –

Salman Ali on Jinnah, Mountbatten, and Gandhi

"Mountbatten and Jinnah were bound to clash: they were both on the same 'level'. Although their opinion might be opposed, their approach, as two persons, was similar.

But with Gandhi, who claimed always to be guided by his 'inner light', Mountbatten was never equal. Gandhi could raise or lower himself in relation to Mountbatten, because his approach, whether sincere or insincere, was not worldly.

Gandhi once made a promise to Jinnah and then went back on his word. He excused his action by saying that his 'inner light' had permitted him to change his mind.

Jinnah was angry and said, 'To hell with his inner light. Why can't he be honest and admit that he just made a mistake'."

'Pakistan'

The word *Pakistan* was apparently invented by the Hindus, some time about 1940. They began to say, 'Oh, these Muslims want a Pakistan — a sacred state — a state of their own'. It was derisive, but the Muslims were quick to adopt the word. Then, if a Muslim wished to pick a quarrel with a Hindu, he would say, 'Pakistan Zindabad', meaning, 'Long live Pakistan'. The Hindu would say the equivalent to, 'To hell with Pakistan'. Then, the fight.

In wrestling matches, games, races etc., where a Muslim was taking part, the other Muslims would shout, 'Pakistan! Pakistan!' The word came to be used rather like a college cheer, but it soon became the cry of a nation.

Quaid-i-Azam

Noman[1] and others tell me that Jinnah was just called Quaid-i-Azam (The Great Leader) by Gandhi. This sounds rather vague. Noman said also that when Jinnah fell ill in Karachi, x-rays were taken by a Hindu specialist, and his disease was diagnosed as Tuberculosis. It was then decided that he would not last more than six months. One copy of the x-rays was sent to Delhi, where the opinion of the doctors influenced the Indian government in their decision to invade Hyderabad.

Note

Although Mr Noman was a fairly reliable source of information, this story seems almost absurd. It apparently refers to Jinnah's illness in Lahore, during November 1947—only three months after Partition; and it is extremely unlikely that the Pakistani doctors would have then allowed their Governor-General to be examined by a Hindu specialist.

– **4 December 1951** –

Dear Mr Bolitho,

Thank you very much for your letter of 19th November. I am very glad that you have accepted this important task, and I wish you every success in your work. I hope to see you after your arrival, and will be glad to have a talk with you then.

Your visit has already been written up in the Pakistan Press, and whilst I will readily say a word to Miss Jinnah if I have the opportunity, I am sure that she will be only too anxious to help in a matter such as this, and that you need not expect anything but friendliness and goodwill.

I am so glad to have news of Michael Killanin—remember me to him if you see him.

Yours Sincerely,
Gilbert Laithwaite

H. Bolitho, Esq.,
the Athenaeum,
Pall Mall,
London S.W.I.

– **4 December 1951** –

Derek Peel and I dined with Habib Ibrahim Rahimtoola, the High Commissioner, and his wife, at their house in Avenue Road. They were eager to make us like Pakistan and they talked of Jinnah as if he were a prophet. Rahimtoola said, "He gave up racing to devote himself to the cause of the Muslims". He told us also a story of Jinnah's arrogance.

"One day, about the end of 1944, I was with Jinnah in his study in Bombay when the telephone rang. Jinnah answered it. The voice at the other end announced himself as the Governor's private secretary—with a message from the Governor. Jinnah answered, 'If His Excellency is too busy to come to the telephone so am I'. The result was that the Governor himself came to the telephone.

"When the telephone conversation was over, I said to Jinnah, that is one quality you must never give up—arrogance. It makes a hero of you to the students. Jinnah just smiled."

Mazhar Ahmad on Jinnah

"He always gave the most work to the people he liked best. Then, he was so repelled by Gandhi's emotionalism—praying in public, and the sort of thing, it made him doubly cautious in showing any feeling in the speeches he made to masses of people."

Chaudhri Khaliquzzaman on Nationalism

"You must remember that the Muslims in India, for some generations, hated the idea of nationalism because, under the Hindus, they would have to suffer complete subjugation—greater than what they had to endure under the British. In Pakistan, it is still the nature of the people to dislike the idea of nationalism, because of its meaning in the past. They are, therefore, torn between two ideologies—that of nationalism and that of Islamism."

– 26 December 1951 –

Still at Sea

Mazhar Ahmad, who is a passenger on board, was naval ADC to Jinnah at the end. He said, today, "Jinnah died like a Shakespeare [an] character who, when he turns his knife into his own breast, declares, dramatically, 'I die.' Jinnah said at the end, 'My work is finished. I die!'"

Abdul Wali, another young naval officer on board, said, "Audiences sometimes laughed at the mistakes Jinnah made when he tried to speak to them in Urdu. Jinnah always said that English was his 'mother tongue'."

Mazhar Ahmad said to me, "Jinnah wrote very little and he kept no day-to-day diary. But there was a book in which he wrote occasional notes. One day I turned over the pages. I wanted to read it, to know his innermost thoughts. I stole it and kept it for two hours. My conscience pricked me so I took the book back. I am sorry now.

"Sometimes when I was working alone with him in a room, he would say, 'I think we ought to open a window'. No matter what important work was occupying his mind, he would not permit the informality of my opening the window for him. I had to ring for a servant. All [work] would be delayed for this."

Mazhar said, "Jinnah was rationally but not emotionally kind. One day he was on a platform with some other people when a little child walked through the audience towards him. Jinnah said to the official next to him, 'Is this your child?' and when the man said, 'No', Jinnah rejected the child's hand."

"There was a similar incident at a garden party. An old Pathan Muslim chieftain from Baluchistan advanced towards Jinnah and held out his hand. Jinnah said, 'If I shake hands with you, I will have to shake hands with all the people here. And for this there is no time'."

Lieutenant Wali said, "When Jinnah came to our ship, the Dilawar, he came to the wardroom and some of us became excited about the plight of Kashmir. One officer spoke passionately against India and all Jinnah said was, 'My boy, be patient'."

Wali said, "When he signed our guest book, he placed his monocle in his eye with a gesture so exquisite, so beautiful."

While we were talking, Mazhar Ahmad twisted a button, nervously, on my coat. Then he said, "But don't you twist buttons when you are nervous". I answered, "No". I put both hands in my pockets hoping that it will seem that I am not.

– 5 January 1952 –

Mazhar Ahmad told me of his Service with Jinnah as Naval ADC

"I joined Jinnah in May 1948, four months before he died. He died on 11 September 1948, when he was almost 72. I had my first interview with him in January 1948. He sat at the far end of the room to assess me as I walked in. He stood up and shook my hand. I had heard of him as a man who was hard, who drank too much, and never said his prayers. This was the usual Hindu criticism of him—that he was not a good Muslim—that he was ruthless and intolerant.

"I soon learned that this was not true. He did not say his prayers, but I never saw him drink socially. All I ever saw him drink was one double whisky, at night; I believe that his doctor ordered this.

"In June, towards the end of the month, we left for Ziarat, 75 miles from Quetta, for a rest in a small English house in a compound. Miss Jinnah was there. She was possessive and watched his every move, and everyone else's. She knew everything that went on in the house.

"When Jinnah's health improved, we returned to Karachi for the opening of the State Bank. Jinnah looked upon this as of great importance. He was still not well and I said, 'If you write the speech, the Prime Minister could read it for you'. But he was insistent. The Bank meant that Pakistan would have its own currency.

"There were two thoughts in Jinnah's mind as we flew from Quetta to Karachi. That he would not live very long, and that the opening of the Bank was a rebuff for those who thought that Pakistan would be an economic failure. He insisted on the greatest possible show, that he should be received with a public demonstration—diplomats and all. Miss Jinnah went with us. Jinnah wore a *sherwani* and astrakhan which has become the official headdress in Pakistan.

"The opening of the Bank was his last public appearance. When I brought him back to Government House afterward we climbed the stairs together...after a few paces he dismissed me...I turned back and saw him staggering towards the door and I was afraid for him.

"We returned to Ziarat. On 11th August it was obvious that he was seriously ill. On 12th August, at night, the doctor told me that Jinnah would have to be moved to Karachi next morning. I asked, 'How?' and he answered, 'That is your business'.

"Miss Jinnah ordered that the move must be kept secret. I sat up all night making arrangements. I could not obtain a proper ambulance. I got a big Humber car and had one seat lowered so that we could stretch a mattress for him. Miss Jinnah was insistent that no one was to see him lying helpless on the stretcher. Although it was obvious he was dying, Jinnah insisted on being dressed for the journey—a new *sherwani*, pump shoes, his hair perfectly arranged—monocle and white handkerchief.

"I lifted him in my arms from the stretcher to the car. He was light as a child. I put him on the mattress but not exactly in the centre. His cheek was next to mine. As I was still holding him, he smiled and said, 'Mazhar, your are out of breath, and I am also out of breath.' So we paused; then I moved him again. I asked, 'Are you comfortable, Sir', and he smiled as he said, 'Where is my handkerchief?' There was one in his pocket. I placed another in his hand. Miss Jinnah and the nurse—Nurse Dunham—got into the car with him. I sat in front and as we drove slowly towards Quetta, I prayed. We arrived at the Residency and I carried him to bed. As I tucked him in, he smiled.

"That was the evening of the 13th. The eve of the Pakistan Day celebrations. About 12 o'clock fireworks began in the town. I sneaked out to see the celebrations, for only five minutes, but Miss Jinnah knew. Next morning she asked me, 'What were the fireworks like?'

"We stayed in Quetta almost a month and did not leave until 11th September. We arrived at Mauripur at 4:15 p.m. in the Viking. We had asked for an ambulance to be at the end of the strip. I looked out and saw only a 15 cwt. truck, ramshackle, open and without curtains. We put the stretcher into the back of the truck. Miss Jinnah sat with him. Just before entering Karachi the truck broke down and the five cars following were held up. Finally an ambulance came. We took him to Government House and at 10:15 that night he died."

Mazhar said that Jinnah despised Gandhi's "vague philosophical absurdities; they distressed him so much that Jinnah weighed every opinion before he spoke. He once called Gandhi, 'That Hindu revivalist'."

Mazhar said also that Jinnah insisted on his sister sharing his prestige. That he was sometimes short-tempered when he was ill. Mazhar used a good phrase in describing Jinnah—as "a cold, celibate man, with all his passions in his mind". He said that Liaquat Ali Khan knew better how to handle men. Jinnah was impatient and inclined to bully.

Once in 1946, the year before Partition, when Jinnah still went to race meetings, Begum Rahimtoola invited him into her box where Mazhar's elder brother was also sitting. "I'll give you a tip for the next race", said Jinnah. "Put your money on Hindustan". "But, Sir", said Mazhar's brother, "How can you say a thing like that!"

"Never mind", said Jinnah. "It's only a horse."

Hindustan came in first and the young man won sixty-nine rupees for his ten.

* * * *

Mazhar said that as Jinnah grew old, he liked to have young men about him. His secretaries and ADCs were all young. He came to enjoy the stimulus of young people and seldom refused to speak to them in audiences, no matter how busy he was.

In the last days at Ziarat, he saw the ADCs one afternoon, playing tennis. He said to them, "Oh, I wish I had some tennis shoes. I play too." This was only a few weeks before he died.

* * * *

Mazhar spoke again of Jinnah's dislike of touching or being touched. "He would devote his mind and even his life to helping the poor, but he did not wish to shake hands with them."

* * * *

Suleri told me that when he was in London he went to the airport to see Jinnah taking off for Pakistan [India?]. There arrived an old, devoted Muslim, who lived in the East End of London. He had hired a taxi cab for the journey to the airport and it cost him about £8. Suleri said to Jinnah, "This devoted old man is poor, but has spent £8 to come and see you".

All that Jinnah said was, "You Muslims! You are so extravagant."

– 8 January 1952 –

We arrived in Karachi and I was immediately worried of what I shall have to endure. A Pakistani named Mr Haris burst into my cabin and gave me a pamphlet on this subject of Jinnah's date of birth. He bombarded me with argument.

– 10 January 1952 –

We are settling into the fantastic Metropole Hotel. Yesterday morning, when I was just out of bed, a reporter came into my room, handing me a card which claims that he represents the '*Daily Mail*' and the '*Sydney Morning Herald*'. He asked for my impressions and I answered, "But I haven't even had my bath yet; I can't even find a cake of soap". My idle words did harm. The Suleri, anti-Government and therefore anti-Bolitho newspaper came out, with big headings, "Mr Bolitho complains that there is no soap in Metropole Hotel". Within a few minutes, the manager appeared with some ordinary hotel soap; a little time later an official from the Ministry came with a box of expensive Mornay cakes of soap—bought at Government expense. Well, it is a lesson I must learn: not to make remarks to newspaper reporters.

S.N. Baqar, Director General of Civil Defence said to me, "Jinnah was not always infallible in choosing his lieutenants. He was therefore sometimes disillusioned. Whenever he found that he was deceived he gave no quarter. He was without pity if ever he was betrayed."

His attitude towards the poor. "You must be saved. But I do not want you to come and thank me." Baqar said, "The emotion of gratitude was repulsive to him."

At Simla, in June 1946, when Jinnah and Gandhi were being photographed together:

GANDHI: "You like this, don't you?"
JINNAH: "You like it better than I do."

* * * *

Baqar said, "To Jinnah, the Koran was a system of life, not just a religion".

* * * *

Dacca, March 1948. Jinnah had to take salute at march past. The Commander-in-Chief was with Jinnah, on the dais. Jinnah stood up, but three feet too far back. The Commander-in-Chief said, "You must stand here, Sir". Jinnah asked, "Why?" The Commander-in-Chief answered, "Because this is a military parade and you must do as you are told". Jinnah said, "Very well", and stepped up.

* * * *

At Calcutta, February 1946, Baqar said to Jinnah, "What of the economic situation? We have no iron, coal, hydroelectric power, industries, etc." Jinnah answered, "I am fully aware of this. Our people have had no opportunity to develop these things. I have every faith, and so should you. Thus, given the opportunity, our people will achieve all these things. Remember, I am going on, even if it kills me."

* * * *

Baqar said that Nazimuddin, the present Prime Minister, was afraid of Jinnah.

* * * *

Jinnah, to some young men, "Don't enter politics until you have made your pile".

* * * *

Baqar said, that Dr S.A. Hamid, a barrister, was in London, 1920–1921, where he went to hear Jinnah give a speech. Jinnah was then 44 years old. He wrote to his family in Bombay. "There is a young man whom I have met. His name is Jinnah. I feel that he will play a great role in shaping the future for Muslims in India."

Baqar talked also of Jinnah's honesty, while he was practicing law in Bombay. He was once overpaid for conducting a case. He returned the extra money with a note, "This is the amount you paid me. This was my fee. Here is the balance."

* * * *

Two Stories told me by Col. Majeed Malik

In 1946, when Malik was Director of Public Relations in the army, he was suddenly sent to England on duty. Jinnah asked Malik to take a message to Pethick-Lawrence, then Secretary of State for India. Jinnah wished to tell Pethick-Lawrence that the Muslim sepoys (rankers) did not share the view of their officers, that Partition would not be welcomed by the army.

This was an important message at the time, as Jinnah wished to make the British government realize that the mass of Muslims, including those in the armed services, were all in favour of partition.

Malik did what Jinnah asked and was back in Delhi, where he lived in a house next to Jinnah. But Jinnah was away, in Bombay. Believing that the message from Pethick-Lawrence was important, he went all the way to Bombay. Malik spoke to Jinnah on the telephone and went to see him, several times. Every time Malik raised the subject, Jinnah would say, "Don't talk about it. Things have changed since then and I am no longer interested."

The second story concerns two of Malik's friends who were unhappily married. Jinnah also knew them and was fond of them both. Malik suggested to the wife that she should seek Jinnah's help in persuading the man to give his wife a divorce. Jinnah would not help. He said, "What passes between a man and his wife no third person can understand, therefore, I cannot help you".

Jinnah then spoke of his own marriage, which was unlike him. He said, "I loved my wife and she loved me, but we could not get along together—and no outsider had the right to judge us."

Malik said that, in spite of this, he had good reason to believe that Jinnah did see the husband as, two weeks later, he suddenly agreed to a divorce.

* * * *

Mazhar Ahmad

"When I was at Quetta with Jinnah he sent me into town to get him some ties. I chose thirty of the best for him to take his pick. I took back and showed them to him, he said, 'No I don't like any of them. Take them back and tell the shop to let you know when they have some new ones'."

* * * *

– 11 January 1952 –

Karachi

I was taken to see Fatima Bai, who married one of Jinnah's cousins. She was a beautiful old lady, with fine bones, and a black scarf over her head. The room, up some stinking stairs, with scaled blue walls, rocking chair, cupboard in which family souvenirs and photographs are kept. The son was there, Mohammed Ali, a sort of businessman and very full of himself. It was not easy to make him talk of Jinnah, or to allow his mother to talk. They gave us tea, made by a daughter in a silvery sari, in a squalid kitchen.

Fatima Bai went to live in the Jinnah House in Karachi, when Jinnah was still a boy; aged 8 years. She was then only 14. He would make her sit while he studied by the light of a lamp. One night when he was studying very late she protested, and he answered, "Let me study. One day I'll be a great man."

I think that he believed this of himself. As Governor-General, more than sixty years later, when he was a great man, he rode in his carriage with outsiders, like a viceroy.

I remember being told by one of the British officers that, just after Jinnah settled in as Governor-General, the British Naval Commander called and signed his name in the book; Jinnah refused to return the call. He said, "He is the commander of only one part of the British Navy. I am head of a state."

The pride had endured. On the way — in the year that he [Jinnah] first joined the Indian National Congress, he refused to sit on the floor with the others and he demanded a chair.

Another curious picture of him, of his earlier life in Bombay. The story was told to me by someone who knew him then: "If he offered you a cigarette, you felt welcome. If he offered a second one, it was a sign that he was pleased. If a third cigarette was offered, then you could be certain that he was delighted.

"His housekeeping was strictly parsimonious. The exact amount of food for each person was measured out and each person would be served with that amount. Nobody was ever asked to dine at the last moment.

"I remember, in Bombay, when Jinnah gave a party for the young Raja of Mahmudabad, of whom he was very fond. Bombay was amazed — Jinnah, of all people, asking four hundred to dine. It was said that old men in their eighties were astonished and left their sickbeds to be carried to the party. One of them, with a temperature of 104, was from his bed and said, 'This is the first time, and certainly the last time, that we are likely to be asked'."

* * * *

A reporter from *Dawn* said to me, 'We had to join the people with some plea, and religious ideology seemed the most convenient at hand.'

* * * *

Question and Answer

HECTOR BOLITHO: "May I know whether Communism is a serious menace in Pakistani colleges."

PROFESSOR MAHMUD BRELVI: "Western Pakistan seems to be devoid of any large communistic activity, but Eastern Pakistan is affected by it to some extent, mostly due to its close proximity to West Bengal, which is well known as one of the centres of Indian Communism. The educational institutions of West Pakistan are, therefore, free from any active Communistic influence, but educational institutions in East Pakistan seem to be considerately influenced. Faith in Islamic ideology prevents most people from falling a victim to Communistic ideology."

Brelvi is the busy professor, in a topee, who has been lent to me to help with research. I suspect that he is wordy and not very reliable. And he is nosey, and likes scandal.

He said, "Miss Jinnah would never allow her brother to enjoy himself. If there was a bit of a party, she would try to stop him having fun; she would say, 'Come along, it's time you went to bed'. But, when he was given a chance, Jinnah knew how to relax. He would sit, completely relaxed, with a glass of whisky or brandy, and just be content to listen."

Our Bearer, on the British

"The poor people, like myself, who work hard for their living, prefer the days when they were ruled by the British. When the British made up their minds or took a decision they stuck to it. The Pakistanis change their mind all the time."

Mr Allana

We have made friends of Mr Allana, a rich follower of The Aga Khan, and once Mayor of Karachi. Also of his son and daughter. There is a similar gap between the generations to what you find in better class English families. He said of his son, aged 22, "I say to him, at your age, you have the opportunity of having all I knew when I was 44".

I had met his pretty little daughter, aged 16, in a lovely sari. Two pushing Pakistani men came afterwards and sat beside her on a sofa, at the end of the dining room, asking her permission. Their manners were unpleasant. I said to her, afterwards, "I hope that when you grow up, you won't subscribe to the idea that women are inferior to men — or allow them to be rude to you like that". She nodded her sixteen-year old head, prettily and wisely, and said, "Oh, I won't do that! You can be certain." I said to her father, afterwards, how charming she was, and that she had ideas of her own. He said, "I don't know, I never talk to her."

– 23 January 1952 –

I have met the arch humbug, Ahmed E.H. Jaffer, who wears a red carnation and haunts the Metropole to meet anyone important, in the hall. He is a big businessman. He asked me to go this evening to the Yacht Club, to see the film of Jinnah's funeral. I thought it a solemn occasion and put on a black tie. I arrived to find about thirty people drinking dry Martinis and whiskey, and no film. He said that there was a "hitch". I feel prim and disapproving that he should make light of Jinnah's funeral. The truth is that they do not really care. I can gather endless, gossipy stories, for they love gossip. But getting facts, and serious stories that help me into Jinnah's mind, is the devil's own business. I do not believe that they care about a permanent record of Jinnah's life. Liaquat cared, and would have helped me. It is my tragedy also that he was shot, between my agreeing to come here, and my arrival.

Two Stories

Noman said to me, "As an indication of how this Government works, it took a Cabinet meeting five hours to decide what colour the new railway carriages should be".

Then: "At one of the annual meetings of the Muslim League, one of the members proposed that Jinnah should be permanent President — instead of holding annual elections. Jinnah opposed this motion, saying, 'Annual elections are important. I must come before you each year, to seek your vote of confidence'."

A Comment

An Englishman who has been here many years said of the Pakistanis, "They are never happy unless they have a grievance. You must realize that kindness as part of human relationship is unknown in the subcontinent."

I do not believe this. I sense a different form of business. However, how many Europeans are kind without seeking some return, within or outside themselves.

Karachi

While we were staying at the Metropole Hotel, the Grand Mufti of Jerusalem arrived to stay. It was strange to be in the same hotel with such a violent enemy. There was a meeting of Islamic divines in the late afternoon—a tea party, and then a great, beautiful rug was spread in the hotel courtyard, for prayers. I watched the Grand Mufti take off his shoes and then kneel to pray, his forehead towards Mecca, his back towards the American Bar.

While this was going on, the builders were busy, adding a new storey to the end of the hotel. Just as the Grand Mufti was deep in prayer, a basket of rubble landed on the ground—sounding like a rifle shot. The Grand Mufti looked up, alarmed. People stood on the balconies surrounding the courtyard. Most of them smiled.

Told me by George Galitzine

"When Jinnah and his sister attended a gathering of chieftains near the North West Frontier, there was grave disorder. Some of the chieftains had ridden two days to be there; when they saw that Miss Jinnah was unveiled they turned their backs. When Jinnah addressed them in English, because he could not speak Pushtu, they spat on the ground and walked away.

Chief Inspector of Police, Sheikh Abdul Qadir

While Jinnah was Governor-General, he sacked his driver because be failed to stop when ordered by a police constable. The police constable was new and he did not recognize the Governor-General's car. He waved it to halt, but the driver went on. Jinnah said, "The law is the law and you must respect it".

"In the morning, Jinnah would sit down with all the newspapers. Then he would summon his secretaries and dictate letters and press releases. When they were typed he would check them and send them straight off, without any change of mind."

The Metropole

The restaurant manager of the Metropole Hotel has the commercial name of Mr Soso. He was once manager of the restaurant of the Carlton Hotel in London and, I believe, of the Hotel de Paris at Bray. He told me that he knew Jinnah for many years in England. Jinnah used to go to the Carlton Grill, and to the Hotel de Paris at Bray. They were always meeting, at the various hotels where Soso has worked during his decline [?]. The Hotel Imperial at Delhi, the Cecil Hotel at Simla. Soso surprised me by saying that even in the early days in London, Jinnah was luxurious in his taste in food. When he became Governor-General, in Karachi, he would send over to the Palace Hotel, where Soso was then working, for special dishes.

M. Ashir, News Editor of "Dawn"

"The Islamic religion is nebulous. Because it claims to be the final religion of the world, it must be, and is adaptable.

"It is contrary to the religion of Islam that one man should condemn another. 'He is not a good Muslim because, so-and-so.' Only God may be the judge of whether a man is a good Muslim or not. God may overlook the weaknesses of a human being because his goodness is sufficient to ensure his salvation.

"The great weakness of Muslim people is that they could more readily respect, trust and follow a rich man. Jinnah was incorruptible; he could afford to be, and therefore he attracted a big following.

"Islam orders five prayers in each day. Some people, if they are especially religious, say an extra prayer, about 4 o'clock in the morning. This is the Tahajjud prayer."

Mr Ashir then said that an ADC, or secretary of Jinnah, told him that he often saw Jinnah up about 4 a.m. and presumed that he was saying his prayers.

I wonder if this is true. Most people deny Jinnah's religious habits. And I like the claim that it is contrary to the religion of Islam for one man to condemn another. I find that they thrive on rumours and malicious gossip.

– 24 January 1952 –

(I made pencil notes of this and am not certain of the date). I lunched with the Aga Khan and his lovely Begum, in a blue sari. The Aga Khan knew Jinnah well; said he was instinctively and essentially an aristocrat. That he was greater than Hitler or Mussolini, because he had no forces, whatever behind him.

I suggested that Jinnah died at the right time. Hitler and Mussolini lived too long and began to undo what good they had done. I suggested that had Jinnah lived there might have been war over Kashmir instead of the long struggle of mere argument.

The Aga Khan has promised me every help with my book and has asked me to stay with him in the South of France on my way home. He told me that he has smoked only one cigarette in all his life—once, when he went to see King Edward VII. "He offered me one and I felt that he was so courteous; he would not have smoked himself, if I had refused. So I did it, but it was a very untidy business."

The Aga Khan said that he considered Edward VII was a great King. I remarked that the fashion now was to decry him and write of him as a vulgar man.

"What does that matter!" said the Aga Khan. "What if he ate five dinners a day and drank too much? It makes no difference." I lost my heart to the Begum. Her gentle watchfulness over him, and her kindness to the servants. Delightful to watch.

– 26 January 1952 –

The noises in this vast, ridiculous hotel are especially terrible at night, but I am yielding to eastern tricks and chicanery to fight them. A few days ago an important police officer came to my room. He said that he controlled all the traffic for this part of Karachi. But his real purpose was to tell me that he had saved Jinnah's life some years ago in Bombay, when an assassin tried to stab him. I knew this cannot be true as, on the only occasion when Jinnah was attacked—and not very much hurt—the other person in the room was his secretary. The police officer no doubt arrived later.

Now promoted to authority and power, in Karachi, the man wished to be mentioned in my book. A devil of astuteness came to my aid. I said to the police officer that the noise of the traffic outside my hotel bedroom was so terrible at night that I could not sleep. "And how", I asked, "can you expect me to write a good biography of Mohammed Ali Jinnah when I cannot sleep?"

He promised to divert the traffic from the street that passes my window, every night after 10 o'clock. And I really believe that he has done so. The last two nights have been very quiet.

Encouraged by this success, I made war last evening against a dog that howls to the moon, the whole night through. I complained to the assistant manager, twice, but nothing was done. Last night I picked up the telephone, got through to Mr Ansari, and did my best at speaking like Mr Haji, the Aga Khan's secretary. I said, "How do you expect His Highness to sleep while that dog howls in the courtyard?"

Mr Ansari said, "Yes, Sir". A few minutes later the dog stopped barking and I have not heard it since.

– 27 January 1952 –

Conversation with Dr L. Soldinger at Hotel Metropole, regarding Lt.-Col. (Dr) Ilahi Bakhsh's Book on Jinnah's Illness and Death

Dr Soldinger said it was quite apparent that Ilahi Bakhsh had no justification for not calling in expert European advice during the critical days of Jinnah's illness. Dr Soldinger said Ilahi Bakhsh should have insisted on the opinion of an outside specialist and that his conduct was unprofessional where the life of so important a person as Jinnah was at stake.

I asked Dr Soldinger if he believed in the rumour that Jinnah was already dead when he arrived in Karachi. Dr Soldinger said that after reading Ilahi Bakhsh's book, he did believe that Jinnah might have died in the aircraft—possibly even before Miss Jinnah and the staff officers left Quetta. I let him ramble on, realizing how careful I must be with all that I am told.

I know, from Mazhar Ahmad, that Jinnah was still alive when he arrived at Government House in Karachi. And from Begum Liaquat Ali Khan.

– 29 January 1952 –

I talked with Nanji Jafar, a crinkled old man with tousled snowy hair. He was 8 when Jinnah was 14. Jinnah's father gave him a cricket set and, from this time, he taught the boys in the street to play. Old Nanji Jafar recalled Jinnah saying, "Don't play marbles. It dirties your clothes. Stand up out of the dust and play cricket."

It is the most important episode of Jinnah's childhood so far; the desire to stand up out of the dust. Nanji Jafar said that Jinnah taught them to play, but he was not a bully. He was a thin boy. When Jinnah went to England he gave Nanji Jafar his cricket bat. He said that Jinnah went to school in a carriage, but that the other boys walked.

* * * *

N. came to my room today and was angry at my good opinion of Mountbatten. He answered, "He is the poor relation of kings, with all the dangers this implies—the frustrated wish to rule—the ambition to create his own kingdom".

He told me a story of Jinnah's incredible exactness on facts. It was in Delhi where a reporter from the *Sind Observer* telephoned and asked for an interview. Jinnah answered, "Yes, come tomorrow at 5 o'clock, but telephone first".

At ten minutes to five next afternoon, the reporter telephoned and was told that Jinnah was "sleeping". The reporter came five minutes late and, finding Jinnah waiting for him near the door, he said, "I'm sorry I am late but your bearer said that you were sleeping."

Jinnah said, "I was not; I was lying down, reading a newspaper". He then sent for the servants and questioned them, one by one. He carefully explained the fine difference between "lying down to sleep", and "reclining to read a newspaper." Then he directed the reporter to a chair and the interview began.

Col. Majeed Malik on the Differences Between Jinnah, Gandhi, and Nehru

"Jinnah rose to his high position and gained esteem with virtually no contact with the masses. He was essentially a private person— essentially an aristocrat in his attitude towards the people. Whereas Gandhi and Nehru spent their whole life in public and toured the entire country, making themselves known to the people. Gandhi even prayed and washed and slept in public"

* * * *

Two months or so after Pakistan, Jinnah went through the Khyber Pass, as far as the Afghan frontier. The Afghan guards had orders not to show any consideration to the Pakistanis, so the sentry merely scowled at Jinnah. But Jinnah put out his hand and said, "Come on, shake hands". The sentry succumbed to Jinnah's smile and a photograph was taken of them, hand in hand.

This story was told to me by a reporter who was there; he said that when the photograph was reproduced in a newspaper, the wretched sentry was "sacked".

– 1 February 1952 –

Poor [Mahmud] Brelvi has turned out to be the donkey I suspected from the first. He has broken appointments, given me wrong information all the while, been busy writing his own book, on the sly. He is a sad and miserable man. The real trouble, at root, is that so many of his kind pretend to English scholarship with not even a simple, honest knowledge of the language. I had to complain to the Ministry, that Brelvi was not giving me the help I was promised. My silly, punctual habits will bring too much misery before I am finished. To digress from Brelvi—the young editor of one of the Pakistan languages, whom I have come to like, is Yunus Said. He is civilized, charming, and intelligent beyond the average. But his sense of time is whimsical, in spite of his gifts. I had an appointment for him to come to lunch a few days ago. He did not appear at 1 p.m., as arranged. Next day, he came at 1:20 p.m., and said, "I am sorry, but I am twenty minutes late". I smiled, and did not tell him he was one day and twenty minutes late.

Back to poor old Brelvi. He is hiding behind sickness, since the ministry apparently scolded him for being remiss. Perhaps they threatened to sack him. I do not know. But he wrote me his feelings, emotional letter, and sent it to me by hand [*Letter deleted*].

– 4 February 1952 –

At 11 o'clock this morning I went to see Miss Jinnah, at her request. Her home—Flagstaff House—is guarded by four rusty cannons. I was kept waiting in a room full of incredible furniture—it looked as if it had been collected from a dentist's waiting room in the north of England. Then I was shown into Miss Jinnah's presence. The conversation was not easy. She has definitely refused to help with the biography, because the government—Liaquat Ali Khan—approached me first without consulting her. All very tiresome and narrow. Miss Jinnah puts herself first, even before her brother's memory. I believe that she is dominated by her resentments. Not one kind word about anybody, or anything. And not a phrase or story of use to me in my book. I doubt whether she really has any important documents. Jinnah wrote so little—never saw life in terms of the written word.

Miss Jinnah gave me a cigarette and, as I soon realized that only curiosity had prompted her to ask me to come, I used the cigarette as hers (*sic*) I could to end the interview. I saw by her hands—restless on the arms of her chair, that she was likely to end the visit when she chose. So I rose quickly and stubbed out the cigarette in an ashtray. I took so long over this that she simply had to rise and be polite. Then I departed, past the rusty cannons and back to the hotel.

My opinion is unfair because I began by disliking her for refusing to help over the book. She wore native dress and my prejudice being what it is, I saw her as a cross between a vulture and a camel. I had written her a charming letter, from London, the moment I agreed to write the book, but she had ignored it. She even tried and told the Karachi reporters that she knew nothing of the plan for me to come here and write the biography. Then she admitted to me that she had received the letter.

I am told that Jinnah and his sister bickered, constantly. One little, searching story, told me today. She came into his study one morning and began to fiddle with some newspapers. His secretary was there and repeated the conversation:

JINNAH: "What are you doing, Fatima? Why are you so restless?"
FATIMA: "It is so warm."
JINNAH: "It is not warm. It is sultry."

She left the room and returned ten minutes later, to fiddle again with the newspapers.

JINNAH: "What is wrong with you, Fatima? Why are you so restless?"
FATIMA: "It is so warm."
JINNAH: "Ten minutes ago I told you that it is sultry—not warm. Let that be an end of the matter."

* * * *

It is interesting to seek for the roots of Miss Jinnah's dislike of Begum Liaquat Ali Khan.

Begum Liaquat told me these stories during one of my different visits to her house—with flowers instead of cannons at the gate—music, and cocktails. When Jinnah and Pethick-Lawrence were talking one day in Delhi, Jinnah suddenly said that he would like to make a note of something that Pethick-Lawrence said. Begum Liaquat and Miss Jinnah were also in the room and Begum Liaquat said, spontaneously, that she would take down the notes. Afterwards, when the women were alone, Miss Jinnah said, "You should not have done that".

Once a year, the four of them dined and played bridge. On one of these occasions, as the Jinnahs were leaving, Liaquat chaffed Jinnah about his lonely bachelor state. Miss Jinnah had gone out of the room and Jinnah did not realize that she had returned and was within hearing as he answered, "I would marry, if you could find me another Ra'ana".[2]

The challenge was not all on one side. One night at a dinner party, some of the guests got up to dance. One of the men was F.M. Khan, who was a good dancer. Begum Liaquat insisted on Fatima Jinnah getting up and dancing with him—probably the first time she had ever dared. Thus petty[?] the story is at its roots.

Begum Liaquat also said that Fatima Jinnah suffered under her brother's reproofs. He despised her intellectually and would say, in front of other people, "Be quiet Fatima. You do not know what you are talking about."

* * * *

Ata Rabbani, former Air ADC to Jinnah, talked to me of life at Government House in Karachi, after Pakistan. I asked if Jinnah ever broke through his reserve with him; he answered, "Yes, once, when Miss Jinnah went to Bombay for four days. He suddenly seemed quite happy".

* * * *

M. Ashir, news editor of *Dawn*, said that Fatima Jinnah was partly responsible for Jinnah's death. She insisted on such strict secrecy regarding his illness that he was denied the proper attention that might have prolonged his life.

Another story of Jinnah's pride, at a viceregal reception. Jinnah was tired and he summoned a young officer to go and tell Mountbatten he wished to go home. The young officer was horrified so he went first to ask Liaquat Ali Khan's advice.

"What am I to do?" asked the officer. "Your duty", answered Liaquat Ali Khan. So the officer went to Lord Mountbatten, who rose from his chair and said, "Oh, all right. It's getting late." So he said his farewells, left the room and thus left Jinnah to take his leave also.

– 6 February 1952 –

Conversation with Mohammad Noman

He told me that he said, "Did you ever dance, Mr Jinnah", to which he replied, "No, I don't, because it means asking a favour of a lady".

Noman continued, 'It was the same with Jinnah's second marriage. Ruttenbai Petit was considered to be the No. 1 Parsee debutante in Bombay. Everyone was interested in her, except Jinnah. Because of his aloofness, she became interested in him and got to know him. It was she who asked, 'Will you marry me?' He is said to have answered, 'It seems to be an interesting proposition'."

Noman then spoke of January 1948, the year in which Jinnah died. He said, "I went to see him, but he was not his old elegant self. His tie was hanging away from his collar and he looked untidy. I dared to say to him, 'Mr Jinnah, you don't look like a man whose expectations have been realized in his life time'."

"Jinnah answered, 'What I hoped for has been exceeded. But I never expected what happened in East Punjab and Delhi.[3] They used to call me Quaid-i-Azam[4] but now they call me Qatil-i-Azam'."[5]

One day—January or February 1940—Noman found Jinnah sitting up in bed reading a speech that Gandhi had made. Jinnah said to Noman, "I have not slept a wink, examining this speech to find out exactly what is in his mind". Noman added, "He knew what was in Gandhi's mind".

* * * *

While talking to a group of Muslim workers at Mr Ispahani's residence [in Calcutta] on 1 March 1946, Jinnah said, "I am an old man. God has given me enough to live comfortably at this age. Why should I turn my blood into water, run about and take so much trouble? Not for the capitalists, surely but for you, the poor people. In 1936 when I was in Bengal I saw the abject poverty of the people. Some of them did not get food even once a day. I have not seen them recently, but my heart goes out to them. I feel it, and in Pakistan, we will do all in our power to see that everybody can get a decent living."

* * * *

Noman spoke of Jinnah's days of prosperity, when he was living in Little Gibbs Road in Bombay. When he arrived home from his chambers, each evening, he would sit down and take a book from his desk. In it he would enter the fees he had received during the day. Then he would call Fatima Jinnah and ask for details of what she had spent on housekeeping during the day—fish, so much; chicken, so much. Then he would deduct the total and tell her how much she should have left for the rest of the week. Then Jinnah would send for the chauffeur, who would give him a note of the mileage run during the day. This would also be entered in the book. One day Noman said to Jinnah, "How do you find time for all this?" Jinnah clinched his fists and said, "This is hard-earned money! This is hard-earned money!"

– 7 February 1952 –

Stories of Jinnah told by A.B. 'Sonny' Habibullah and his Brother, Ibrahim

'Sonny' Habibullah said, "Jinnah was delighted in the company of young fashionable people. He was refreshed and seemed to become a different person." I reminded Sonny that Mrs Naidu wrote of Jinnah as being very sensitive. He said, "Yes. Jinnah's brusque, sometimes almost rude manners and autocratic ways were merely a defence for his sensitiveness". "But", he added, "Jinnah changed very much in 1940–41. He no longer seemed to enjoy argument or discussion; he became almost offensive in getting his own way."

Sonny Habibullah told me how his brother Ibrahim Habibullah met Jinnah and went to work for him. It was during the Spanish Civil War and they were together on a platform at a meeting[6] with Pandit Nehru and Subhash Chandra Bose. Afterwards, when Jinnah and Ibrahim Habibullah who had recently returned from Oxford, after completing his studies were alone, Jinnah said to him, "Don't you think Nehru was talking nonsense?"

Ibrahim Habibullah answered, "No, I agree with his views". Jinnah, "The laws of the jungle must always prevail, unless you understand that you are a madcap."

Ibrahim Habibullah, "We call ourselves human beings because we have emancipated ourselves from the jungle. If you do not appreciate this, then, Sir, it is you who are the madcap."

'Oh', said Jinnah. "I need men like you. Come and join me."

– 8 February 1952 –

Mohammad Noman told me a story of Jinnah, Mrs Naidu and a French clairvoyant. Some time in 1919, at the Taj Mahal Hotel Bombay, Jinnah never mentioned to anyone that he had trouble with one of his arms. He had been to Vichy for treatment. Mrs Naidu and the Frenchwoman were together in the hotel. The clairvoyant asked Mrs Naidu to ask Jinnah if he had ever had trouble or pain in his arm. Mrs Naidu went over to Jinnah and asked him.

Jinnah answered, "Why do you want to know? Who told you? Yes, I do have a pain in my arm, at times."

Mrs Naidu went back and told the Frenchwoman, who said, "That man will one day create a state of his own".

Mrs Naidu told Jinnah the story. Some time later, after partition, Jinnah met Mrs Naidu at a party. He asked her the name of the Frenchwoman and said, "I never forget that story".

– 8 February 1952 –

Conversation with Mohammad Noman the same Evening

He said, "Although he would not admit it, Jinnah acted as secretary, for some time, to Dadabhai Naoroji who was MP for Finsbury and who helped to bring Jinnah into public life, in England, before he returned to India." (This is interesting as a sign that Jinnah never liked having to be grateful to anyone. He was not big enough for that emotion.)

Noman said, "Fatima Jinnah's role was confined to looking after her brother's creative comforts. She deprived him of his emotional happiness, but she did not try to interfere with his public life or position."

I do not believe this is true. I think Noman exaggerates. She did look after his creative comforts and, after his separation from his wife, she no doubt stood between him and any further emotional happiness. But I believe that she *did* try to interfere in his public life. Her jealousy of Begum Liaquat Ali Khan might have done terrible mischief—as it actually *does* now, after Jinnah's death. The enmity between these two women—one the remarkable, talented widow of the murdered prime minister; the other, the sister of the dead Jinnah—is a lively poison here in Karachi. People talk of it; they repeat bitter stories, so that I am almost sorry for Fatima Jinnah, fighting, like a fiend in the straitjacket of her limitations.

Noman said, "Just after Partition, everything in Pakistan was very shaky; there was hardly any money in the Treasury to pay salaries. At that time, Gandhi sent a letter to the Pakistan Government, requesting permission to come on a visit to this country. Jinnah asked why. Many members of the Government thought that it was most important that Pakistan should come to an understanding with India, both economical and political. They said, therefore, that Gandhi's request should be met."

"Jinnah stated that he, as Governor-General, would, if necessary, veto the decision of the entire cabinet. Jinnah stood up, pointed, and said, "Look at the sea! If you wish and decide to invite Gandhi to Pakistan, I wish you God-speed. But if you should invite him, you may lift me up and throw me into the sea, rather than that I should have to witness Gandhi coming to this country."

Noman spoke of Jinnah's parsimony. "Jinnah had a cook for ten years. During the war when there was a shortage of food, people in

Bombay were asked to grow as many vegetables as possible. Jinnah grew some in his own garden. The cook stole from the garden, but charged two rupees for them on the housekeeping account, pretending he had bought them from a shop. He was sacked immediately." Jinnah said to Noman, "So far this has been an honest man. There is no place for a dishonest man in my house."

This parsimony continued even when Jinnah was Governor-General. A cup of tea would arrive in the ADC's office with the milk and sugar already in it. One day, when the ADC had a visitor, he asked for a second cup of tea, but it was refused.

Noman is well known as a mimic. One day Jinnah sent for him and said, "I hear that you mimic me with great skill. Show me how you do it." (This was some time in 1938). At the end, Jinnah said, "Very good, but these will help you." He handed him both his astrakhan hat and his monocle. Noman said, "The first and last present he gave me, in all the years that I knew him."

Noman spoke of the parting between Jinnah and his wife. She became seriously ill, in Paris, and Jinnah, who was in London, went over to see her. He called at the hospital with flowers, but out of visiting hours. He left the flowers, with a card, "From M.A. Jinnah".

Noman added, "He signed all his letters to her "M.A. Jinnah'."

Notes

It would be easy to fall into the dangerous habit of using the servants in this country, as slaves. I have to watch myself. This morning, I had put a muddle of newspaper cuttings on the floor. I found myself thinking, 'the bearer will pick them up'. I hate this attitude, so I hurriedly picked them up myself.

I gave a talk to the Karachi Union of Journalists, and told, on the way, the story of a stone which I carry with me. It came from the Temple of the Moon God in Ur of the Chaldees and bears a date about the time that Abraham was a boy. Some of the reporters took down my talk in shorthand and one newspaper came out with 'oracle of the Adelphi' instead of 'Ur of the Chaldees.'

This pretence at knowledge of English can be alarming. I spoke also for the British Council, with Fareed Jafri, a journalist, as my chairman. During my talk I described the span of Queen Victoria's life, "from the days of the gibbet, to the day of the moving picture machine". In his speech of thanks, Fareed Jafri said, "Mr Bolitho has described Queen Victoria's life, from the days of the giblet...."

Mazhar Ahmad

Mazhar, who has been seconded to me as a sort of ADC, is a temperamental young man. He is a naval officer and was Jinnah's ADC, but he developed tuberculosis and was sent to England for a cure. He came back to Pakistan on the same ship with me. He is a strange confusion. One day last week, he arrived an hour late and explained that he had been writing a poem. He read it to me. It was sour with introspection and self-pity. Next day he said that he wished to commit suicide. And I found him out in a strange little piece of deceit. On the same ship coming from England was another Pakistani naval officer, but from the North West Frontier. His name was Abdul Wali and I liked him. When Mazhar and Wali arrived in Karachi they were sent to the same naval barracks. I asked Mazhar, day after day, "Where can I find Wali?" He would not tell me that they were in the same barracks. Eventually I found out, and Wali came to see me, carrying a bunch of flowers. He is as uncomplicated and direct as Mazhar is confused.

* * * *

Jinnah's Birthplace

Soon after I arrived in Karachi, I asked to see the house in which Mohammad Ali Jinnah was born. I was taken by Mohammed Hussain, of the Ministry of Information, but to the wrong house. I even took samples of the broken plaster and of some worn wood, hoping that I might hunt out a scholar who could put a date to the house. Then came this extraordinary admission. Mr Hussain, of the Ministry of Information, did not know where the creator of his nation had been born.

Then someone took me to the right house. It was a three-storey building, rather tumbledown, in a poor, crowded area of Karachi, Newnham Road, in the district known as Kharadar. The ground floor was given over to little shops. There were wrought iron balconies. What annoyed me was that I could not make any Pakistani official interested in the birthplace. I put up the idea to Dr Qureshi, Minister of Information, that the house should be bought and made into a museum—a shrine. I pointed out that young Pakistanis might feel inspired to patriotic emotions if they were taken there and told, "Here was born the creator of your country". Dr Qureshi is a man who is apathetic about even his own ideas; he received mine with a weak smile and did nothing. I was annoyed by his apathy. I had the home photographed; I tried to awaken the interest of every official I met, but nothing happened.

About this time, the Mir of Hunza arrived to stay in the Metropole Hotel. A delightful, forthright ruler, came from his wild kingdom in the north, with his cousin. I met His Highness the Mir, who is a follower of the Aga Khan, speaking perfect English, with a slight touch of Sandhurst in his accent, learnt from officers who have been his guests, while on leave. He told me that before Pakistan, he always had plenty of officers to stay in his kingdom, which has Russians and Chinese for neighbours. He is forthright. The best story revealing this! He lunches in the dining room of the hotel and I see him almost every day. We were walking out of the dining room one day when Mr Soso, the restaurant manager, bowed very low and said, "I hope your Highness enjoyed your lunch."

The Mir answered, "No, I did not! Every day, the same damn thing."

Well, back to Jinnah's birthplace!

One Sunday I went to the beach to swim. As I was coming out of the sea, I saw Mr Allana, the ex-mayor of Karachi, also a follower of the Aga Khan, and very rich. He came down the beach towards me and said, "Mr Bolitho, I hope you will honour me by lunching in my bungalow. I have also his Highness the Mir of Hunza." I accepted and we walked up to the beach towards the bungalow. On the way, Mr Allana said, "Mr Bolitho, His Highness wishes very much to swim but he has brought no bathing clothes. You are about the same circumference as His Highness and it would be a great kindness if you…"

Of course, I agreed. I dried my swimming shorts on the fence, dressed, and was delighted. The Mir's wife was there, ignoring purdah, and the talk was easy and often amusing.

After lunch, the Mir went off to swim and Mr Allana said, "Mr Bolitho, it is a great kindness that you lent His Highness your swimming suit, and it is an honour that you have come to Pakistan to write the biography of Quaid-i-Azam. If there is anything I can do for you while you are in Pakistan, you have only to ask me."

I thought of Jinnah's birthplace, and my dream of a museum. I said, more or less, "Mr Allana, I seek nothing for myself in Pakistan. But I have one ambition—to see the birthplace of Quaid-i-Azam purchased and turned into a museum and library—a shrine, Mr Allana, so that you may take young Pakistanis there and say, 'Here the creator of Pakistan was born'."

Mr Allana agreed. I only know that the house was purchased within a week or so. Of course a great many people claimed that it was their idea. But I'd had my way and I don't mind two hoots who enjoys the credit. But I must add that it was not through any feat of scholarship or cleverness on my part. It all comes from the fact that I was more or less the same circumference as His Highness the Mir of Hunza.

– 15 February 1952 –

I was alone in the hotel when news came of the death of the King. That was nine days ago. I feel strangely isolated—thinking of the day when I first met him at Glamis—when he was still Duke of York. I drove over with Lord and Lady Kinnaird, to tea, with them. Afterwards, when we were leaving, he came down and opened the door of the car. And the little girl, who handed the bread and butter, is now my sovereign.

I went today to the memorial service in the Anglican cathedral, in Karachi. It was moving, because there were all the English there, and one felt that one was in a church, in England. But not one Pakistani said a word of sympathy. In my heart of hearts, I dislike them. As Muslims, they are so different from the ones I knew in Trans-Jordan; the ones in King Abdullah's court. I came near to some of them. I came near to none of these.

Told by Sajjad Raza

In July 1947, just before Partition, Sir Francis Mudie, who had been Governor of Sindh, was appointed Governor of the Punjab. The next Governor of Sindh moved into the house for a while. (He was Sir Ghulam Hussain Hidayatullah.) After Partition, Hidayatullah moved to a new house and Jinnah moved in, as Governor-General.

Sir Francis Mudie's Military Secretary had taken the house croquet set with him to Lahore, without marking the inventory. And Hidayatullah had made off with the books from the library, leaving the shelves empty.

Jinnah immediately checked the inventory. He saw the empty shelves and said, "What is this?"

"This is the library, Sir", answered his secretary. "Where are the books?" asked Jinnah. When he was told he said, "Go and bring them back." And they were brought back.

Later, in Lahore, when Jinnah was staying with Sir Francis Mudie, Jinnah said, "You know, a theft took place in the house after you left. The croquet set was stolen." Sir Francis Mudie had to explain that his staff had taken them and that he was very sorry.

– 1 March 1952 –

Metropole Hotel, Karachi

The second anniversary dinner of the Karachi Chamber of Commerce. The Governor-General, Sir (*sic*) Ghulam Mohammed was the guest of honour. Fifteen minutes before he arrived at the hotel, two lorry loads of police, half of them in steel helmets and with rifles, arrived outside the hotel and more or less took it over. The unarmed police took up their positions behind the hollyhock clumps in the garden. Then the Governor-General arrived, followed by a police constable with a sten-gun at the ready. After the speeches, and after the formal dinner, the Governor-General came into the main hotel dining room where we were all sitting, and he sat at an unprepared table, to watch the cabaret. The man with the sten-gun, still at the ready, sat down at an empty table near by, with his eyes shared between the Governor-General and the stage. During all this the band played "Lollaby of Broadway".

– 1 March 1952 –

Admiral and Mrs Jefford, and Wendy, to lunch. He is a delight. He stood up to Jinnah and therefore earned his respect — and got it. He has created the Pakistan navy. He is preparing a report for me, to use in my book.

* * * *

– 10 March 1952 –

Notes on Talk with Jamshed Nusserwanjee

A dear old Parsee gentleman. A theosophist who came to see me at the Metropole Hotel. He wore a long white coat and check grey hat. He recommended me to see Kanji Dwarkadas when I go to Bombay. He said he was an old friend of Jinnah and then used a nice phrase; he said, "His memory is very beautiful".

He said of Jinnah, "He was emotional and affectionate, but he was unable to demonstrate it. All was control, control!"

Then, "I saw him once in tears. It is a fine thing that I can tell you. It was in 1927 [1928], during the Congress session in Calcutta."

He paused then and said, "I shall write it out for you".

Again, of Jinnah, "There was some kind of loneliness about Jinnah. A lonely man."

Next day, Jamshed Nusserwanjee bought me the following notes:

'The Parting of the Ways'

During the Congress session at Calcutta in 1927 [All Parties National Convention in December 1928], a telegram came from Mr Jinnah, who was in Delhi, saying that he and six other colleagues of the Muslim League would like to meet and discuss certain points with the Congress committee—these were their demands for a settlement with Congress. Mr Jawaharlal Nehru was President of the Congress. Most of the leaders were against the plan, but Mahatma Gandhi prevailed upon them to invite Mr Jinnah and his party to Calcutta. They came and Mr Jinnah placed the demands of his party before a special committee, but they rejected them. There were eighteen against and two for: those two were Mahatma Gandhi and myself. Mr Jinnah returned to his hotel in tears. Mahatma Gandhi went to his room, sadly, at 3 a.m., and span on his spinning wheel until 6 o'clock in the morning. About 8:30 next morning, Mr Jinnah and his party left for Delhi. I went to see him off at the station. He shook hands with me and these were his words, "Well, Jamshed, this is the parting of the ways".

"Thereafter, Mr Jinnah rejected all proposals, even the All-Party resolutions, consistently. He would not trust the Congress leaders. He attempted to reach reconciliation at the Round Table Conference in

London, but there again he was disappointed. But these are matters of records.

"Twice, actually, it had seemed that reconciliation was fairly close, but Mr Jinnah was absent from India and he would not consider such reconciliation.

"Then came the suggestion of a separate Pakistan. Many of his own colleagues believed that it was an impossible idea, but Mr Jinnah was one who did not budge and he got what he wanted.

"Mr Jinnah was a thoroughly trained constitutional person; when the Radcliffe Award was given, defining the border lines of Punjab and Bengal, between India and Pakistan, he was advised by all his colleagues not to accept it. But he stood firm, saying that once the arbitration was accepted, then the award must be honourably accepted also.

"Mr Jinnah wanted the minorities to stay in Pakistan. He promised them full protection, and he kept his promise. But, unfortunately, trouble began in West Pakistan and most of the Hindus left. I saw him in tears on 7th January 1948, when he visited a camp of minorities in Karachi. Mr Jinnah did suggest, at one time, the peaceful transfer of population between India and Pakistan. He said that if two could not live together peacefully, the best way was the exchange of population, organized in orderly ways.

"It is not true that Mahatma Gandhi and Mr Jinnah had any ill feeling between them, or that there was any dislike for each other. Mr Jinnah never accepted the saintliness of Mahatma Gandhi, but he knew that Gandhi was agreeable to settlement with Muslims and that he supported Muslims whenever they made political demands. It is true, however, that Mahatma Gandhi was consistently against Partition up to the last, and that Partition was accepted by Congress against his wishes.

"Mr Jinnah was never a demonstrative person. He always controlled and held back any kind of emotion. He was reserved, dignified and lonely...

"Mr Jinnah was for Independence since 1916 and he served India as a staunch Nationalist. But he could not accept Mahatma Gandhi's satyagraha [sit-down-strike] or non-cooperation, and he remained aloof from this part of Congress activities, as Mrs Besant did. He would not break laws or court jail-punishment. Mr Jinnah was too refined and had presumably to win over Muslim leaders and he did manage to get many Muslim leaders out of the Congress. Mr Jinnah had no friendliness for the activities of Muslim priests or ulema [religious heads]. He had never any kind of outward show for Religious ceremonies or Prayers. He had no ill feeling for Hindus. He was a type of constitutional ruler."

* * * *

At last, I was invited to lunch by the British High Commissioner. After being entertained to curry struggles in Pakistani houses, with not one object worth looking at, it was a delight to eat at a table with good silver and see pictures and furniture that brought some of the beauty of England into this parched, ugly city—all camel dung and sand.

* * * *

News from Nagpur that a Mr Awari wishes to have Queen Victoria's statue removed from in front of the Madhya Pradesh Assembly buildings, because it "reminds us of our past slavery". What half witted nonsense! And, in London, arrangements are in hand to put memorial plaques on the houses where Gandhi and Jinnah lived when they were students. One purrs with the warmth of civilization.

– 3-8 April 1952 –

It was refreshing beyond measure to leave the agitated, tree-less port of Karachi, teeming with merchants and refugees, and swollen with civil servants—to make the journey six hundred miles inland, to Lahore. The cool train carried us away from the harshness of the Sindh desert, towards the trees, the gardens and the tombs of the old Mughal city. Here the trees have deep roots, for the earth is well-watered, wet food for the trees instead of the stingy dryness of sand. Where trees have roots, the people also have roots. The moment you arrive in Lahore, you lean towards the vast trees. When it is dark, they seem like fabulous elephants, moving against the sky. You are immediately conscious of the rich earth beneath you, from which all this life springs, and you imagine that even the voices of the people have a peace and security in them that you do not find in new places.

Just as you sense the depth of the earth, you also sense the depth of its history. Alexander the Great must have passed quite near, after he defeated Porus, ruler of the Punjab, in 326 BC...

It is a pity that Mohammed Ali Jinnah was not interested in the voices of history…"How shall I treat you?" Alexander asked the warrior, and Porus answered, "Like a king". Even Jinnah's cool blood might have been quickened by valour; such examples from these giants of behaviour.

It is attractive to think over this; that, within a few miles of where Alexander rode, at the head of his army, the monumental 'Pakistan Resolution' was passed in 1940. At the great meeting in Lahore, within the bowl called the Wrestling Ring, the decision was made, that the Muslims would save themselves from the Hindus and form their own nation…. But there was no sign that here Jinnah had hypnotised the multitude with the promise that they would be free, strong and great. The words of the stubborn, brave men, who dare to turn the tides of history do not alter very much. Alexander said, "It is sweet to live with courage". Jinnah said, "Failure is a word unknown to me".

…He [Jinnah] was more remarkable than the traditional heroes in that he was not a soldier and unaware of battle. All his victories came from his mind. [Cf. see below General McCoy's comment.]

* * * *

Conversation with Abdul Wahid, 'Dawn' Representative in Lahore

ABDUL WAHID: "Jinnah had no contact with the masses, but somehow he was able to feel the pulse of the people—their reactions, dissatisfactions and ambitions. His lieutenants—Liaquat Ali Khan, the Khan of Mamdot, etc., also had no contact with the masses. They were well-educated landlords or industrialists, with no weight behind them, like a trade union leader or a socialist who has risen from the ranks. Jinnah's choice of such people was deliberate."

MAZHAR AHMED (interrupted): "Jinnah picked men whom he considered to be on his intellectual level."

ABDUL WAHID: "Particularly in the Punjab, the great stimulus to Jinnah's power over the Muslim people was provided by the oppression of the Sikhs and Hindus. Thus, before Partition, when Muslims were outnumbered and dominated by Sikhs and Hindus, everything that Jinnah did for the independence of the Muslims was a step in the right direction.

"After partition, when the Muslims had their own country, Jinnah's opinions and decisions began to be doubted by some of his own people. I feel, as many others do, that Jinnah died at the right time."

MAZHAR AHMED (interrupted): "Jinnah's process of thought and leadership were interrupted by his death. Had he been allowed to complete his programme, the finished result might have been entirely satisfactory. As it was, his death cut it short—thus, any complaints against him are like the dissatisfaction of an audience which suddenly sees the curtain rung down in the middle of the last act."

ABDUL WAHID: "Just prior to Partition, in Lahore, the British I.C.S. officials—completely out of tune with the aims of the socialist government in England—and still keeping to their own ideas—became callous and indifferent to the rape, slaughter and destruction that were taking place. They stayed in their clubs, throughout the night, drinking and dancing with Anglo-Indian girls, and staggered out into the morning, over the corpses that lined the road, to return and sleep in their homes."

HE SAID: "I owe everything to the British; my education, thought and way of life. I am grateful for this. But the brutal indifference of the majority of the civil administrators in Lahore, in the last days, was comparable to everything I have read about the last days of Rome."

MAZHAR (interrupted): "It is unfair to generalize. Many British service officers were so devoted to their duty and their responsibilities that they were killed in trying to help refugees."

* * * *

Note by Derek Peel

Abdul Wahid's comments are very melodramatic. It is perhaps true that some of the wartime civil servants were not of the same calibre as their predecessors; true also that it is easy to appear callous—as many doctors appear callous—in the face of mass human suffering; especially in a country where human life itself is counted for so little. But it is obviously not true that within the disciplined pattern of a British administration a man would be allowed to sleep of his "drunkenness" during normal working office hours. Perhaps some Britons were seen standing helplessly on the sidelines during the "last days" while savage butchery—often highly organized—went on before their eyes; but it must be remembered that most of the British troops had been withdrawn, and that civil authority was then in the hands of the Indian and Pakistani police. The "rape, slaughter and destruction' continued for many months after the "Transfer of Power" to India and Pakistan.

Begum Shah Nawaz[7]

I talked to her alone and thought her superior to any other woman I have met in Pakistan, because she has no rancour in her. She said:

> I was born in 1896. I can remember the night when my father thought of the words, "Muslim League". It was a hot, summer evening, after dinner, and we young ones had gone to bed. My father suddenly called out, "I have thought of the name. 'Association' is no good. The only word that appeals to me is 'League'."

The butchery in the Partition massacres broke my father's heart.[8] He came to Lahore for two months after partition. He said to me, "You are a legislator and I want you to stick to it". This was when I was asked to go on a lecture tour in America.

Jinnah arrived in Karachi after partition without even an inkstand.

When I was in London I arranged a dinner and theatre for Jinnah to meet Dr Buchman. That was in 1946. It was to see a play by the Moral Re-armament people. We had supper in Dr Buchman's house afterwards and Jinnah was full of fun and anecdotes and stayed to the end.

Jinnah once said to me, after talking of the failure of his marriage, "I have my grandchildren to play with." Jinnah needed understanding and patience. His wife had neither. She was gay and impressionable and liked to shock him.

– 6 April 1952 –

Wing Commander M. Ata Rabbani, former Air ADC to Jinnah[9]

"In July 1947 I was on leave when I received a telegram ordering me to report at Delhi. I was then 27. On my way back in the train, I read in a newspaper that Jinnah was to fly to Karachi with his ADCs and I thought to myself, 'How wonderful it would be if only I could fly him. I had met him only once.'

"I arrived in Delhi and I was summoned by Liaquat Ali Khan. He said, 'How would you like to be ADC to the Quaid?' I answered, 'I would love to!'

"He said, 'You had better go in and see the old man. He wants a chat with you!'

"I went to the Quaid's house, and after he had asked me a few questions, he said, 'Tell Liaquat I approve of his choice'."

"So, on 7th August, with Ahsan, the Naval ADC, Miss Jinnah, and the Quaid, we flew from Delhi to Karachi, in Mountbatten's white dakota. There were only a handful of people to see him off. Before leaving the house Jinnah had given me a cane basket full of documents to take to the aircraft. Before we took off, he went out to be photographed, but he did not speak. As we taxied out he made only one remark; he murmured, 'That's the end of that', meaning, I supposed, the end of the struggle on Indian soil.

"He was perfectly dressed, as ever, in a white *sherwani*, and his Jinnah cap. Dark glasses. Miss Jinnah sat in the front and I sat opposite the Quaid. He had an immense bundle of newspapers which he read immediately and during the entire flight. Only once, he spoke. He handed me some of the newspapers and said, 'Would you like to read these?'

"This was his only remark during a journey of 4 hours—all he said in what one might describe as the greatest hours of his life.

"We reached Karachi in the evening, and as we flew over Mauripur, Jinnah looked down and saw thousands of people waiting for him, including many women—waiting on the sand, to greet him.

"Even then there was no change in his expression and he did not say a word. He was the first to emerge from the aircraft, followed by Miss Jinnah. All the Muslim big guns were waiting for him. He shook hands with a few of them, and then got into the motor-car.

"The thousands of people were cheering, 'Pakistan Zindabad!' 'Quaid-i-Azam Zindabad,' still he showed no signs of pleasure. He was very tired and he entered Government House, for the first time, without a word. After two or three days he changed his apartment from the left to the right side of the house.

"The day I remember best was the day when the members of the Cabinet were sworn in. When everything was ready, I went up to him, in his room, and told him that the ministers were waiting. All he said was, 'Shall we move?' He walked downstairs, and when we came to the first floor, he paused and went out of the balcony, to look at the crowd.

"It was the first time that I ever saw him show that he was happy. He made only one remark, when I said to him, 'It is becoming cloudy outside. It might rain.' He answered, 'No, I know them well. Karachi clouds do not have any water in them.' He went through the ceremony without sharing any emotion, but when I escorted him back to his apartment, he seemed happy.

"I became fond of him as my leader, and as a symbol. It had been my fond desire to be his pilot and I had come closer than that."

* * * *

Notes Regarding a Private Luncheon Party, at which Jinnah was Present, made by then Lt. Col. (Now Maj.-Gen.) H.I. Ahmad

"During the summer of 1945 when I was an instructor at the Staff College, Quetta, Mr Jinnah, President of the All India Muslim League, and Miss Jinnah came to stay with Qazi M. Isa, President of the Baluchistan Muslim League. All the time there was a good deal of discussion between the staff and the students of the staff college regarding the proposed plan for the establishment of a separate state known as Pakistan. The consensus of opinion, particularly among the senior British Army officers, was that this was rather an impractical step. The most they would admit was the possibility of autonomous Hindu and Muslim States with a combined Defence and Foreign Policy.

"The then Comdt. Staff College, Maj.-Gen. S.F. Irwin, OBE, expressed a desire to meet Mr Jinnah and accordingly a luncheon was arranged at my residence. During luncheon the Quaid, in very measured tones and with a wealth of detail, gave his reasons for the establishment of a separate Muslim State. There was a good deal of questioning by Maj.-Gen. Irwin, and Col. Crocker, the deputy commandant and there was a discussion regarding the Army. The Quaid said that no state could be called independent unless it had its own Defence Services and its own Foreign Policy, and he was convinced that once Pakistan was established, these things would come into being. Maj.-Gen. Irwin said that he had never before heard so clear an exposition of so intricate and difficult a subject and that he was now convinced of the necessity for Pakistan."

Mazhar Ahmad's Notes after Listening to Me Talk with Prof. B.A. Hashmi, Principal of the Central Training College, Lahore

"Professor Hashmi first met the Quaid at the Muslim University in Aligarh. When Jinnah's wife died, Hashmi went, with a friend, to visit him and offer condolences. They were shown into a room and Jinnah walked in. There were no signs of grief on his face. Hashmi was with Jinnah for a whole hour, and they talked on every subject under the sun, but not one word was said about the recent bereavement. Hashmi left Jinnah without being able to get in one word on the real purpose of his visit. The only sign of death in the house was the formal black armband on Jinnah's sleeve.

"Professor Hashmi told us of a girl in Quetta who confessed to Qazi Isa, now Pakistan ambassador in Argentina, that she found Jinnah's hands very attractive. Isa told Jinnah. A few days later, Jinnah found himself sitting next to the same girl at the races. Catching her off guard, he said, 'Now, now! don't keep looking at my hands.'

"Professor Hashmi believes that Jinnah relaxed with younger people who were not directly related to him and who had no political axes to grind."

* * * *

Stories told by Two Masters at the Govt. Training College, Lahore

"The Quaid was asked to unfurl a flag at a school in Larkana, in Sind—long before Partition. He advised the school authorities, 'open rifle clubs'.

"As a boy of ten, Jinnah once stole a free ride on the footboard of a gharry, with another schoolboy. The driver shoved them off with his whip and said, 'The urchins! They must be Musalmans.' Jinnah said to himself, 'Is it so bad to be a Musalman?' (I do not believe this last one)."

* * * *

Conversation with Farrukh Amin, former Secretary to Jinnah

"Jinnah never read very much for pleasure. A few American magazines lay beside his bed, but his main, insatiable interest was newspapers, from all over the world. For many years he kept books of newspaper cuttings, filed and annotated with his own abbreviations. These are, presumably with Miss Jinnah."

I said that I doubted, whether Miss Jinnah had any really important documents, as Jinnah wrote so little. I remarked also on her own innocent, rather schoolgirl knowledge and use of English.

Farrukh Amin agreed, then said, "Jinnah annotated the books he read, in the margins and on the blank pages. These annotated books would be of interest if you could use them."

* * * *

Miss Jinnah

Someone I cannot very well name said to me this morning, "Fatima Jinnah! She is a sour old fascist. And she was beastly to Jinnah. After his daughter moved, he had to keep the photographs of her in his bathroom. He told a friend of mine that she insisted on them being moved from the rest of the house."

* * * *

The Government

Robert Hack, of the British Council, told me a story of his journey by motor-bicycle from Karachi to Lahore. He stopped to lunch, near a well. An old farmer with a fine face, 'almost sanctified by his good living' invited him to go to a local meeting. Hack found a number of elderly, respectable men, one of whom complained that the present government of Pakistan would not tolerate any opposition. He said, 'The British, even in their Empire, were liberal.'

* * * *

The Museum

I went to the museum in Lahore because I was told that there were some interesting objects associated with Queen Victoria. Most curiously, the folding spectacles, given by the Queen, to Fakir Syed Nooruddin, were stolen on the day of my arrival in Lahore. There were few labels on the objects. But I saw a little grey clock, also a gift from Queen V. to Fakir Syed Nooruddin. There were some charming miniatures paintings, presumably Mughal. One was delightful and labelled, "A Lady with her maids enjoying rains". They were in the open, extending their hands to enjoy the cool showers. One realizes how climate influences the painter. One cannot imagine an English artist painting a lady and her maids enjoying the rain in a Sussex garden. Rain, a pleasure and a luxury in the Punjab, is a damned nuisance in England.

* * * *

A responsible old follower of the Aga Khan told me that Jinnah once chided the Aga Khan for the life he led in France and for being photographed with so many pretty girls around him. He asked how this life could be reconciled to his life as the religious leader of millions. The Aga Khan is said to have answered, "In India, 200 million Hindus worship cows. Am I not better than a cow?"

* * * *

Someone said to me, "Jinnah was strangely free from showman's tricks: when he arrived at Lucknow for the important meeting [to preside over the Muslim League session] in 1916, he stepped off the train, wearing an English suit, an English hat, and a malacca stick. The secretary of the Muslim League said, 'You cannot possibly face the crowd dressed like that.' He kept Jinnah waiting while he hurried to the market where he bought a tarbush and brought it back for him to wear."

* * * *

This story was told by a man who was in the room at the time of the incident. One day Jinnah said to Liaquat Ali Khan, "If we were in

England, I would elevate you to the House of Lords". Liaquat, an aristocrat at heart, did not realize until afterwards what Jinnah implied.

* * * *

– 2 April 1952 –

Conversation with A.B. (Sonny) Habibullah

"I was one of Jinnah's first disciples in the revived Muslim League and I was with him four years, from 1936 to 1940. In 1938 or 1939, a rather Nazi-minded man addressed Jinnah as 'The leader of my Nation'. Jinnah said, 'I may be your leader, but not of a separate nation'.

"Jinnah had a tremendous ego and was always susceptible to flattery. His marriage flattered him—the *crème de la crème* had fallen for him. Up to 1943 he would tolerate, even enjoy argument. But after that, when his health began to fail, he became impatient, refused to argue, and preferred 'yes men'. But his smile was always infectious, and his movement, when he threw his head back and laughed, was quite charming.

"His impatience—he discarded Mahmudabad for saying, 'My leader must not be the ablest politician, but the man who is closest to God'. He put Jehangir down when he became too powerful, even though he was devoted to Jinnah. He eliminated Ismail Khan, President of the UP Muslim League, because he would always oppose Jinnah when he thought him wrong.

"Jinnah never, or seldom, kept his servants more than a year. He also never kept his political friends. In the first Pakistan Cabinet there was not one single man who had been with him at the beginning.

"Jinnah's light reading was mostly Victorian literature, though he read little—Dickens, Macaulay. He was no scholar; he was culturally mediocre and very down to earth. He never had Nehru's culture, or his humanity. His English was not good, but when he spoke, you would forget that he was making mistakes. His greatest gift was a sort of sixth sense for appreciating a situation. But he never thought big; he was limited, within his singleness of purpose.

"Jinnah loved young men. If someone worshipped him, he would take them up like a puppy."

HECTOR BOLITHO: "His loneliness is an interesting theme. I think it is related to frustration and being hurt when he was young. He was poor after the death of his father and returned, from a certain recognition in London, to the humble life in Karachi. He went to Bombay and it was a long time before anyone believed in him, as he believed in himself. I see him during that period as a lonely, introvert dandy, antagonistic to society. Thus his marriage to the daughter of a Parsee knight was a triumph: His rudeness to Governors is all part of that early frustration. He bullied his inferiors and could not relax with his betters."

SONNY HABIBULLAH (continued): "When Jinnah was asked to lunch by Lord Willingdon—he was then Governor of Bombay—Jinnah was flattered and he accepted, for himself and his wife, although he loathed Lord Willingdon. Mrs Jinnah was dressed very daringly for those days, low neckline and all that. Lady Willingdon said to an ADC, 'I am sure Mrs Jinnah must be feeling cold. Will you bring her a shawl?'

"The ADC brought the shawl. Jinnah, in anger, rose from the table and said, 'When Mrs Jinnah feels cold, she will say so, and ask for a wrap herself.' Then he stormed out, with his wife, and never went to Government House again."

HECTOR BOLITHO: "Lady Willingdon is a very silly woman. She should have known better. It is a pity, because Lord Willingdon was a great gentleman. It is a question, you know—how much were the wives of Britons appointed to India responsible for our losing her. Wives of senior army officers often lose the battles their husbands have won."

Sonny Habibullah told me about an important by-election at Jhansi, in the southern part of the UP [in mid July 1937]: "Nehru challenged Jinnah that the Muslim League would never win this election, which was regarded as a key election in the province. Jinnah ordered me down to Jhansi, to organize. Mahmudabad gave 10,000 rupees and a car. The collector of Jhansi said that the Muslim League had not got a hope, as votes were bought and sold. Heavy campaigning brought the Muslim League and Congress neck and neck in the towns, but the country people were to be swayed only with money.

"In one village, I saw 1000 Muslims outside a polling station, not voting. They wanted 10 rupees each, to vote for us. The priests harangued them, but to no avail. Suddenly, as I was talking to the headman, a man ran up and told him that his son was bleeding from the nose and mouth and was dying.

"Look what you have done, I said to the headman. Because of your wickedness, God is punishing you by taking away your son. The headman was very distressed and begged one of the maulvis to pray for his son.

"I told one maulvi to stay there and 'pray like hell' and I took another maulvi and the headman in my car to where the son was lying. I always carried ice and antiseptics etc. in my car. When I saw the boy I realized that he was only suffering from sunstroke. But I told the second maulvi to get down and 'pray like hell' also. I told him to ask God to forgive the father for his wickedness in wanting money for the votes of his village, and to save his son. I made an ice pack, which did the trick, and after twenty minutes the boy came to.

"The poor father was so overjoyed that he rushed to the villagers and said, 'This is an act of God.' He told them that their wickedness had been absolved only by the prayers of the priest, and that they were to go in and vote, without demanding money.

"Thus the Muslim League got a clear thousand votes and we won the election."

* * * *

Owain-Jones[10] on the Radcliffe Award

"The award was not made known until one week or so after Independence, and Radcliffe had returned to England. The original Mountbatten line had been messed about as much that even sub-districts had been divided, and India had been given one small but vital stretch of road that opened the way for them to Kashmir." Owain-Jones said that when Radcliffe returned to Delhi, before going home, he saw Mountbatten many times and that this concession to India was an afterthought, insisted on by Mountbatten.

* * * *

In Lahore we met D. Peel-Yates. He said that Jinnah used to wear a small badge on his lapel, showing India, with the Muslim areas marked in green—the areas now roughly embraced by Pakistan. (Others have told me that this is not true.) Peel-Yates said that Jinnah had three ambitions. 1. To become the highest paid lawyer in India. This he did. 2. To marry the most beautiful girl in India. This, so far as Bombay society was concerned, also came true. 3. To become President of Congress. Peel-Yates said that Jinnah's interest in the Muslim League, his later opposition to Congress, and his desire to establish Pakistan, was the outcome of the denial of this third ambition. (Pakistanis to whom I spoke all denied this third point. But the opinion is interesting as that of an Englishman who has lived in this country for many years, but not concerned with its internal politics.)

* * * *

Jinnah, Speaking to Punjab Muslim Students' Federation, 2 March 1941

"I am not a learned Maulana, or a Maulvi; nor do I claim to be learned in theology, but I also know a little of my faith, and I am a humble and proud follower of my faith."

* * * *

Jinnah to the Journalists' Association, Allahabad, 5 April 1942

"I hope that I will see it [the creation of Pakistan] during my life time and, if I do not see it—I have no son to succeed me—perhaps one who succeeds to the ideal for which I am fighting, which is in the best interest of everyone, would see it an accomplished fact." This is described to me as a 'badly reported' statement by Jinnah to the Journalists' Assn. [Association] Allahabad, 5th April 1942.

* * * *

There is one change in the monuments in Lahore that saddens the heart of the Briton passing by. Queen Victoria's statue has been removed from under its ornate stone canopy near the Punjab Assembly, and it is now in a cellar in the museum. Muslims are taught to abandon all effigies and graven images, so there was a convenient argument for those who insisted on the removal. But someday, when tempers are quiet and life in Pakistan admits the value of gestures, I hope that the Queen will be brought out of her dark store; and that some Punjabi boy who has studied his history, might carve on the base of the bronze the words Queen Victoria used when the draft of the Indian Proclamation was placed before her, in 1858. She thought that the phrasing was wrong in spirit that, as a "female sovereign", speaking to "a hundred million Eastern people on assuming the direct government over them", the proclamation should "breathe feelings of generosity, benevolence and religious toleration".

* * * *

Before leaving Lahore I met Peer Tajuddin, barrister-at-law, of 7 Queen's Road, Lahore. On the way to Rawalpindi, Mazhar Ahmad who was also present at the interview wrote these notes on the conversation.

Peer Tajuddin said that though Quaid-i-Azam led a very active life, he was essentially a very lonely man. Quaid married Ruttie, the beautiful daughter of the multi-millionaire Sir Dinshaw Petit, when she was still in her teens. But Peer Tajuddin says it was she who "chased" Jinnah. Jinnah at that time was a smart and fashionable man-about-town. His reputation as a brilliant lawyer and a man of integrity was beginning to form. As a comparatively older man, he excited Ruttie's young imagination. "She hero-worshipped him." The Parsee community would have been against marriage with a Muslim, but Ruttie did not care. "She took her umbrella under her arm and went straight to Jinnah's house."

Jinnah loved his wife but she did not live very long. From her he had only one child—a daughter: Dina. But she returned to the Parsee fold "much as the Roman Catholics do". Dina married a rich Parsee in Paris called Wadia who had a French mother and who was a Roman Catholic by faith. The Parsees were very happy to get Dina back into the fold through her marriage to Wadia even though the texture of their religion had changed. To Jinnah the loss in marriage of his daughter and the death of his beloved wife meant the end of family life. When domestic happiness was lost and family felicity disappeared, it left a scar on Jinnah's mind and the sadness was reflected in his character. But Jinnah was not inclined to be soft, and to admit defeat in love and domestic affairs was not in his nature. Deprived of a family life, he was able to devote all his time and energies to work for the good of the Muslims. He stopped accepting any briefs which would entail going out of Bombay and generally he began to lose interest in his profession. This coincided, in 1937, with the rejuvenation of the Muslim people.

Peer Tajuddin once had to give evidence before the Sandhurst Committee on which Mr Jinnah sat as representative of the Muslims while Pandit Motilal Nehru represented the Congress. The same evening at the Maiden's Hotel in Delhi, Quaid saw the Peer Sahib sitting in the lobby and asked him over to his room for a friendly chat. Peer Tajuddin was with Mr Jinnah from 10 p.m. to 5 in the morning. The talk was friendly and animated. Mr Tajuddin asked Quaid-i-Azam "do you know of any honest men in Politics?" Quaid-i-Azam answered, "Yes Sir Pherozeshah Mehta and Gopal Krishna Gokhale." (Mehta had helped Jinnah to become a presidency magistrate in Bombay during his early judicial career and for Gokhale, of the Servants of India Society, Jinnah had worked as Secretary—both these men Jinnah admired).

Peer Tajuddin said, "They are both dead. Can you name any living?" But Mr Jinnah could not though Gandhi and Motilal Nehru were both alive and active in the field of Indian Politics.

Peer Tajuddin said, "Jinnah could not be purchased by anybody."

* * * *

– 11 April –

Visit to Liaquat Gardens [Rawalpindi] with James Hardy, Assistant District Commissioner of Police, who was present when Liaquat Ali Khan was assassinated—at Rawalpindi. Hardy described the scene: We walked to a bare stretch of ground, with a few thirsty trees and some flowering shrubs in tin tubs. The ground has since been called Liaquat Gardens. Hardy told me that half a lakh [50,000] of people were gathered on the ground to hear Liaquat speak. There were 300 policemen. Liaquat walked towards the dais, under an arch of spears, held by fifty Muslim guards. By his own orders, Liaquat sat alone on the dais, with the military [political] secretary behind him. He was to make an announcement, probably concerning Kashmir. The address of welcome was read and then presented to him. It was placed on the table before him. Then the president of the local branch of the Muslim League went to the dais and said that Liaquat would address the crowd. There were cheers and the president stepped down again.

Hardy said, "Liaquat stood up and took three steps forward. He had said only, 'Brothers of the congregation', in Urdu, when there were two shots. He fell, dragging the rostrum with him. There was pandemonium. I was sitting on ground level. As I leapt up on the dais, another shot was fired. I went down on my knees, leaning over him. I said, 'where have you been hurt?' He said, 'I feel pain in my back, on my left side.' I said, 'Would you like some water? I will get a doctor.' There was another volley of shots, from the police, fired indiscriminately. I lowered myself over Liaquat's body, on my hands. I could hear him reciting the Kalma—the Muslim creed. I unbuttoned his coat and saw blood, as I reached the fourth button.

"Sadik [Siddique] Ali Khan, the military [political] secretary, had caught Liaquat as he fell. A doctor appeared and I pushed to find a car or an ambulance. Liaquat had lost consciousness: his eyeballs had turned upwards, and his mouth had fallen open.

"The pale-skinned little Afghan who had fired the shot with a 38 Inger, was set on by the crowd, who were out of control. His ribs were broken by men who smashed at him with the heavy palm post. There were spear wounds and four revolver wounds in his body.

"From the Liaquat Gardens, I went to the broadcasting studio. There was a recording machine and microphone on the dais and as Liaquat fell, he must have dragged the microphone with him. I heard the pathetic record, played for me at the studio—the shots, the moans, a gasp, and, faintly, the prayer."

* * * *

10 April, Conversation with Lt.-Gen. Sir Ross McCoy, an Australian, now Chief Military Advisor to Pakistani Army

General McCoy, speaking of Pakistanis, "They are like an adolescent who does not know what to do with his hands. He is terribly anxious to be taken notice of, but he does not know what to do where he is."

General McCoy was Commander of Peshawar Area at the time of Partition. He said, "Jinnah never spoke to me of the problems of the Army. In no sense was he a soldier, nor had he much knowledge of military history. Other creators of countries, like Cavour, Garibaldi, and Bismarck, considered their triumphs and strategy from a military point of view. This did not seem to enter Jinnah's head, and it might be said that, from a military point of view, Partition was a foolhardy act. Jinnah left to Liaquat Ali Khan the task of Minister of Defence."

* * * *

Brigadier Sir Hissamud Din Khan called on me at the hotel [at Peshawar]. An absolute pet. He said, "I am descended from King Ahmad Shah Abdali, and my ancestors came from Persia in the mid-eighteenth century." I said that I was pleased to be away from Karachi and that I was happy when I was in country where trees were growing.

I said that cities built in sand, where there were no trees, did not endure. He quoted an old Persian saying, "The roots are the people and the branches are the King—and the tree cannot live without the roots"— A tree cannot live without its roots, nor a king without his people.

He said, "For eleven years I was in the Council of State during which I saw Jinnah very often. I was CGS to the Nawab of Bhopal, and Jinnah used to come to see him. They were real friends. Jinnah had the best brain I have ever met in my life. The spirit he left in Pakistan is unbelievable, especially in the army. They would go through fire or jump into the sea for him."

(I did not interrupt to say how much Jinnah would have despised them for doing so.)

"I am a Frontier man. Karachi does not suit me. When Jinnah came to stay with the Nawab his tastes were very simple. When I asked him what sort of food he wanted, he said 'Dal and rice'."

(I thought of the special dishes he used to order from the Palace Hotel in Karachi, his liking for the Savoy and the Carlton in London, and his appetite for caviar).

"When he spoke, everyone listened with heart and ear. He was very careful in choosing his words."

(Of course I did not interrupt, but I thought the old soldier was imagining a little).

Then he spoke of himself. "My father was the first Indian to hold the Queen's Commission, and at that time, he was the only Indian who held it. He had the KCVO, and the KCIE. My uncle, Colonel Nawab was ADC to Prince Albert Victor in Queen Victoria's time. I knew Queen Victoria. She signed my commission. I went to the coronation of King Edward VII and have served in the army forty-seven years. (This seems muddled, as his commission was signed by Queen Victoria. I saw it.) I hope to go to the coronation of Queen Elizabeth II. I was ADC to King Edward VII and King George V. I still shoot in the hills and go fishing."

Then followed a nice incident, which shows how natural these proud Pathans are, and how free of the pretences and self-consciousness of the politicians and officials in Karachi.

Sir Hissamud Din Khan said, "What are you doing this evening?" I told him that I was expected to dine with the great Khan Abdul Qayyum Khan, Chief Minister of the North West Frontier Province government. He said, "Oh, I am giving an evening garden party. Come there instead. I'll ring the Chief Minister and ask him to come too."

And so it was. We went to an incredible night garden party, with a pipe band playing *The Green Hills of Tyron* and merry English and Scottish airs, as if Independence had never happened. Every now and then, Sir Hissamud Din Khan took us into the house, past the souvenirs of his Englishness, into a little room, where we were given secret whiskies and sodas of terrifying strength. I remember everything through a delightful haze, and, when someone made a speech, in Pashtu, the very English voices of the Pathan officers, trained at Sandhurst saying, "Here! Here!"

* * * *

Notes on Talk with Khan Abdul Qayyum Khan, Chief Minister of NWFP Government

A big, round man, with the sharp-edged method of a lawyer. I went to see him in his room at the Ministry. There was a photograph of Jinnah on his desk, and not one, untidy paper. It was absolutely clear. The Minister for Education told me afterwards that the Chief Minister has a mania for being rid of papers and that he works on files in his motorcar. No eastern laziness here.

The Chief Minister compared Jinnah's visits to the North West Frontier. "When he came here in 1937 [1936], Congress was at the height of its power. He wished to win leading Frontier men over to the Muslim League, but he had a poor response. He argued long hours, but failed.

"Shortly after 1937 I was elected to the Central Assembly of India and I saw a great deal of Jinnah. I was bitterly opposed to him at the time. But we gradually discovered that the Hindus aimed at domination. We had to think whether, in creating our own Muslim ideal, we would be falling from the sky and getting stuck on top of a dead tree. Jinnah knew what was right and what was wrong. No one could influence him.

But his Pakistan slogan was mocked at the time. Here in the NWF Province we thought it an idle dream. Jinnah used to say to me, 'There is no alternative but to join the Muslim League'. He would fight the world rather than yield. He had a deadly effect in debate—always tried to speak last, after the leader of the Congress Party.

"In 1944 or 1945 [1944] I saw Jinnah in Kashmir on holiday. He asked me why I did not join the Muslim League...that the bulk of the Hindus only wished to use us and to dominate us.

"In 1945 I was in Lucknow and there I wrote a letter to Jinnah and said that the only way of saving the Muslims was in the creation of Pakistan. After writing this letter, and seeing it published, I left for Peshawar—by train from Lahore. I was garlanded everywhere we stopped. The change had come. I was elected and we went into opposition. After that the people were all for Pakistan. Congress lost its hold on the Frontier and when Nehru came, to awaken, or re-awaken the power of Congress, he was stoned beside the road of the Khyber Pass.

"I was arrested and sent to jail for four months. Then came the plebiscite, with a British General in charge. The result was 52 per cent for Pakistan. In 1946 [1945], when Jinnah came, again, he was splendidly received—so different from 1937."

I did not feel that I would learn much of Jinnah as a man from Khan Abdul Qayyum Khan, but I was aware of his own hard talents.

* * * *

The Khyber Pass, 13 April

We drove as far as the Afghan frontier, to the road that leads to Kabul. When we were in Karachi, the Pakistani politicians were angry with the Afghanistan politicians. On the frontier, where the Afghan sentry stood within a few yards of the Pakistani sentry, there was no anger; indeed, there is such friendliness between the two outposts that the Afghans brought troops from the far northern part of the country to man the post. They hoped that this would break down the neighbourliness that even enemies might enjoy standing in the oven heat all day, with only a frontier between them.

So the Afghan sentry had a Mongolian look and the fair-skinned Pakistani Pathan on guard had an English look. (The romantic traveller might believe that his fairness and his apple cheeks are an inheritance from one of Alexander's soldiers who paused here, more than 2000 years ago.) Both the Afghan and Pakistani sentries are Muslims and, above the tempers of their politicians and the commands of their officers, they can hear the voice of the Prophet who is no small power over their minds. They brew their tea in the same pot and keep a peace their betters cannot achieve, over their inkpots and conference tables.

The chains between the two sentry posts is but a symbol; it is lowered frequently to allow mules and water carriers to pass, on their peaceful journey.

* * * *

Karachi, Metropole Hotel, 19 April 1952

Back to this incredible hotel. The band in the courtyard playing the same tunes, the sound of the donkey bells, and the little birds. While I have been away, one of them has come into my bedroom and made its nest above the electric fan. Now, as an English animal lover, I cannot turn on the fan and have arranged for a separate one, to be stood on the table. It is picturesque—but a damned musician. The bird, not the fan.

We have three rooms each with its own bathroom. The bathroom to the sitting room is therefore not used—except to store our suitcases. There I carry on a deck business. I can order what food I like and merely sign for it. I order piles of sandwiches and the bearers and servants are fed on them, in the bathroom. I have even smuggled little parcels of them out of the hotel, for the poor on the road. There is no end to my dishonesty. I love the experience of robbing the rich to feed the poor.

My ethics were more staunch when I arrived than they are now. Two episodes frighten me and make me feel that I am yielding to the easy ways of the East and that it is time I went back to London, SW. My hotel is paid by the Government and, as Suleri and others are against my appointment, I am scrupulous in watching every item charged on the bills, which I sign and I found that they were charging about £1 a bottle for lime juice. So, I immediately arranged to buy my own from the shop, for a few shillings. But, the other evening, Mr Soso came to my table and said, "We have some caviar from Teheran". The very words were beautiful, so Derek Peel and I helped ourselves splendidly to "Caviar from Teheran". When the bill came for me to sign, the charge for the caviar was about £6. I had a vision of some clerk in the Ministry processing on my extravagance. I told Soso, "I simply cannot sign that." So he cancelled it and is making the amount up slowly, day by day.

My second sin. The secretary, who comes to help and hinder me each morning, reads my letters, on my desk, when I am out of the room. I saw him, twice, but he did not see me. Three days ago I became angry at certain delays in the Ministry, so I typed a letter, with a carbon copy, to my publishers in London, saying that owing to the delays I was seriously thinking of giving up my task and returning to England by the next ship. I left the carbon copy of the letter on my desk overnight. The secretary arrived in the morning. I left him alone in the room and everything worked as I hoped. He obviously read it because, within an hour of his leaving, Brelvi appeared, with the answers to all my questions, and the documents I had asked for. Well! It is time that I departed. The awful thing is that I felt more elated than ashamed.

I think that I should keep the following letters, as showing the difference between Miss Jinnah and Begum Liaquat Ali Khan. About 10th February I wrote Miss Jinnah a letter, asking if I might come to see her. I had been trying to locate the house in which Jinnah lived as a student, in London, with the hope that the London County Council would put a memorial plaque on the Wall.[11]

This is Miss Jinnah's reply.

FLAGSTAFF HOUSE,
15th Feb. 1952

Dear Mr. Bolitho,

Thank you for your letter dated 13th instant. Please let me know the subject matter which you desire to discuss with me.

Yours sincerely,

(Sd) Miss Fatima Jinnah

This is my reply to Miss Jinnah. I received no answer.

Hotel Metropole
Karachi
Pakistan

February 20, 1952

Dear Miss Jinnah,

I think I can achieve my purpose without seeing you. I have just received a letter from the London County Council, in reply to one from me. I suggested that it would be a pleasant and suitable memorial to Quaid-i-Azam if a plaque could be placed on the house in which he lived as a student in London. You may know that this is done in the case of men of fame and importance who have lived in London. The Chairman has written to me, asking for the address at which your brother lived during his student days. Perhaps, if you are interested in such a memorial, you would be so kind as to send me the address and the dates of his residence.

Yours sincerely,

About the same time, I received the following letter from Begum Liaquat.

18 Feb. 1951 [1952]

Dear Mr. Bolitho,

The book you so kindly sent has kept me going—I am very busy at the moment with Mrs Roosevelt's programme and hence can't get along as fast as I wish to finish it. I find it fascinating and easy reading. Do let me know how soon you want it back.

I have been praying for you to have better luck—my sympathies are with you. May be some day, you will help me with the late Prime Minister's Biography.

I was glad to have met you. It's very rare nowadays to come across people with such a fund of humour and deep understanding of the human mind. Your visit was exhilarating, to say the least.

Wishing you the best of luck in your future programme.

Yours sincerely,

Raa'na Liaquat Ali Khan

* * * *

In Anger

I sit here in this ridiculous hotel, hour after hour, day after day, the victim of dilatoriness, of their arrogance and their broken promises. I am told that I must expect this; that our standards are not the same, because east is east and west is west—I am bored with that argument. I was bored last night when Jafri came and said, "of course, I must expect to be let down by my own people, but I don't expect to be let down by the British".

I don't see why the British should be the sole nurses of ethics in the subcontinent. Really, I have tried to meet all this evasion and crookery with polite ethics, but it is wearing me out.

* * * *

Commander Ahsan,[12] Royal Pakistan Navy, formerly Naval ADC to Mountbatten and then to Jinnah, for ten months, from August 1947

Ahsan was in the aircraft—Mountbatten's Dakota—which brought Jinnah from Delhi to Karachi on 7 August 1947. (The following notes should be compared with those I made often taking to Rabbani, the air ADC.)

Ahsan said, "Contrary to his usual habits, Jinnah shook hands and said 'Goodbye' to all those who had come to see him off—mostly junior members of the staff, servants and stenographers. As he stepped into the plane he turned round and said, 'I suppose this is the last time I'll be looking at Delhi'.

"We took off just before lunch and Jinnah asked for his food soon after we left Delhi. The picnic lunch had been prepared by the Viceroy's servants. Jinnah complained bitterly—about the quality of the food, the inferior china and cutlery—and the thermos which had been provided.

"Jinnah read all the newspapers he had brought with him, then he passed them to us and dozed off. When we were approaching Karachi he suddenly became buoyant when he saw the milling masses of people below. At the airport, the huge crowds surged around the plane. Jinnah did not say very much, but he looked pleased—a sense of fulfilment. He handed me two packages—a despatch case and a sort of hold-all, and said, 'Now, I want you to make sure that you look after these'. They apparently contained important documents.

"There was the official welcome at Mauripur. Jinnah, who usually expected discipline from people, and who would refuse to greet them unless they formed up in an orderly line—this time cheerfully shook hands all round. He inspected the local Muslim guards in a very relaxed manner and he was most genial.

"The streets were lined with people all the way to Government House, except in one section where the welcome was not what he expected. He complained to me and I pointed out that it was probably a Hindu section, and that they had not got much to be jubilant about.

"At Government House he inspected the Guard of Honour. Later, he said to me, 'Do you know, we have to be very grateful to God for what we have achieved. I never expected to see Pakistan in my lifetime.'

"On that first day in Government House, he selected his own quarters. He said, 'This wing will not be occupied by anyone except myself and Miss Jinnah'. Then he went toward two other, big rooms and said, 'These will be for very important people. I don't want any governors of province or ministers in these rooms. Only very important people, such as the Shah of Persia, or the King of England.'

"He then asked for a radio, immediately. I said, 'You are tired, Sir. Why not leave it until tomorrow!' Jinnah replied, 'Don't have any of those delaying tactics with me'.

"He was very triumphant, yet, I think, humble for what he had achieved.

"I often went with Jinnah and Miss Jinnah, for the weekends, to Malir, (near Karachi) to the Amir of Bahawalpur's palace. One night at dinner, Jinnah hurried to me and said, 'Nobody had any faith in me. Everyone thought I was mad, except Miss Jinnah.' Then he paused and said—in front of her—'But, of course if she hadn't been with me all along, she wouldn't be sitting here with me now'.

"When Lord Mountbatten, as Governor-General of India, flew to Lahore to see Jinnah—on his way to England [This was when Mountbatten came to Lahore on 1 November 1947 to discuss and resolve the Kashmir issue, and not on his way to England]—Jinnah did not meet him at the airport; he did not even meet him at the front door, did not rise to greet him when he walked into the room.

"Afterwards, Mountbatten said to me, 'If he ever comes to Delhi, I shall greet him with all the ceremony and courtesy I can'.

"At the opening of the Constituent Assembly, Lady Mountbatten came with her husband. Mountbatten said to Jinnah that he would like

Lady Mountbatten to sit on the dais with them. Jinnah refused and said, 'My sister will sit in the distinguished visitor's gallery. Your wife will sit with her.'

"Before partition, when Lord Mountbatten was still Viceroy, Jinnah often annoyed him by just calling him "Mountbatten'. The Viceroy resented this, but never showed it."

Ahsan talked of Jinnah's relationship with Sir Zafrullah Khan, the Foreign Minister. "One day he went to a reception, in a lounge suit. He had just arrived from abroad or was just leaving, and his clothes were packed. Jinnah said, 'This is the last time you will come here improperly dressed'."

Ahsan said, of Jinnah's inability to keep his friends and trusted colleagues, "I believe that even Liaquat would have been dismissed had Jinnah lived for a few more months". (I did not tell Ahsan that I had seen the letters exchanged between Jinnah and Liaquat, in which Liaquat resigned after a scene at dinner, in which Jinnah was very rude. He saw Liaquat afterwards and persuaded him not to resign.)

* * * *

Colonel Majeed Malik said, "Mountbatten was the only Viceroy whom Jinnah really trusted or respected. He said so; he said, 'Mountbatten was the only Viceroy I ever liked and I gave him my confidence. But he betrayed me'."

* * * *

Noman said that it was nonsense to credit Iqbal with the idea of Pakistan and that he, Noman, has documentary evidence to prove that Partition, as it came in 1947, was thought of in 1921, by a Hindu politician. I asked him if I might see the "documentary evidence", but I doubt if I shall hear anymore.[13]

* * * *

Nobleness of purpose, and loneliness, being akin, Jinnah suffered because of his rigid principles. They formed a wall between himself and warm, human friendships—a relationship he never really knew in all his life.—H.B.

* * * *

It is hard to expect ethics and tranquil government from a nation of people who, because of the climate, have to sleep in the afternoon, with their bodies so vulnerable to diseases—so occupied with flies, heat, ants and dysentery. Think how dysentery detains them from ordinary habits and behaviour. How can they organise themselves into a vanguard when their needs must, in a moment of argument, rush to the sloot. Seriously, I thought of this as I drove the streets in the heat of the afternoon and saw men sleeping on the pavements, in little segments of shade. How can they be expected to respond and click their heels to the cry of 'Pakistan Zindabad', with the temperature at 109. People are subservient to climate and geography, and I think history and geography should be more closely related, in study.

I suggested to silly old Brelvi that the Pakistan Government buy an estate in a cold country and fly its officials back and forth, so that they would be braced for their task. He blinked. I am at a loss in dealing with them, because I am impatient with compromise. I deal in black and white and I have no subtlety. I am shocked one moment and delighted the next, and don't seem able to steer between the rocks. I am drawn to Jinnah because of this. He was completely un-oriental in his ethics. Odd, I dislike his rudeness, but must relate it to his honesty. I dislike his class-consciousness, but understand it. Sometimes, when I am harassed by the incompetence I endure, I look at the photograph of Jinnah on my desk and almost pray to it for help.

If I had known him and worked with him, we might have got over his barbed-wire of arrogance: or we might have parted, quietly, after a flaming row. I would never have put up with his remark to Ahsan, "Don't have any of those delaying tactics with me". Insolent old warrior. But he was forced into it by the sleepy, dishonest people he led into freedom.

* * * *

To Karachi

Thank you, Mr Jinnah,
For our pleasant land,
A thousand tons of camel dung
And twenty miles of sand.

* * * *

The letter on the opposite page [deleted] will tell more of Atiya Begum than I can write. She lives with her husband in an arty-crafty elegance, with one hand stretched towards her grand ancestors and one towards the literati. She breaks in two under the strain. She and her husband told me only gossiping stories about Jinnah and his sister. I set them down, but I know enough of the facts now to reject them in considering my book and what I put in it. Atiya Begum's husband said, "Miss Jinnah played a very small part in her brother's life until the beginning of the last war. I blame Mrs Naidu for destroying Jinnah's marriage. She made the match by introducing them. I have heard that Ruttenbai Petit threatened to kill herself if she could not marry him. Her parents forbade it, because she was so young.

"Mrs Naidu, who was afterwards in love with Jinnah, herself, did all she could to break up the marriage. Miss Jinnah had no part in this, although in later years, when his daughter Dina was married, Miss Jinnah did all she could to destroy the relationship between her and her father."

Then this story. "Some time in 1939 or 1940, when Jinnah was living alone in Bombay, he left to attend a Congress meeting [the Muslim League session in April 1941] in Madras. As usual, he travelled alone in a first-class coupe, attended by two servants who would come around at each halt to see if he wanted anything. At 4 o'clock in the morning, the servant knocked on the door and there was no answer. He got the conductor to unlock the door. Jinnah was lying on the floor, unconscious. When Jinnah returned to Bombay, the doctors said someone should come to look after him. It was only then that Miss Jinnah, who had previously been working as a teacher in a convent came to look after him.' (The above statement is, I am sure, only half true, and must be checked carefully.)[14]

* * * *

– 30 April 1952 –

Lunched with the Governor of Sind, Din Mohammed, who was a member of the Radcliffe Commission and who has promised to write a report, on his point of view. The lunch was really for me to meet the romantic little Pir of Pagaro. There was a nice touch of graciousness and efficiency on entering the Governor's house—cool, spacious, with silent servants moving about with iced drinks. I was shown into a sitting room where two youngish men were sitting in deep chairs. One was splendid, in immaculate white, gold shoes and a fez. The other was in an English suit and English shoes. He wore three fountain pens in his outside coat pocket. I bowed to the gentlemen in fez and gilt, thinking he was the Pir. I was wrong; he was only an uncle, and editor of a little newspaper—the *Sind Observer*.

The Governor came in. Charming and easy. Lunch was not the usual curry struggle—everything beautifully done. I sat next to the Pir and made slow conversation. He talked about his education in England, having lived at Pinner, of all places. I had the impression of stubborn, fierce will, behind his schoolboy manner. The veneer was Pinner, the essence, untouched. His eyes extraordinary: slumbering anger and sadness. One would never know him.

After lunch, the talk was rather against the English.[15] They thought that the English quit India too quickly. I told them that the English were very weary at the end of the war, and after; that 2,000,000 English homes had been bombed and the people exhausted. They were in no mood to care over much what was happening elsewhere. And I said, frankly, that many people were rather bored by India. I became a little angry. The editor man [Pir Ali Mohammad Rashidi] with the gold shoes said, "But you are interested in Pakistan, Mr Bolitho". I said, "I am interested in my task, which is to write a biography of Mohammad Ali Jinnah".

He went back to the subject of our leaving India too quickly. I answered, mildly, "If I may say so, the word 'Quit' was written on the walls by your people—even when the Prince of Wales was your guest." Then I realized that I must not answer.

Then they attacked the British for the way they treated Indian antiquities. This was really too much, but I kept my anger. All their museums grew out of British care—what of all that Lord Curzon did? Schools, universities, museum—all British—all created by the British. And, look at the Lahore museum, how it has deteriorated—neglected—since they took over.

The Governor calmed the editor of the *Sind Observer* and all was well in the end. It was the little Pir of Pagaro who fascinated me. That strange and savage inheritance—and the villa at Pinner, where the English tried to refine him.

* * * *

– 1 May –

I went to Begum Liaquat, at 6, for cocktails. Dear me, how I smile every time I pass into her garden, with the flowers, and remember those horrible guns at Miss Jinnah's gate. Begum Liaquat looked delightful, in a pale pink dress and scarf. She described meeting Jinnah, in July 1933, when he was in Hampstead. She said, "My husband and I pleaded with him to come back and work for his people—to lead them. I was young then—it was the first year of my marriage—and I promised him that if he would come back, I would organize all the Muslim women to support him. He smiled amiably, as if I were just a young girl who did not know what she was talking about."

A nice remark that I did not note at the time. Talking of Miss Jinnah and her early training as a dentist, I said, "What nice woman ever really wished to be a dentist!" Begum Liaquat answered, "Yes! All those extractions!"

* * * *

– 1 May –

Sonny Habibullah. He was very frank about the faults in Muslim character. I put forth my argument that people in a very hot climate are exhausted and need the discipline of people from colder countries. I said, "You might have an official class, trained in a colder climate and flown to Pakistan for spells of three months, for administrative duties. Then flown back again."

He answered me with a serious comment. "The fault goes deeper than that. Muslims lack the sensibilities and gifts of character that come from equality in marriage. There are few love marriages among Muslims. After marriage, they still go on saying 'I' instead of 'We'."

* * * *

– 6 May –

Dined with Mr and Mrs Van Dusen, Americans who have lived here a long time. Begum Liaquat came—a vision, all in white—a white mist of a dress. She came into the drawing room carrying a little bouquet for Mrs Van Dusen. How one pounces on the gestures of manners!

Everything polite and beautiful. There are these oases of pleasure, in this vast thicket of political get-at-your-throat. Mr and Mrs Van Dusen have been home to Begum Liaquat and her children: There was no anxiety at dinner; no feeling that anyone had a cause, a government, or an argument up their sleeve. And I admired Begum Liaquat for her serenity. I have seen the shadow of grief pass over her when she mentions Liaquat's death, less than seven months ago. But the value is there. There are flashes of bitterness, against Fatima Jinnah, and against the dilatoriness that still leaves her husband's assassin and the plotters, rather, unpunished. But who would judge her—especially when once sees her alone with her children.

She was beautiful and intelligent and unselfish, all through the evening, and I feel flattered that Mr and Mrs Van Dusen had asked Derek and myself, with no one else.

* * * *

M. Ashir, News Editor of 'Dawn'

A rather bitter, more intelligent than most. I deplored the lack of documents and archives. He said, "You can't have archives in this country. The white ants would eat them."

* * * *

– 7 May –

A great, selfish day for me. In September 1938—fourteen years ago, my play, "Victoria and Disraeli" was produced by BBC, with Mary Tempest as Queen Victoria. Of course, I sat back, grateful, but frustrated, because I saw myself in this part as "Dizzy", and have done so, ever since. Here, in Karachi, there is a company of amateurs, with Mr and Mrs French-Thompson, of the BOAC (British Overseas Air Company) as the leaders. They call themselves the Clifton Players and they produce English plays, every so often. Today, over the Pakistan Radio, we presented my "Victoria and Disraeli", with myself as Disraeli—at last. We stood before the microphone, in a circle, and I sweated—there were actually spots of sweat on the tile floor—as I over-acted, and enjoyed myself beyond measure. They are giving me a set of records of the performance so that I may take them home and remind myself of my personal victory and, I suppose, my artistic shame. As a matter of fact, I think I did quite well. I had practised Dizzy's voice day and night—making the stomach notes rich as possible. Well! There it is. I enjoyed it. What Pakistan thought, I was not told.

* * * *

– 8 May –

At night, I dined with Commander Ahsan and his wife. Admiral and Mrs Jefford there. And their daughter Wendy. She always seems to know what I have been doing the day before, so I call her 'The Spy'. It is so nice being able to say, "oh, you spy", to an English girl, knowing, that she won't be offended.

* * * *

I forgot to make a note on my talk with Sir Shah Nawaz, in his garden, a day or two ago. A dear old man, with geese and goslings busy about us as we sat in the garden. He was perfectly dressed and had quiet manners. He talked of Jinnah, but had no love for him. He said that now, in India as well as Pakistan, there is a wave of nepotism, selfishness and place-seeking that is very dangerous. He admitted that it would have been checked in Pakistan if Jinnah and Liaquat Ali Khan were still alive.

* * * *

An Englishman now employed by the Pakistan government: "In Chittagong, some time in 1948, the Commissioner gave an informal lunch party for Jinnah. The Prime Minister of East Bengal—Khwaja Nazimuddin (now Prime Minister of Pakistan)—was there, but the other guests were not chosen as officials, but as friends. There was one Englishman and he was warned, before lunch, by the Military Secretary, 'You may not address the Quaid unless he speaks to you!'

"Jinnah was dressed, in English clothes; very thin but rather handsome. He teased Nazimuddin mercilessly, in front of his subordinates, on the subject of purdah, because Nazimuddin's wife is still in purdah."

* * * *

I was told of a wealthy Hindu who approached Jinnah—while he was practicing as a lawyer. Jinnah suggested a fabulous fee at which the Zamindar protested. Jinnah answered, "You can't travel in a Pullman on a 3rd-class ticket."

* * * *

I must remember the story of Mountbatten, Nehru and Jinnah, all speaking on the radio on agreement to Partition. The speeches were introduced by Chopiris Polonaise. Mountbatten spoke in English, Nehru in English and Hindustani, and Jinnah in English. Mountbatten, who had checked Jinnah's speech beforehand, gallantly wrote the words, *Pakistan Zindabad* at the end.[16] Jinnah, unable to tell his people in their own language, they were free, had to be "translated" by one of the announcers at the radio station.

* * * *

– 9 May –

I lunched today with Khwaja Nazimuddin, the Prime Minister—alone. This, on the eve of my departure. I have had no help from him whatever. I can only repeat, these ambitious ones don't care two hoots for the memory of Jinnah. Nazimuddin said, "I asked no one else so that we could talk". He told me nothing of value—whether because he is too clever to commit himself, or because he is not interested in remembering Jinnah, or because he is an amiable ass, without the depth, that might retain an impression, I do not know. I thought him quite incapable. He could not even cut his melon properly and I leaned over and said, "Let me do it for you". He seemed quite pleased. A child at heart. Most dangerous in a Prime Minister.

* * * *

– 10 May –

All is arranged for us to sail to Bombay in an Italian cargo ship, carrying only a handful of passengers. I feel that I need the mental holiday, away from anyone who is likely to talk about Pakistan.

We lunched with Terence Creagh-Coen[17] and dined with Begum Liaquat Ali Khan. She made every possible gesture and Miss Miles, her companion, brought in Begum Liaquat's children and they played for us—violin and piano. They played "Sonny Boy".

Then we went into the garden where the elder son played with his toy aircraft. Begum Liaquat told us that his aircraft got out of hand a few days ago, sped over the neighbouring gardens and landed on someone's green house. Begum Liaquat made every effort to make us feel this was our friendly farewell to Karachi. It was very generous and touching.

* * * *

Copy of a Letter to Colonel Majeed Malik

Karachi
Pakistan
m/v Risano
Keamari.

15th May 1952

Dear Majeed,

It seems that we are to sail at 10 o'clock this morning. The delay is a disaster for me as I cannot be in London in time to take over my house. But it has also been an opportunity. I have come to know the harbour. I have bathed again at Sandspit; seen turtles and their eggs; wandered among the remarkable houses of Baba island, caught a fish, eaten curry on the floor with the customs officers, and, during long hours, I have observed the boats on the water. Please arrange to have photographs taken of all the various little craft: Bunder-boats with one-boy, two-boy, three-boy and four-boy winds—and all the others. I saw one today, being rowed by two men while two others stood up, holding small sails fixed to their waists and held aloft in their hands. There is a whole book to be written on the harbour—in three sections: a) the foreshore, b) the craft on the water, and c) the fish and animal life below. However, if you have the photographs taken, send me a set to England as I am sure I could place them with a magazine.

Thank you for your letter and for the addresses in Bombay. This will make all the difference as I know nobody there.

I must love Pakistan after all. Yesterday, on the wharf, I talked with three boys from the Sind Madrassah School. They did not know what was written over the gate of their own school. So I gave them a 20-minute lecture on Quaid-i-Azam and on the emotions that must stir in all Pakistanis. One of them believed that if he went to England he would have to obtain permission from the Indian High Commissioner. This made me furious, and, with pebbles set out on the wharf, I explained the relationship between Pakistan, England, and India.

I may be a tiresome visitor, but my emotions are of the right kind.

The agent now threatens a strike in Bombay. What hell life has become since the masses come to think they have rights and no responsibilities:

Can your research department tell me anything about these two names:-

Richmond Crawford II
Sydney Thurbron

They are the names of two tugs in the harbour. I thought it a sad kind of fame—having one's name sprawling across the end of a squalid tug.

Thank you for all you have done to pour oil on the very troubled waters. I confess that I have been unhappy and often bewildered. I have never dealt with a government before—only with individuals—and the impersonal element is something I do not understand. Your laugh, your tact, and your "good morning to you", have made a great difference. Please remember me to your wife and thank you again for that perfect evening.

Two things. Please do not forget the airmail numbers of *Dawn*. And please keep Brelvi up to the mark over those forgotten tasks.

* * * *

– 18 May –

I always wish to see the home in which a man lived—to associate him with the walls, objects and garden. The birthplace of Jinnah, in Karachi, did not help me, but I expected much from Jinnah's house in Bombay.

Yesterday afternoon, and this morning, everyone has been helpful. It might have been Gandhi's life I was writing: more helpful than Jinnah's own people.

The homes! For many years, including the time of his marriage, he lived in an old Goanese bungalow, in Mount Pleasant Road. After his wife's death, 1929, he lived in there, until he went to England in 1930. Then, when he returned to Bombay, in 1934, he must have begun to wish for change, and grandeur. He demolished the Goanese bungalow and built the present, 'mansion', which is now the home of the deputy British High Commissioner. The building began in 1939 and, during the two years of building, he lived in a rented home in Little Gibbs Road, higher up on Malabar Hill. These two years were important ones in Jinnah's life. I went, first, in search of the house in Little Gibbs Road. We drove—it was Sunday evening—(yesterday, as I am recalling this next day) we drove along the promenade by the sea—an oriental Brighton. The merciless heat of the day was lifting and an uncertain, cooler breeze, came in from the Arabian Sea. There were thousands of people, mostly dressed in white, moving gratefully towards the water's edge—with just a few beds of scarlet geraniums, incongruous as poppies in snow.

I went towards his house with a deeper sense of dedication than I had when I began my trip, almost a year ago. I have read of little else, but Jinnah, and Pakistan: I have talked to at least 100 people who knew him. From the quiet, impersonal interest in him, as the subject of my book, I have warmed to my task. I felt at first that his seeming rudeness, his iceberg aloofness and his almost tiresome celibacy, would make the book dull. As I dig deeper, I, myself, saw deeper. The amalgam of loneliness, mental and moral celibacy—the integrity, so intense that it was a form of self-torture. His virtues were so intense and his faults so trivial that I was afraid that, from a writer's point of view, there would not be enough struggle and contrast to make the book come alive. But I am afraid no longer. There is a touch of affection coming to my task.

We climbed Malabar Hill, to the hanging gardens. Standard roses, erect and stiff as if they had been trained at Sandhurst. And plants, cut into elephants, a giraffe, and a plough with its oxen. Perfect, but not my kind of garden. Then to Little Gibbs Road. I came to an open gate, leading to the lawn of a big house, on the lawn were three Parsee ladies, like fabulous butterflies, in their saris, taking the evening air. I asked them, "Do you know in which house Mohammed Ali Jinnah lived in Little Gibbs Road?" One answered, "Oh, they have pulled it down. It was up there!" She pointed to a pile of rubble, higher up the hill. I explained my errands and she said, looking at the others, "I knew him quite well. I used to see him—almost very day. So erect and so charming. He always took off his hat and said 'Good morning'."

I walked up the hill, to the rubble in the neglected garden. Jinnah must have enjoyed this eminence, with its view over the water. It was a view for a conqueror to deserve, with the ocean framed in golden mohur trees, and the noise of the waves beating on the rocks. How different from the horrible flatness of Karachi! But the house had gone and in its place were what looked like the foundations of a block of flats. There was only one sign that Jinnah—or anyone—had ever lived there: some twelve, cracked bathroom tiles, salvaged by the housebreakers, were stocked against a pile of bricks.

* * * *

When I compare the apathy of Karachi, over Jinnah, and the eagerness here, I am bewildered. I don't have to ask. In the evening we dined with Sir Cowasjee Jehangir, a fabulous Parsee, with his grand house called Ready Money Mansions. We ate at his club,—the Willingdon Club— where we met two or three important men who had known Jinnah. They all said, "Oh, if I can be any help, do come and see me". Then back to Sir Cowasjee's mansion—overlooking the vast sea, and the coast of black rocks. The house is vast, with statues and, on the first floor, a big drawing room like an antique dealer's fair. Then the splendid gallery which he has built, for his early Indian bronzes (?) and Mughal and other paintings—Persian. It was a great experience, to sit with a cultivated old man, who has cared enough, to bring this fine collection together. He gave us a number of reproductions of some of the pictures and we sat, comfortably, sipping whiskey and soda and talking.

Sir Cowasjee Jehangir said of Jinnah, "He came here often, but he was never interested in the paintings or the sculpture. He had no sense of history: he would walk past all these things that I love so much, find a chair and talk of nothing but politics.

"I knew Jinnah as far back as early 1901. He was poor then, but his clothes already had distinction. He was a member of the Orient Club and I used to see him there. He was even more pompous and independent during those lean years than later on. He had four years of struggle without briefs. He would never do an unjust thing. He was no lawyer. He had no university education and he had to be briefed for a case with great care; but he was a brilliant advocate.

"He was what God made him, not what he made himself. God made him a clear thinker and a brilliant advocate. He could see around corners, with his sixth sense. But he was not an educated man and he had little sense of literature or style in his writing. And he was no orator. He was all logic, and no magic. He never made an oration. He drove in his point with slow delivery, word by word, all pure cold logic."

Then, 'The greatest English lawyer we ever had in India was Inverarity. He was of the class of F.E. Smith or Symon. I once called Jinnah a 'bloody fool' and Jinnah walked out. But he called everyone bloody fools, from judges down.

"He had a great regard for Jinnah's talents."

Hector Bolitho to Sir C. Jehangir. "Did you merely admire Jinnah or did you also like him?"

"Yes, I was fond of him. Genuinely fond of him, because of his sense of justice and because, with all the differences and bitterness of political life, he was never malicious. Hard, maybe, but never malicious."

I enjoyed meeting Sir Cowasjee Jehangir. Interesting; as we were leaving, I noticed a sketch of Ruskin on a wall, and a Hogarth print.

* * * *

– Monday, 19 May –

Our only formal introduction in Bombay was to Kanji Dwarkadas, through dear old Jamshed Nusserwanjee whom we met in Karachi. Our introduction to Sir Cowasjee Jehangir came from him. The arrangements he has already made are incredible. He came to lunch today, having already arranged for me to see Morarji Desai, the Chief Minister, Raja Sir Maharaj Singh, former Governor of Bombay, Lady Petit—Jinnah's mother-in-law, and Neville Wadia, Jinnah's son-in-law. All this is to happen before we sail on Friday.

I went to the Law Courts this morning, hoping to find the rooms in which Jinnah worked. Actually, the High Court Chambers. My luck was incredible. I wandered among the vast, formidable, ugly buildings and then asked a man if he could help me. "Oh, I knew Jinnah quite well", he said. He was Mr C.N. Joshi, a most important man. When I told him that I was actually writing the official biography of Jinnah he said, "Then you must come and must see Motilal Setalvad, the

Advocate General". Without any fuss, this was arranged over a telephone. So, I sat with these two kind helpers and made my notes.

Joshi said, "There is one picture of Jinnah that stays in my mind, when I think of his ultimate success. We were all at the Round Table Conference which was held in St. James's Palace. At 12:30 each day, the other delegates would go off in their Daimlers and Rolls Royces, to lunch richly. Jinnah would stay and eat the 1/- buffet lunch. One day he said to me, 'I have no future in politics in India. I am not going back.' You will remember that he did stay in England: that is when he began to practice at the Privy Council Bar."

When our talk was over, Joshi led me past the police in their gold and blue turbans—past iron bars and chairs, and a sort of cage of prisoners. Then to the legal chambers and the actual rooms in which Jinnah worked. There were betel nut juice stains on the walls.... "Very different from when Jinnah worked here", said Mr Joshi. "Everything was spotless. You know that his wife furnished the rooms for him and made them very grand. Look at them now!"

* * * *

A reporter came to see me in the hotel. He told me a story of the Press Conference in Delhi, in July 1947. In a small, hot room—100 journalists and only one fan which was trained on Jinnah. One of the reporters asked Jinnah, "Will Pakistan be a theocratic or a democratic state?" Jinnah answered, "Get that dirty nonsense out of your head", and the reporters were so furious that all the 100 walked out.

This is the reporter's story. I do not know if it is true.

* * * *

In the afternoon I went to see Lady Petit—old, rather blind, and lovely—in a big, cool drawing room. It was a glimpse at the polite, elegant and very different life of these rich Parsees, compared with the curry struggles of those Karachi houses. She did not speak much of Jinnah, which I understood. We drank tea and talked lightly. Young Lady Petit was there; she came to the door with me and said, of Jinnah, "He was always so gracious to ladies. He would compliment us on our saris. The other politicians were grand and swept one aside."

* * * *

I saw Kanji Dwarkadas in the early evening. He is most attentive. He said, "When Lord Linlithgow arrived as Viceroy, Jinnah was summoned to meet him. Linlithgow felt that Jinnah was being obstinate and that he was utterly opposed to him. Jinnah arrived 15 minutes late. When Lord Linlithgow told Jinnah why he wished to speak to him, Jinnah answered, "There is no point in any discussion. You are a double-crosser.' And he left the room!"

I wonder how true these stories are—how much they have been embroidered. They sound too slick. I have come to the conclusion that I must suspect all these anecdotes until I have heard them confirmed by a Briton. And what a monstrous admission this is! And yet, I wonder. I think that Englishmen tell the truth—all things being comparative. At least, they are seldom malicious.

* * * *

We dined with the British deputy High Commissioner, in the grand house that Jinnah built, on the ruins of his Goanese bungalow. Before we left Karachi, even responsible officials said, "You will get no help from the Hindus". One even said, "You may have trouble being allowed to land in Bombay, as you are writing about the Quaid". What nonsense!

We were driven to the house in Mount Pleasant Road by an ordinary Hindu taxi driver. I gave him the number of the house and he answered, "Oh, you mean the Jinnah house". He was no sour partisan.

We walked down a steep, short drive, towards a grand portico, a marble terrace, balconies and then, within, high rooms. I suppose that ambitious men, born in little houses, require these assurances. It is very natural.

This was the house, built on the ruins of his marriage, in the first years on his unbridled, worldly success.

We had an English evening in an Indian setting. The High Commissioner and his wife were tranquil and we talked of cricket, Hampton Court and Runnymede. After dinner we drank coffee on the terrace and forgot Jinnah and Pakistan.

The idea of Jinnah expressing his ambitions in a big house, with big rooms came back when I saw what was his library. Wow! Yet he was no reader, except for his smattering of Dickens.

* * * *

– Tuesday, 20 May –

In the morning I went to his home in Mt. Pleasant Road again to talk to the gardener—the only servant left from Jinnah's time, The High Commissioner's wife said she would act as interpreter. What other people in the world are capable of such nice unpretentiousness! Or do I imagine this. She was so nice about it, but we got very little from the man. He was away to be brought from his wheelbarrows. He grinned and showed his betle nut stained teeth. He said that Jinnah's favourite flowers were petunias and phlox. He liked the garden to be very tidy: if there were too many plants he would say, "It's like a jungle!" He would walk through the garden quietly and never pause to pick a flower. "Miss Jinnah?" I asked. The gardener said, "She managed all things." He said that Jinnah was kind to his servants.

Dwarkadas came to lunch. He told a superficial story of Jinnah meeting Dr Annie Besant. He arrived in the room smoking a cigarette, which she hated. Dwarkadas said to Jinnah "Please put it out", but Mrs Besant said, "Never mind". But Jinnah was gallant and he put it out.

Curious, these endless, trifling stories.

* * * *

In the afternoon I went to see Mr Claude Batley, the architect who designed Jinnah's grand home in Mount Pleasant Road. I went to his rooms and found a round-tummied man, bent over his *Times* crossword puzzle. On the wall beside him—in a crowded room—was a watercolour sketch of Ipsurch, painted, he told me, by his father. And some fine, early Indian drawings. He said of Jinnah, "He had a taste for cigars and wine, but none for architecture or furniture. Yes, I designed the house for him. He wanted a big reception room and a big verandah—and big lawns for garden parties. The house was begun in 1939 and finished in 1940. He appointed a Muslim Clerk of works, an English builder and a Hindu plumber. He insisted on choosing the colours of the marble for the terrace, and standing by when the pieces of stone were fitted, much to the annoyance of the Italian stone masons doing the work."

Then, "Jinnah had no feeling for craftsmanship. So long as the house did not leak, he did not mind. Unfortunately, as so often happens in a new house, there was a leak. He was furious. When I passed the certificates for the contractors, Jinnah would not pay. He haggled with the contractors and insisted on reductions when the work was finished."

"The fittings and furniture were Jinnah's own and were very poor." Then Mr Batley sighed and we gave up talking about Jinnah. He gave me a splendid drink and he produced books and drawings to show me similarities between Akbar and Elizabethan architecture. Then he gave me a copy of his book on the subject. I liked him very much.

* * * *

I went also to see Dr D.K. Mehta, of the Nature Cure Institute, Little Gibb Rd. He had attended Jinnah. He said, "Jinnah was a good patient and a good friend. As a politician, he kept his distance. Gandhi was naked before his disciples, in every way. Jinnah was always clothed... There is the difference. As a psychological entity Jinnah was an introvert—and an introvert thinker. He was a thinker, not a feeler. He was too conscious of himself. Jinnah was a source of power. Gandhi was only an instrument of power. Jinnah was a cold rationalist in politics—he had a one track mind, with great force behind it." Then, "Jinnah was potentially kind. I am sure of that. He built walls to protect himself. But the kindness was there."

"Gandhi said cleanliness was not only next to Godliness; that it was Godliness. Yet he would do dirty work and soil his hands in helping the squalid poor. Jinnah! No! He did not wish to touch the poor."

* * * *

– 21 May –

I spent an hour with Mr Shantilal L. Thar, a partner in the firm of Devkaran Nanji—brokers. Mr Thar looked after Jinnah's investments from 1937. He said, "Jinnah's mind was clearly decisive in making investments. He never cared to bother unnecessarily. When he had spare funds to invest, he would send for me. He would say, 'Suggest a few investments': I would offer him perhaps five and he would make his choice. Once he had made the investment he would not bother to ask their price thereafter—this was curious in him—unless he had made up his mind to sell. If any of my suggestions did not yield a good result, he never referred to it, even casually.

"Jinnah loved talking to people who were not Muslims. But he preserved a distance between himself and his equals. With me he talked politics and he propounded his faith in Pakistan, but without ever being bitter against the Hindus. By nature, he was not anti-Hindu, but he whipped up hatred against them for his own political purpose.

"At the time of Partition his fortune must have been from 6 to 7 million rupees. Although he was thrifty, he never pursued money in a cheap way. One instance of this. A client was sent to him and he told Jinnah that he had limited money with which to fight his case. Jinnah took it up and lost. But he believed in the case and that it should be taken to the Appeal Court, so he promised to fight the case, without being paid. He won, and when the client offered to pay, Jinnah refused; he had agreed to take no fee and he would not have the conditions changed just because he had succeeded."

Then, Mr Thar said, "Jinnah was an epicure, to the finger tips".

I smile as I think over the kindness, of both Parsees and Hindus, in recalling Jinnah. And those unstable officials at the Ministry in Karachi thought I would find only bitterness. It is not so. Mr Thar said also, "Jinnah talked to me once, of the Indian princes. That was in 1946, before Partition. He said, that the late ruler of Baroda[18] (The Gaekwar or Maharajah) stood head and shoulders above all the other rulers. That the late Maharajah of Mysore was a great gentleman; that the late ruler of Gandol was all head and no heart and that the Nawab of Bhopal had both head and heart."

Shantilal Thar said that after Partition, Jinnah telephoned him three times, from Government House in Karachi, regarding the sale of his shares.

* * * *

– 22 May –

We have arranged to be transferred to the P&O ship sailing tomorrow, so that I may be in London sooner, and go to the south of France to see the Aga Khan.

I talked again to one of the lawyers who worked with Jinnah in the High Court. He said, "Jinnah could never be wrong. He was no lawyer, but his clear-headedness in a case was remarkable. His advocacy was all the more remarkable because of his want of English—all because he lacked a university education. He would hoodwink judges by grandiose references; he would say, 'This has already been decided' and usually get away with it. When one counsel challenged him and asked, 'Where?' Jinnah could not give the reference."

This lawyer said, "I became interested in a relief fund and I began to raise money for it. I went up to Jinnah in the Bar Library and I showed him the subscription list. He put it back and said, 'I am not interested'."

* * * *

I am pleased to be going home—to be escaping from the terrible mischief of the sun that sends everyone to sleep. I could never live in a country where the flowers wither in a day—where one can actually see the petals curling and dying. It is the same with the people. They seem cooked and brown at the edges.

Heaven knows if I shall ever make a quiet, thoughtful book out of all the conversations I have shared, in Pakistan and here.

I feel a strange weariness after all the enmity in Karachi. Looking back, I recall endless conversations that were hostile—anti-Afghan, anti-Hindu, anti-British as if enmity and enemies were a real and positive delight. I was so willing to trust, and anxious to be twisted. However, Jinnah is very clear to me. There is a touch of dedication now, in putting down his story.

* * * *

Notes after Returning to England

18 July 1952. K.H. Khurshid came to dinner. Eight months ago, when I just met him, with Salman Ali, he was belligerent. Yet he knows more of Jinnah than almost anyone. It is interesting: he is still cautious with me, but willing to help. He has promised to read the manuscript and this means a great deal to me. I like him. I like him for explaining his unwillingness to help. There is something of Jinnah's honesty in him and I shall make a friend of him if it helps me.

24 July. Admiral Jefford and Mrs Jefford came for drinks before we all went on to the party given for him by the Pakistan High Commission. We sat on the balcony and the Admiral told one or two stories of use to me—but one or two I cannot put in my book. He told me that, through carelessness, for one year after Pakistan, the Indian service intelligence reports were still sent from Delhi, through Bombay, to Karachi—as they had always been *before* partition. The reports, written, of course, from India's point of view, were both interesting and helpful.

When Admiral Jefford was retiring he went to see the Prime Minister, Nazimuddin, who had decided not to invite and appoint another British Admiral in Jefford's place. Jefford said to him that he did not think that the Pakistani senior naval officer was ready for the appointment of C-in-C. Nazimuddin answered, "you have only yourself to blame. If you had stayed, the situation would not have arisen. I cannot risk—politically—inviting another Englishman out as C-in-C. You will have to ask the British Admiralty to give us a good Chief-of-Staff."

I said to Admiral Jefford, "I cannot see much hope for Pakistan, there are only a handful of good men at the top—not enough to keep the country from disaster."

Admiral Jefford said, "I am sure they will survive. They have an excellent 2nd Eleven. So long as Pakistan can survive the next ten years. you will find some very able man coming to the top of Government."

* * * *

Two stories I must remember. Sometime after Partition, Jinnah addressed a meeting, in Dacca, in the open air. It was at the time of the language controversy and when he said, "Urdu is to be the state language of Pakistan," the students booed him. And Mrs Naidu's remark, in the early days, when she was supposedly in love with Jinnah. "*Hai-hai* what has happened to this beautiful boy? Why has he muddled in politics?"

* * * *

– 30 July –

Colonel Geoffrey Knowles to Lunch

He was Jinnah's Second Military Secretary, after Colonel Birnie. He joined Jinnah early 1948. One, typical story, when the Duke of

Gloucester was about to visit Jinnah. "It was important that the programme for the visit should be passed by Jinnah and handed to the BOAC pilot before 4 p.m., so that it world arrive at St. James's Palace before the Duke left England. I had drawn up the programme and my only chance of talking to Jinnah was just as he was going upstairs to lunch.

I said, "May I talk to you, sir about the programme for the Duke's visit?"

"After lunch" Jinnah answered.

I said, "But, Sir, this is urgent."

He answered, "Mr Knowles, nothing is urgent."

"However, he agreed that I should send the programme up to him. It was back on my desk, approved by Jinnah, at 2 o'clock".

Colonel Knowles said, "Jinnah always called his service officers 'Mr' when he was a bit fussed".

* * * *

On 1 July 1948 Jinnah drove, with Miss Jinnah, in State, without ADCs or secretaries—to the opening of the Pakistan State Bank. Jinnah was seated in the state coach, with eight horses. He turned to Knowles and said, "Colonel Knowles, I hope the horses have been exercised sufficiently". Colonel Knowles said, "I liked Jinnah, and Miss Jinnah. He was always polite to me and, if disagreed, it was always in a pleasant way".

* * * *

Jinnah once described Muslim enthusiasm as being "like soda water".

* * * *

Ispahani, the High Commissioner

Jinnah said of himself, "I am an ordinary man, full of sin". But this the people would not believe. They wished to deify him.

* * * *

– London, 1 August –

Meeting with Sir Feroze Khan Noon in the house of the Pakistan High Commissioner, Avenue Road, Hampstead. He said, "I knew Jinnah from 1920. At that time the Muslim League was a weak association, with a handful of members in each of the various cities. When 1920 reforms came in, we formed the Muslim Conference, which then had some authority. Jinnah kept on with the Muslim League when we formed the Conference [the All India Muslim Conference was formed at Delhi on 1 January 1930]. He was very tenacious and incorruptible and would not accept office.

"I used to go and see Jinnah, before Pakistan, in Delhi. An illiterate servant would bring the letters in, open them, and hand them to Jinnah. Then he would answer them immediately."

(Note: Before partition, Sir Feroze Khan Noon was Indian High Commissioner in London, 1936–41. I believe that he was always opposed to the separate ambitions of the Muslim League, and a reluctant associate of Jinnah, until the division of British India became inevitable. – H.B.)

[On the contrary, he was Jinnah's 'man' in the Viceroy's Council and kept him informed about the official policy till 21 August 1945, when he resigned to join the Muslim League and did electioneering on its behalf, seeking to 'upset' the Unionist apple cart in the Punjab.–Ed.]

* * * *

Conversation with Nasim Ahmed, London Correspondent of 'Dawn', 7 August 1952

"Jinnah's greatest achievement was in managing to survive as head of the Muslim League without being discredited. All the previous leaders had been discredited." Nasim Ahmed recalled the first speech Jinnah made to the Constituent Assembly, as Governor-General: he said, "The Constituent Assembly has got two main functions to perform. The first is the very serious and responsible task of framing our future constitution for Pakistan..."

Nasim Ahmed agreed that Jinnah had probably been working on the framework of the constitution for some months — probably on the lines of that of France. Jinnah realized that the constitution was of prime importance to Pakistan, and that the country would not begin to run properly until there was one. Nasim Ahmed said that he believes, however, that Jinnah was not prepared to risk the violent opposition and controversy which would come from certain quarters of the Assembly; and that he decided to wait until the time was opportune. Jinnah, however, died one year later, and Pakistan still has no Constitution.

Nasim Ahmed said, "Although Jinnah did not observe the religious rites of Mohammedanism, Sir, by his creation of Pakistan he furthered the cause of Islam more than any of the religious leaders".

Nasim Ahmed said, "Jinnah created Pakistan, in spite of the Muslims."

* * * *

Sir Cowasjee Jehangir, whom I met again in London, said, of the massacres at the time of Partition, "If the rest of the world was shocked by the Hindu-Muslim massacres, it is perhaps convenient for them to forget that this was an unpremeditated horror, as opposed to the premeditated horrors of Belsen—of Europe and Japan'.

One day in August, Major Haji and his wife came to my house in London. He was secretary to the Aga Khan and I saw a good deal of him in Karachi. He said, of Jinnah, "You must remember that he was the only Mohammedan lawyer of consequence in Bombay in his time. There were one or two other Muslims practising but they were insignificant. It is not fair to say that Jinnah was merely a good advocate. This opinion is held by Hindus, who will not credit a Muslim with the facility to 'know' law, and how to interpret law. As an advocate, Jinnah outshone his fellows. His appeal to a judge and jury was very dynamic, but he certainly also knew the law.

"I first met Jinnah in 1920. I had been a member of Gray's Inn, I had served in the war and then, in 1920, my father took me to see Jinnah in Bombay. My father said, 'Here is my son. Make him as brilliant as you are'."

"Jinnah replied, 'He can come and work in my chambers, but he must shine with his own brilliance'.

"A Hindu with another Hindu, or a Muslim with another Muslim, would ordinarily have pushed him on, as a protégé, and would have used his influence to gain him a favourable position. But Jinnah was impartial, and did not give favours."

I spoke to Major Haji of the many times I had been told, in Pakistan, that it had been British policy to keep the Muslims in second place. He answered, "It is not in the least true. Certainly, at the beginning, before the mutiny, Britain had to 'defeat' the Muslims, in her conquest of India, because the Muslims were the ruling power. But, after the mutiny, the trend of British policy was to please the Muslims."

* * * *

General Sir Frank Messervy[19] came to see me at the Athenaeum. He said, "Forming the Pakistan army was not a very difficult task. The regiments were there: they had Islam behind them, and this force bound them together in no time. Jinnah was not really interested in the army; he had no ideas. He would say, 'I have had no military experience. I leave that entirely to you and Liaquat.'

"Mountbatten really wished to be Governor-General of both India and Pakistan. He said to Jinnah, 'You would like me to be Governor-General of Pakistan' and Jinnah answered, 'No, I am going to be G.G.'

"Two weeks after Gandhi's death, I went to stay with Mountbatten, to say 'goodbye'. My term was over. We were alone without our wives. I assured him that Pakistan and its leaders were genuinely sorry that Gandhi had died: that they realized he had genuinely tried to stop the killing. Mountbatten put his profile to me, as he always does when he wished to pronounce something, and he said, 'Gandhi will go down in history on a level with Christ and Buddha'. It shows how partisan he had become! 'Kashmir obviously belongs to Pakistan, except the south eastern bit', but Nehru said, 'In the same way as Calais was written on Mary's heart, Kashmir is written on mine'."

Sir Frank Messervy on Jinnah and Nehru: "Jinnah, being over honest, thought everyone else dishonest; Nehru, being highly intelligent, thinks every one else stupid".

This theme developed as I talked with Sir Frank Messervy. Jinnah had long decided that although the British were to leave the subcontinent, his forces must be commanded by British officers. It is incredible to realize that this indomitable man had dared envisage, and form Pakistan, without considering the part armed forces would necessarily play in assuring order among a distraught, illiterate population. When the time came to think on this, Jinnah clearly realized that British officers were necessary to his bewildered forces. He had a few ships, but not a drop of oil to send them to sea; his air force and his army were similarly impoverished and disorganised. He is said to have said to General Sir Douglas Gracey, "Ten years is the time I have fixed for asking the British officers to leave. When that time comes, I shall think about it again." The next task was to prevail upon British officers to stay. This was not easy. Many of them were out of sympathy with the policy of the divided countries. But there were some for whom service in India had been a work of dedication. The army had been all their lives and, come what may, they loved India. Thus it was that a British admiral stayed to create and command the Navy, an RAF officer came out to create the Air Force, and General Sir Frank Messervy remained, to command the army.

* * * *

Begum Liaquat

Twice after returning to England, I saw Begum Liaquat Ali Khan. She was kind and helpful to me in Karachi, and going to her house was pleasant. But here in London, I did not like having to sit in silence while she talked of "that Mountbatten woman". It was insulting and I was angry.

* * * *

K.H. Khurshid

Khurshid, Jinnah's secretary, who has become a friend after our first meeting, said of Jinnah's marriage: "It opened, for the first time and closed thereafter, forever, the door of his emotions. Never again did he trust all his heart to a human being. From then on, even his warmth was calculated. He was by nature celibate. Marriage was alien to his nature".

"When I was in London with Jinnah [December 1946] we dined one night with Anthony Eden. Eden saw my name on a card and said, 'Khurshid—that is Persian for sun'. Jinnah said he did not think so. When I arrived, I confirmed what he had said. He surprised us by writing my name in Persian characters. Apparently he knew both Arabic and Persian".

Liaquat once offered Khurshid a drink, but Jinnah said, in a fatherly way, "No, not yet. He is too young; when he is older".

"I was staying with Jinnah in Sir Cowasjee Jehangir's country house. Jinnah worried lest I was bored. He asked, 'Do you read Shakespeare?' I confessed, 'Not since school.' He went into town and brought back a whole set of Shakespeare, Shelley and Keats, for me to read. But he read only newspapers. The ever abundant stream of newspapers; he gave all his time to them".

* * * *

– 24 August 1952 –

Raja Sir Maharaj Singh, former Governor of Bombay came to lunch with me at my house in London.

"I first saw Jinnah in the winter of 1911, when he was a member of the Imperial Legislative Council, which had been formed after the Morley-Minto reforms of 1909. Jinnah was a prominent member and always sided with the progressive element.

"Jinnah strongly supported Gokhale in advocating the introduction of free and compulsory education in India. In an impassioned appeal to the Finance Minister, Jinnah said, 'Find the money! Find the money! Find the money!'

"Jinnah was a good debater, but he had a weak knowledge of English, because he had no university education. He had no interest whatever in literature, music or painting."

Of Jinnah's religion: "The Muslims are divided, in India, into two sects—Sunnis and Shias. The Sunnis are in vast majority. Jinnah came from the Khoja—Aga Khani sect of the small Shia sect. It was incredible that Jinnah, who came from a tiny division of a small sect—an unorthodox sect—should have been the man eventually to lead all the Muslims of India.

"The Aga Khan might rather have resented Jinnah as, at the beginning, the Aga Khan was supreme in importance among the Muslims of India. He was eventually supplanted by Jinnah. [As a political, rather than religious leader. —H.B.]

The great mistake made by the British in India was that they paid more attention to university and secondary education than to rural and primary education. Technical and industrial education were neglected, but this the British can hardly be blamed for as England herself made little progress in that field by the beginning of the century."

I asked Sir Maharaj if he thought that India's demand for self-government was in any way related to similar demands elsewhere in the Empire, about the same time. He replied that Lord Curzon had mentioned that "the victory of Japan over Russia had reverberated through the whispering galleries of the East".

* * * *

I must remember the remark said to have been made by Lord Mountbatten, "I do not mind what is said about me and my work in India, now: I care only for what my grandchildren will say and think".

* * * *

I went to Pakistan, willing to believe in all of them. After six months I believed in two of them—Jinnah and Liaquat Ali Khan—both dead. In this unhappy state I returned to England and wrote my book.

* * * *

Bombay Municipal Corporation
No MCR/5445 of 195-195
Date 29/8/1952

Shri Hector Bolitho
6, Lowndes Place, London, S.W. 1, (England)

Subject:- Information regarding Miss Fatima Jinnah

Dear Sir,

Reference: Your letter dated 30-5-1952

Miss Fatima Jinnah a Licentiate in Dental Science (L.D.Sc.) of the Calcutta Dental College worked in Municipal Girls' Schools of the Bombay Municipal Corporation from 20-12-1927 to 31-8-1930. She was entrusted with the work of treating only girls in the Municipal Schools for all dental troubles.

She resigned Municipal service as she could not be granted six months' leave to proceed to England on account of her indifferent health.

Yours faithfully,
(Sd) B.K. Patel
Municipal Commissioner
for Greater Bombay.

* * * *

Dina Wadia

Dina Wadia, Jinnah's daughter, came to see me in my house in London on 2nd October 1952. I recall these remarks from her conversation. "My father was never rude. He was intolerant of weakness. I remember him reading *Grey Wolf*, when I was very young and living at Hampstead. He said, 'Read this, my dear, it is good!' He loved my mother. He was celibate; he never loved anyone else. He had absolute contempt for all the politicians. Although Liaquat and Begum Liaquat were not loyal, he would say, 'They are the best that I have'.

She spoke of the "ingratitude" of the Pakistanis and said, "He gave them a country and their freedom".

Of Miss Jinnah, "She is not very intelligent. Simple. She loathes the present Government. Loathes Begum Liaquat. You know that Begum Liaquat did not go to my father's funeral [but Nurse Dunham (*see below*) had a different story]. My father loved nobody but my mother."

'He needed teasing. I used to call him Grey Wolf. I would make him take me to a pantomime. 'Come on, it's my holidays'.

"The last letter I had from him before he died was to ask me to bring my children and stay with him.

"Years before when he was attacked by that assassin in Bombay, he telephoned me. I found tenderness in him.

"The Pakistan Government of today wish to dispel the legend of him. They hate his memory. They are cut-throat politicians.

"I was with my father until I was seventeen. My mother was beautiful: she wrote poetry; her books, all marked, are in my library.

My mother committed suicide. She was only 30. She was dazzling. My father ... was not so rude and unapproachable as some think."

I quoted the story of Jinnah's rude answer to the judge: and Mrs Wadia answered, "Yes, but the judge was rude first".[20]

"My father was not a rude man. Arrogant, yes. But not rude. I only once saw him have a man thrown out of the house.

"He never worked in front of anyone. Late at night he would pore over his briefs.

"His family in Karachi were rich enough to send him to England to study law.

"My father and Lord Mountbatten were rivals in arrogance and in ambition. Mountbatten had all the frustration that minor royalties suffer. At last, in India, for a few brief months, he was set on a throne."

I thought that Mrs Wadia had shed her father's arrogance, but she has his directness, his vitality, his charm, his eyes, and his almost articulate hands.

* * * *

Nurse Dunham

Stories told me by Nurse Dunham that I could not use in my book. She said that when Nazimuddin appeared at the Frontier, his comic, round, fat appearance delighted the Pathans. They actually saw his tummy appear — then he paused, before they saw all of him. They called him the "Monsoon toad" because he was so round, fat and ineffectual.

She said that the Pathan servants at Quetta, and Ziarat, disliked not only Miss Jinnah, but Jinnah himself. They would mimic Miss J, as she talked proudly about the house, even at her heels, as she walked. One day Nurse Dunham felt that she should protest, she said, "That is Miss Jinnah". They answered, "Ha! Ha! What is Miss Jinnah?" One said to her, of Jinnah, "We do not like him. We do not like that sort of man." Poor Jinnah's aloofness and her pretensions did not go down [well] with the Pathans. One day, when Miss J was particularly unpleasant to some of the Pathan servants, one of them said to her, "You should go on your knees and say your prayers for your sick brother instead of going on the way you do."

Nurse Dunham described the terrible events after Jinnah's death. Miss Jinnah was furious, naturally, when the Government wished to arrange the funeral. She even stamped her foot in the room next to the one in which Jinnah's body was lying. Begum Liaquat sat in the same room as Miss Jinnah, but they sat back to back and did not speak. When the priests came to read the Koran over Jinnah, Miss Jinnah would not allow them into the room where he lay: she insisted on them reading the Koran on the verandah outside.

These notes should be read in association with my biography of Jinnah—the closing pages. Nurse Dunham came to my house in London and told me of his last illness and death—after I had also returned from Pakistan.

* * * *

– 14 May 1953 –

I met Lady Wavell and her son, the present Lord Wavell. Lady Wavell said, "I think Jinnah was one of the most handsome men I have ever met".

"Lord Wavell told me the story of when ex-president Hoover went to India on a food mission: Hoover wished to meet both Gandhi and Jinnah. Congress put out a false story that Mr Hoover would make the gesture of calling on Gandhi. Jinnah heard this and when a car arrived to take him to call on Hoover, he refused to go. He said he expected Hoover to come to him, as he was going to Gandhi. It was all wrong. Gandhi drove to call on Hoover and Jinnah was made to look rather foolish."

* * * *

Khurshid said, "Gandhi said to Jinnah 'You have mesmerized the Muslims' and Jinnah answered, 'But you have hypnotized the Hindus!'" He said, "Jinnah was more practical and more vigorous! Gandhi took refuge in mysticism, and used religion as a whip to his people. Nehru is a dual personality; in him, there is always a conflict between right and wrong."

NOTES

1. Mohammad Noman, author of *Muslim India: Rise and Growth of the All-India Muslim League*, Allahabad, Kitabistan, 1942, Secretary (1937-38) Vice President (1941) All-India Muslim Students' Federation.
2. Begum Liaquat Ali Khan's first name.
3. He referred to the terrible slaughter following partition.
4. The Great Leader.
5. The Great Killer.
6. At a students' moot to found the left oriented All-India Students' Conference, at Lucknow, in mid August 1938, which was inaugurated by Nehru and presided over by Jinnah.–Ed.
7. When I told Ilahi Bakhsh, who had been Jinnah's doctor at the end, that I had met Begum Shah Nawaz, he made a nice or not nice gibberish remark, "Oh, yes, Begum Shah Nawaz's family; they were only Mughal gardeners."
8. She should be referring to Jinnah since her father, Mian Mohammad Shafi, had died in 1931.–Ed.
9. See also Lt. Commander Ahsan's account which differs in some detail.
10. W.R. Owain-Jones, the senior British Council representative in Pakistan.
11. This was eventually done. We found the address of the house on Jinnah's Reader's ticket, still preserved at the British Museum. The plaque was placed on the house, in Russell Road, opposite Olympia. It was unveiled by the High Commissioner for Pakistan. I feel rather pleased because it was my idea.
12. On no account must Ahsan's name be used or quoted in connection with this statement, while he is still alive. Hector Bolitho.
13. I didn't.
14. Miss Fatima Jinnah moved into Jinnah's bungalow and took charge of his house, soon after Rutti's death on 20 February 1929. She was always with him wherever he went, except for Jinnah's visit to London, in December 1946, for talks on the Cabinet Mission Plan and the Constituent Assembly. Jinnah didn't travel to Madras alone, but was acompanied by Miss Jinnah.–Ed.
15. The Pir of Pagaro's father was hanged for treason in 1943, and his two sons taken to be educated in England.
16. When I included this story, of Mountbatten's gesture, in my book, the Pakistani government insisted on my deleting it. I was furious, but it was no use fighting them all at the last moment.–H.B.
17. Terrance Creagon-Coen, an old friend, seconded to the Pakistan government as Establishment Secretary after Partition.
18. I am not very certain of which rulers he referred to. One would have to look up the names and dates, in relation to Jinnah.–H.B.

19. First Commander-in-Chief of the Pakistan Army.
20. Judge: "Mr Jinnah, please raise your voice."
    Jinnah: "I am a lawyer, not an actor."
    Judge: "Mr Jinnah, please raise your voice. We cannot hear you."
    Jinnah: "If you moved that pile of books in front of you, then you would be able to hear me."

PART TWO

Hector Bolitho and Majeed Malik Correspondence

EDITOR'S NOTE

The following abbreviations have been used in the notes:

MS   Manuscript as originally drafted with page numbers from this document.

HB   Means the book, *Jinnah Creator of Pakistan*, as published by Oxford University Press, Karachi, in 2006. HB means page numbers of the published book. If HB comes after *Delete* it means the page number where the surrounding passages are published.

SPF   Means *See Part Five*. It means the excised passages from HB being reproduced fully in Part Five.

Hector Bolitho (1898–1974) was the author and Majeed Malik was the Principal Information Officer, designated by the Government of Pakistan to liaise with Hector Bolitho

6, Lowndes Place,
London, S. W. I.
3rd September, 1952.

Dear Majeed,

I am sending you the opening pages of my manuscript, which comprises the following episodes:-

1. Approach by sea
2. Beginning of a task
3. A game of cricket
4. The Birth-place
5. The beginning of legend
6. Jinnah's English patron
7. A student in London
8. Voices in Westminster
9. A rose, by any other name...
10. Karachi, then Bombay
11. The young advocate
12. Background

This will give you some idea of how I am planning the book. I am anxious to have these back, with the official comments or corrections, as soon as possible, so that I may show them to my publishers. They will wish to have some evidence of the chapters having been passed. May I therefore ask you to enclose a letter, enumerating these episodes, which have been corrected and passed for publication.

With my best wishes and happy recollections to Begum Malik and yourself,

Yours sincerely,

Hector Bolitho.

PRESS INFORMATION DEPARTMENT
Government of Pakistan
Karachi, October 3, 1952

My dear Hector,

I must apologize to you for the delay in sending a reply to your letter of September 3, enclosing the opening pages of your manuscript. This was mainly due to the fact that for a few days I was out of Karachi; and then a few days after my return I fell ill. I am now feeling fit and fine—despite the sultry October weather.

I read your script with great interest and as the last page came nearer and nearer I grew more and more unhappy that you had not sent me a larger chunk. When are you going to send me the next installment? Please make the next one as long as you can. It is a privilege to read your work in manuscript. And this time you have my assurance that saving 'acts of God' I shall write back to you in a fortnight's time. (Did I hear you muttering, 'You Orientals and your promises'. Don't be rude:)

To come to the manuscript. I have a few alterations to suggest:

1. Page 3, last lines of the 1st paragraph of the episode, <u>'Beginning of a Task'</u>.

In five years refugees, officials and businessmen have swelled the numbers to a million and a quarter—and not 1,800,000 as you have said.

2. Page 5, For—
'Mohammed Ali Ganji then surprised me by saying, "In the same year that he was at the Mission School, he married Amai Bai, a Khoja girl from Kathiawar, who was his parents choice."....'
Please consider substituting—
'Mohammed Ali Ganji then surprised me by saying, "In the same year that he was at the Mission School he was married by his parents, as was the custom of the country, to Amai Bai."'

3. Top of Page 9, 'I walked to the corner of the street, through the dust—the dust that is troubled by winds from the desert, so that it forms a melancholy film over all the life of Karachi. It comes in a battalion of hot clouds, invading ones food, ones clothes and ones lungs....'

I may be wrong but it seems to me that this is a slightly overdrawn picture. Would you care to tone it down a little. Or perhaps the sentence may read as follows:-

'I walked to the corner of the street, through the dust—the dust that at certain times of the year is troubled by winds from the desert....etc. The addition of the words 'at certain times of the year' would, I think make the picture more accurate.

4. Last sentence, Page 8,
'......and Fatima who became a dentist and in later years Jinnah's close companion and housekeeper.'
Please omit the words 'and housekeeper'.

5. Page 10, under the episode <u>The beginning of legend</u>, 3rd line of 2nd paragraph: 'He said that his father could remember little Mohammed Ali Jinnah as a boy—so poor that he had to climb a lamp-post and steal the lamp, so that he would have a light by which to study his books......'
The way the story is generally current is that he used to sit under a street lamp to study his books. In actual fact neither your version nor ours could be true because by the standards prevailing in this country during Jinnah's childhood, he belonged to pretty well-to-do family, otherwise they could not have sent him to England. But quite apart from the question of accuracy, my fear is that some of our friends in this country might exploit this little point against us. May I suggest that the sentence may be recast as follow:-

'He said that his father could remember little Jinnah as a boy—so poor that he sat under a lamp-post so that he would have a light by which to study his books.'

6. Consequential changes will be necessary in the next paragraph and for–
'Jinnah was neither Mrs. Naidu's "eldest son of a rich merchant...... reared in careless affluence", nor a poor boy who stole a lamp,'

the following may be substituted:
'Jinnah was neither Mrs. Naidu's "eldest son......reared in careless affluence", nor a poor boy who read by the light of the street lamp.'

7. I earnestly request you to delete the last sentence on page 10, which is as follows:-
'I like best the story of Jinnah, along with a school friend, sneaking a free ride on the footboard of a gharry and being whipped off by the angry driver.'

8. Page 13, episode of <u>A student in London</u>, first line of the 3rd paragraph:—'Dr. Ashraf recalls Jinnah boasting to him that he...... Could you substitute 'telling' for 'boasting to'?

9. Page 15, last sentence of the 3rd paragraph:—'Also, he abandoned his "funny" coat and began the habits of the English dandy, which endured to the end'. What about changing the word 'dandy' to gentleman'?

10. Page 16, last sentence—'......a dying monarch, holding the circle of glass between his almost transparent fingers'. Will you consider changing the word 'monarch' to 'hero'?

11. Page 25, 1st sentence of paragraph 3—'The relationship between brother and sister endured through all differences of temperament and mind that confuse the human heart.' Could you kindly tone down this sentence.

12. Page 30, 'that when he began to practise, he was the solitary Mohammedan barrister of the time;......' 'Muslim' is the word normally used for 'Mohammedan' in this country.

13. Page 37, 'There were terrible outrages in South-East India, for a long time afterwards......' I think you should say 'East India' not 'South-East India'.

Please remember me to Peel.
I hope you are fit and flourishing.

Yours sincerely,

(Majeed Malik)

October 6th 1952.

Dear Majeed,

Thank you for your cables, for the manuscript, and for your letter of October 3rd. There must be a deep sympathy between us because, while you were ill, I broke my little toe. Derek Peel very rudely suggested, 'That's what comes of digging your toes in too much'. I do not know whether you use the expression.

I naturally feel disappointed because I have not received one of the many promised documents and reminiscences. You know, I am sure, that this makes my task very difficult. However, I am very grateful for your kind comments.

Now to your suggested alterations. I have only one or two mild requests to make.

Top of page 9.   I have changed this to 'the dust that, in certain seasons, is troubled by winds from the desert'. I hope this is all right.

Page 16.   Instead of changing 'monarch' to 'hero', as you suggest, I have used the word 'warrior'. I hope you agree.

Page 25.   The sentence now reads, 'The relationship between brother and sister endured through the vicissitudes of half a century'.

I am sorry you wish me to delete the story about Jinnah 'sneaking a free ride on the footboard of a gharry'. I like it because it removes the hint of priggishness and makes him more human. I remember when writing the story of King George VI as a boy, I related the incident of his letting off fireworks in lavatories at school, and of his being punished for it. Nobody objected to such a human story. I would like to induce you to allow me to leave this story of the gharry-ride in.

I enclose two copies of pages 41 to 46. These episodes end the first section of the book, and it would be a great advantage for me to have them passed. One copy is for you to keep: please return the other to me.

My article on Pakistan in 'Everybody's' has had some pleasing results. I enclose a cutting to show you how the good feeling spreads, into the Provinces—the very people one wishes to interest.

I still hope the Prime Minister will write to the Aga Khan. Please use your influence.

With best wishes to you and your wife,

Yours sincerely,

Hector Bolitho.

PRESS INFORMATION DEPARTMENT
Government of Pakistan
Karachi, October 13, 1952

My dear Hector,

Many thanks for your letter of October 6.

I was very sorry to hear that you broke your little toe. I hope you have completely recovered. But, I must confess, I cannot understand how you managed to do it unless you were playing football bare footed, as some of us do in this country—and were playing it with a cricket ball too! But I thought you had passed that age. Or am I wrong?!!

I am in entire agreement with you with regard to the change that you have suggested on page 9, page 16 and page 25. Please do substitute:-

(a) 'The dust that, in certain seasons, is troubled by winds from the desert', (page 9)
(b) the word 'warrior' (page 16) and
(c) 'The relationship between brother and sister endured through the vicissitudes of half a century' (page 25)

in place of the words in your original script.

As for the story of the 'gharry-ride' I have, in deference to your wishes, carefully considered the advantages and disadvantages of retaining it. In fact I have gone to the length of consulting several people about it. The consensus of opinion is that our critics are sure to pluck this story out of its context and exploit it against us when the book is published. I, therefore, request that this story may please be positively deleted.

I hope to be able to return pages 41-46 within the next three or four days.

As for the rest, things are going on pretty smoothly. It may be that we shall meet sooner than you think. There is just chance that I may come to London well within a month. Personally I am not keen at all, as brief visits to places like London, by air, leave me quite unhappy when they end.

Your man, Friday, is regularly getting his Rs. 10/- by the 22nd or 23rd of every month. He is happy—and very grateful to you.

Please remember me to Derek.

Yours sincerely,

(Majeed Malik)

PRESS INFORMATION DEPARTMENT
Government of Pakistan
Karachi, October 31, 1952

My dear Hector,

I found pages 41-46 of your manuscript no less interesting and exciting than the previous ones. My only comment is that in places the picture of Karachi as drawn by you becomes a little too harsh. However, I shall begin from the beginning.

(1) Page 42, 13th line. Would you consider deleting the sentence: 'But I have not been allowed to see them'. Or say instead—'But I have not been able to see them'.[1]

(2) Page 42, 17th line, downwards. 'When he went to see...rather than with him—late into the night'. The picture seems to me to be overdrawn. Mr. Jinnah loved beautiful things and surrounded himself with them. His house was amongst the most tastefully decorated, and he was one of the foremost connoisseurs of carpets in the country. Carpets and Moghul paintings were his weakness. In the light of these facts, wouldn't you like to tone down, or delete, this sentence?[2]

(3) Page 43, line 21 down to the end of the paragraph. 'These dreadful sentinels... bleaching in the sun.' My feeling is that the picture becomes too grim, and I suggest that you might consider deleting this.[3]

(4) Page 44, 3rd line. 'The cotton must be guarded, for this is most of the fortune...'. I suggest that 'besides jute' may be inserted after 'for this'. The re-cast sentence would thus read: 'The cotton must be guarded, for this besides jute is most of the...[4]

(5)	Page 44, beginning of para 3.	Will you consider deleting the words 'All else is harsh', and begin the paragraph: 'So you welcome the cool train...'[5]
(6)	Page 45, last but one sentence.	'One afternoon I stood on the edge of the earth wrestling ring: it was flooded and at least fifty buffaloes were cooling themselves in the water. And children were swimming.' May I suggest that the words 'and at least fifty buffaloes were cooling themselves in the water', may be deleted?[6]

The requests for deletions or alterations made in paras 3, 5 and 6 are based on my reaction that the general picture which emerges appears to be a little too grim. My own feeling is that with these deletions the picture would remain accurate but lose its harsh tone. Do you agree?

By the way, have you seen the November issue of the *'National Geographic Magazine'* (Washington) which has a very good illustrated article on Pakistan by Jean and Franc Shor. I have requested our Press Attaché in London, to obtain a copy and send it to you. Also I enclose a cutting from *'Dawn'*, which contains a reproduction of a write-up on Karachi which has appeared in the *'Christian Science Monitor'*.

    Best regards.

Yours sincerely,

(Majeed Malik)

6, Lowndes Place
London S.W.I.
November 4, 1952.

Dear Majeed,

Thank you for your letter of October 31.

As requested previously by you, I sent you TWO copies of the manuscript, pages 41–46. I asked that one might be returned to me so that I can check the alterations you wish. PLEASE send me one copy back by airmail—by return if possible. I am very much held up until it arrives.

I bow to all your wishes, except that I regret having to cut out the piece about Mr Jinnah on page 42, the 17th line down. This was told me by Sir Cowasjee Jehangir. Mr Jinnah may have developed aesthetic tastes <u>later on</u>; but in these early years, I am assured that he cared little for Moghul paintings or bronzes. All my point is lost if I must delete this paragraph. It wrecks the end of my chapter to delete the paragraph. May I add, 'in these early years', thus inferring that he developed his tastes later on. As a matter of fact, he did not show any interest in painting or sculpture until he married. Then his wife opened up a new world of taste for him. I wish to bring this out when the time comes. So please let the paragraph stand, with the addition of 'in these early years', which will meet your objections, and still be true.

With best wishes,

Yours sincerely,

Hector Bolitho.

PRESS INFORMATION DEPARTMENT
Government of Pakistan
Karachi, December 11, 1952

My dear Hector,

I have not heard from you for a long time. I hope you are fit and well. Did you get the photographs of the bunder-boats? I am referring to the second batch which I sent to you. You will recall that you did not fancy the first batch. I hope the second batch was satisfactory; if not, would you like me to make a third effort.

I am hoping to get a further instalment of the book from you. I trust you have no misgivings about the minor alterations I have been suggesting. Personally I have no doubt in my mind that the arrangement would work very smoothly. Did I tell you in anyone of my previous letters that you are welcome to retain the piece about Mr Jinnah on page 42, the 17th line down? You are.[7]

I hope you are bearing up despite the record fog which has indirectly made itself felt even in far off Karachi! Most of the planes arriving here from London have been hopelessly behind schedule during the last few days.

Please remember me to Derek. I hope both you and he are fit and flourishing.

Best regards,

Yours sincerely,

(Majeed Malik)

6, Lowndes Place,
London, S.W.I.
17 December 1952.

Dear Majeed,

Thank you for your kind letter of December 11th, and for the Bunder-boat photographs which are exactly what I need. Thank you very much for this kindness.

I have conveyed your friendly messages to Derek Peel, who asks to be remembered to you. He is working on a new book concerning the history of weaving in England.

I have not sent any more manuscript, my dear friend, because nobody keeps their promise to send me material. Everyone, from the Prime Minister and the Aga Khan, down to ADCs and secretaries, have broken their word.

How comic it will look if, in the list of acknowledgments, I have to thank only Parsis and Hindus for their generous help in my task of writing a book about Quaid-i-Azam!

Nevertheless, I send you my devoted wishes for the New Year, and may Allah in all His goodness stir your conscience and make you send me the reminiscences you promised.

Yours very sincerely,

Hector Bolitho.

PS. I enclose a copy of my article as it appeared in a New Zealand magazine.

Please reply to   The Athenaeum,
Pall Mall,
London S.W.I.
19th April 1953.

Dear Majeed,

A. I enclose—in duplicate—substitute pages, 35 & 35A for the manuscript already sent to you. You will see that they take the place of the original page 35 and the first five lines of page 36.
I have made an addition which I hope is an improvement. I look forward to receiving one of these copies back, passed by you.

B. I also enclose—in duplicate—three further sections of the book:

Shalimar Gardens
Names on the Land
Background for Pakistan

They occupy pages 47 to 66, inclusive. I equally look forward to receiving one copy of these chapters, passed by you.

In a few days [I] expect to send you a considerable number of chapters, but I thought I would send you the enclosed so that they could be passed as soon as possible.

Begum Liaquat, Col. Knowles and Col. Birnie are being of great help to me in the closing chapters, which will be sent to you in due course.

Please be kind and return the manuscript by air.

With my best wishes,

Yours sincerely,

Hector Bolitho.

21 Wilton Crescent,
London S.W.I.
April 25th, 1953.

Dear Majeed,

I enclose the following chapters of my book, in duplicate:-

In the garden
Morning in Karachi
Ziarat
The last task
The last days

You will see that these form the <u>end</u> of the book. I have written them before finishing the middle, as the story of Quaid-i-Azam's last year of life became so vivid in my mind.

I look forward to receiving one copy of the manuscript, as soon as possible, with your comments.

As you know, my book will suffer from the fact that neither the Governor-General nor the former Prime Minister has given me any tribute, or any stories, regarding the Quaid. Do you think the new Prime Minister would see me when he comes for the Coronation? His recollections of the Quaid would be of great value in recommending the book—especially in America. If he agrees, I would remain in London for the week following the Coronation, in order to see him. But I would like to know as soon as possible.

There is one more thought. Why not appoint Fareed Jafri to make a translation of the book into Urdu—so that it could be published, in Urdu, at the same time as it appears in England. This is, of course, not my affair, but I thought the suggestion might appeal to you.

With my best wishes,

Yours sincerely,

Hector Bolitho.

The Athenaeum,
Pall Mall,
London,
May 3rd, 1953.

Dear Majeed,

I sent you parts of the book, with letters dated April 19th, and April 25th. I have no news of their safe arrival and am terribly afraid lest pirates have captured them on the way.

However, I am sending you a few corrections and additions for the closing chapter, 'The Last Days'.

After searching all over the land I have found Sister Dunham, who nursed Quaid-i-Azam while he was dying. The stories she told me give such a warm and gentle view of him that I am sure you will think them important. The incident in the ambulance, of his touching her arm, is very moving.

And I have now met both his Military Secretaries. One is lending me his diary. The book grows...but the task is not easy because nobody in Pakistan ever answers my letters. Not even the favourite of all Pakistanis, who wears his spectacles in his pocket in such a singular way...which I have since copied.

Please send back the chapters. PLEASE PLEASE PLEASE

May 13, 1953

Dear Majeed,

I have just received your cable, regarding the return of manuscripts sent to you on April 19th and April 25th. I now enclose two further chapters, in duplicate:

Flight into Karachi
The Colonel

I look forward to receiving one copy of these back from you as soon as possible. The delays are very depressing. Fareed Jafri is ill and unable to help me.

But there is something much more important. I lunched with Admiral Jefford last week. As you know, he became a friend while I was in Karachi. I am going to his daughter's wedding next week. He is willing for me to write a chapter on his relationship with Quaid-i-Azam and Pakistan, but he cannot spare the time to help me until after the Coronation. Pakistan has no more genuine friend in this country, and his tribute to Quaid-i-Azam, and to Pakistan, would be an important part of the book. It is very moving to listen to him, speaking with such faith in Pakistan.

The same is true of General Sir Douglas Gracey. A chapter from him is very important, but I cannot see him until late in June. The Coronation is making every one so busy that they cannot help until it is over. This would mean that I would need one more month — to July 20th — to complete the book. Please <u>cable</u> me your decision on this.

I have now written about 50,000 words — making two-thirds of the book. The end would be greatly strengthened by chapters from these two senior officers who have served Pakistan. But <u>please</u> <u>cable</u> your reply as I must change my plans to be able to stay in London for this extra time.

It is within the law for me to ask for this extra time as I was ill for more than a month following the terrible fogs. The agreement with you allows for delay in the case of 'incapacitation through illness'. But I don't want to go through all the dreary business of producing certificates and pressing the point.

I am determined to make the book as good as possible, and I am sure that the extra chapters would enhance it—especially if I can see the Prime Minister also, when he is here for the Coronation.

I am being a good boy and working hard, so please be kind and do your best to help me over this.

With my best wishes,

Yours very sincerely,

Hector Bolitho.

The Athenaeum,
Pall Mall, S.W.I.
14th May, 1953.

Dear Majeed,

I enclose three more chapters of the book, in duplicate.

1906–1910
1910–1913
An Essay in Friendship.

Please correct me in any error of fact. It is not easy for me to be assured over every detail as the authorities I consult vary so much with their facts.

I am writing this letter late at night, after an interesting experience. I met young Lord Wavell and his mother, Lady Wavell, at supper. They are both willing to help me with the book. It is one more reason why I beg you to give me one more month. They are both busy until after the Coronation; after that, they are willing to give me what will be valuable material for the book.[8]

Yours sincerely,

Hector Bolitho.

21st May, 1953

Dear Majeed,

My letters of April 19th, April 25th, and May 14th, remain unanswered and the manuscripts sent with them have not been returned. This all makes it so difficult for me to go on writing as I cannot possibly know what deletions and changes you will make. Please be kind and help about this. The publishers, who have read the first 5,000 words, are repeatedly asking me for more.

What concerns me most is my request for a further month. It is so vital that I should include the material from General Gracey, Admiral Jefford and Lord Wavell. This new and exclusive material will make all the difference to the book and will strengthen the sales in this country. Please cable me about this as soon as possible as I do not wish to engage these gentlemen in giving me material which could not be used owing to the deadline.

I enclose three more chapters, in duplicate. They are
'A Gentleman of "recognised position".'
'The Lucknow Pact'.
'Gandhi, Annie Besant, Samuel Edwin Montagu.'

Begum Liaquat, and Khurshid have both read the book and they seem to like it. In confidence, Khurshid is helping me and checking the manuscript, chapter by chapter.

With my best wishes, but also my entreaties.

Yours very sincerely,

Hector Bolitho

PRESS INFORMATION DEPARTMENT
Government of Pakistan
Karachi, May 28, 1953

My dear Hector,

I am sorry some of your letters were not acknowledged by me but you must have noticed that action was taken on the point raised by you — that of extending the time limit by a month. Ikram's cable must have reached you a few days ago.

As for the script I hope to be able to send one instalment within the next few days and the rest, I hope, within a fortnight after that. You must forgive me for the delay but both Ikram and I have been extremely busy during the last few weeks and are likely to remain so for another few weeks.

With best wishes,

Yours sincerely,

(Majeed Malik)

May 30th

Dear Majeed

I enclose a further chapter of the book:

<u>Jinnah's Right Hand</u>

This has been passed by Begum Liaquat Ali Khan.

I am very unhappy about the delay in returning the manuscript. Chapters sent to you on April 19th have not been sent back to me. This makes my task very difficult as it is not easy to plan further chapters while I do not know what is being cut or changed in the early ones.

And it makes it difficult for me to explain to the publishers. However, I have to work on against this very serious discouragement.

With best wishes,

Yours very sincerely

Hector Bolitho

The Athenaeum,
Pall Mall,
London, S.W.I.

15th June, 1953.

Dear Majeed,

Thank you for your cable.

It all becomes so complicated. My agreement, Clause 9, states:

'The Government shall forthwith appoint one of its officers, to whom the Author shall submit each section of the said book as it is written and such officer shall without undue delay approve or indicate what amendments are required by the Government....'

Ikram—by his word to me—and the late Minister, Dr I.H. Qureshi; both promised that you would be the officer appointed to read the chapters of the book. And I think that two months is an 'undue delay'. The whole shape of the book depends on what deletions and changes are demanded by the Government.

I beg you, dear Sir, to let me have a receipt for the chapters already sent you. I enclose the following additional chapters:-

Jinnah's marriage
The years of disillusionment
Jinnah and youth
Interlude with the doctors

also an additional Page for the chapter, 'Flight into Karachi'—already sent to you.

I attach a list of all the chapters and additions sent to you and not returned. I have included the new chapters mentioned above on this list. I do beg you to sign this list and return it to me. Otherwise I cannot know whether the various chapters arrive safely.

I realize how difficult your task must be, and I am grateful for your personal help in arranging an extension of the time.

My best wishes,

Yours sincerely,
Hector Bolitho.

with my letter dated 19 April:	substitute pages 35 & 35A Shalimar Gardens Names on the Land background for Pakistan
with my letter dated 25 April:	In the Garden Morning in Karachi Ziarat The Last Task The Last Days
with my letter dated 3 May:	Corrections to chapter, 'The Last Days', including Nurse Dunham's notes.
with my letter dated 13 May:	Flight into Karachi The Colonel
with my letter dated 14 May:	1906–1910 1919–1913 An Essay in Friendship
with my letter dated 21 May:	A gentleman 'of recognised position' The Lucknow Pact Gandhi, Annie Besant, and Edwin Samuel Montagu
with my letter dated 30 May:	Jinnah's Right Hand
with my letter dated 15 June:	addition to chapter, 'Flight into Karachi Jinnah's Marriage The Years of Disillusionment Jinnah and Youth Interlude with the Doctors

PRESS INFORMATION DEPARTMENT
Government of Pakistan
Karachi, June 26, 1953

My dear Hector,

I apologise to you most profusely for the delay in returning your script. I return a biggish chunk today and hope to be able to send you the rest in a fortnight's time—earlier rather than later. I am having a hectic time and that partly accounts for the delay. So please forgive a friend for his lapses.

With best regards,

Enclo:- As above

Yours sincerely,

(Majeed Malik)

COMMENTS ON THE SCRIPT
[Attached to Majeed Malik's Letter Dated 26 June 1953]

Pages 35–35A
No remarks,
Pages 47 to 88

Page 50-A	For 'in memory of his favourite dancing girl...' substitute 'in memory of the dancing girl, sweetheart of his son Prince Salim, later Emperor Jehangir'. The change seems necessary in the interest of historical accuracy.[9]
Page 50-B	For the word 'Mughal' substitute 'Afghan'. The gun was cast for Ahmed Shah Abdali who was an Afghan and not a Mughal.[10]
Page 50	I suggest that the clause 'the bhangies being their chief fighting sect' be deleted. 'Bhangies' actually are the sweeper—scavenger class of untouchables. The Sikhs would be offended if we describe Bhangies as their principal fighting sect. I have not been able to ascertain why the gun came to be called Bhangies gun, perhaps the solution lies in deleting the clause.
Page 51	For 'camels' substitute 'bullocks'. There are few, if any, camels in Lahore.[11]
Page 51-A	'The last was the street of cavalry men'. This does not seem to be correct. A *chabuk sawar* is a horse trainer. The sentence should, therefore, read 'The last was the street of horse trainers'.[12]
Page 53-A	It is suggested that any of the quotations may be substituted for this part. The change will in no way affect your argument and would save you and us from hostile criticism here.[13]

'Then the town of Sirhind itself was taken, and pillaged for four days with ruthless cruelty; the mosques were defiled, the houses burnt, the women outraged and the Muslims slaughtered. ... From Sirhind as a centre Banda plundered and occupied the country around.' (*The Cambridge History of India*, Volume IV, edited by Lt.-Col. Sir Wolseley Haig and Sir Richard Burn.)

'Banda now entered Sirhind... He commanded it to be fired, and all the inhabitants to be put to death. While the city was in flames, the followers of this fanatic carried on the work of carnage in the most diabolical spirit. They slaughtered the inhabitants indiscriminately without regard to age or sex. They butchered, bayoneted, strangled, hanged, shot down, hacked to pieces, and burnt alive, every Mohammedan in the place. Nor was this all. The dead, too, were made to contribute their share towards gratifying the rage of these voracious vampires. The corpse of Wazir Khan was hanged on a tree, and left to the tender mercies of the crows and vultures. The sanctity of the graveyards was violated, and corpses were exhumed, hewn to pieces, and exposed as carrion for the wolves, jackals, and other nocturnal visitants to these abodes of the dead. The mosques were polluted and burnt down, and the mullahs, maulvis and hafizes subjected to the greatest indignities and tortures.

'Elated with his success at Sirhind, Banda crossed the Sutlej, carrying fire and sword wherever he went. Towns were devastated and the inhabitants plundered, and driven into the wilderness, or put to the sword. Some of the towns were razed to the ground. At Samana ten thousand men and women were mercilessly put to the sword.'

'Batala had been celebrated from a remote period as a great seat of learning, and a college flourished there at the time. This institution was fired, and the whole city given up to pillage and indiscriminate massacre.'

'From within two or three days' march of Delhi to the environs of Lahore the whole country was ravaged. Mosques and tombs were razed to the ground. Horrible crimes were committed. Treachery and cruelty stalked through the land.'

'His ruling and insatiable passion was that of pouring out Mohammedan blood.' (*History of the Punjab* by Syed Muhammad Latif.)

Pages 54-A and 55-A	It is requested that both paragraphs beginning 'But there are signs,…' and 'There is one change in the monuments of Lahore…' be deleted.[14]
Page 60-A	Delete the words 'and tried to bring the teaching of the Koran nearer to the age in which he lived'.[15]
Page 62-A	Begin the second sentence of the third paragraph as follows: 'When Hindu leaders of Benaras started a movement for replacing Urdu by Hindi he said…'.[16]
Page 63-A	After the words 'English professors and lecturers' the following words may be added if you so desire: 'including Sir Walter Raleigh, the English man of letters, and Sir Thomas Arnold, the distinguished orientalist'.[17]
Page 63-B	Delete the words 'learned by word of mouth, from father to child'. (This is factually incorrect).[18]
Page 65-A	The under-lined clause may be deleted.[19]
Page 66-A	The under-lined part of the sentence may be deleted.[20]

Page 67-A	For the under-lined sentence substitute 'As it was, Jinnah received this enlightenment decades later'.[21]
Page 69-A	The word 'calculating' may be substituted by 'dispassionate'. As a consequential change in the same line the word 'passions' may, perhaps, be changed to 'prejudices'.[22]
Pages 71-A and 72-A	It is requested that the whole paragraph may be deleted. The thread of narrative can be resumed with 'We might take notice of a trifling episode about this time....'[23]
Page 73-A	The word 'arrogance' may by substituted by 'aggressive self-confidence'.[24]
Page 74-A	Delete 'of Jinnah's bravado'. Consequential change for 'he' substitute 'Jinnah'.[25]
Page 75-A	For 'Gopal Gokhale' substitute 'Gopal Krishan Gokhale'. This was his full name.[26]
Page 77-A	For 'Indians' substitute 'Muslims'.[27]
Page 77-B	Please delete 'neither style nor originality of thought—'.[28]
Page 83-A	The words 'obedient to the mind of someone else for the first time' may please be deleted.[29]

Chapter 'Flight into Karachi'

Page A-1	Please omit the words 'the glory, and'. Also comma after the word 'tasks'.[30]
Page A-2	The paragraph may please be deleted.[31]
Page B-1	The underlined sentences may please be omitted.[32]
Page B-2	The paragraph may please be omitted.[33]
Page B-3	The paragraph may please be deleted. This deletion arises out of the deletion of 'B-2'. Also the reference to the land that Alexander the Great conquered is not geographically accurate.
Page C-1	After 'Commander Ahsan' please add 'the Naval ADC'. This change is a consequential one arising out of the deletion of 'A-2'.[34]
Page C-2	The sentence may please be deleted. Apart from other things this is factually incorrect.[35]
Page C-3	The word 'horde' may preferably be substituted by 'throngs'.[36]
Page D-1	The words 'but they were poor and humble' may be deleted.[37]
Page D-2	The sentence beginning 'He was of them......' may please be deleted.[38]
Page D-3	For 'Then he...of victory'[39] please substitute 'Then he permitted himself to indulge in his known enthusiasm for detail'.[40]

122   IN QUEST OF JINNAH

Page E-1   Please omit the words 'or the King of England'.[41]
Page E-2   Please omit the underlined sentence.[42]
Page E-3   For 'their passions' please substitute 'the fervour of the people'.[43]
Page F-1   For 'fussiness' substitute 'attention to detail'.[44]
Page F-2   Please delete the sentence—'He had reached his full stature'.[45]
Page G-1   Please omit 'his equal in integrity, in a continent where integrity is so easily sullied'.[46]

Chapter 'The Colonel'

Page A-1   For 'Quaid-i-Azam' substitute 'anybody'.[47]
Page C-1   Delete the words 'who forced the gate'.[48]
Page C-2   For 'West Punjab' please substitute 'East Punjab'. Obviously East Punjab is meant.[49]
Page E-1   May please be deleted.[50]
Page H-1   This may please be deleted.[51]

The Athenaeum,
Pall Mall,
London, S.W.I.

June 29th, 1953.

My dear Majeed,

Thank you for your letter of June 26th, and for the typescripts of the following pages:

    35 and 35-A
    47 to 88

and the chapters, 'Flight into Karachi' and 'The Colonel'

1. **Page 54.** May I leave in the paragraph beginning, 'But there are signs...' and ending '...on the loan'. Otherwise, the chapter is clumsy and ends in the air.[52]
2. **Page 62.** I attach the correction, for your approval.[53]
3. **Page 67.** You suggest, 'As it was, Jinnah received this enlightenment decades later.' I find this ambiguous and clumsy. May I write, 'As it was Jinnah did not admit this enlightenment until he was a much older man.'[54]
4. **Page 75.** You say 'Krishan'. The Encyclopedia Britannica gives us 'Krishna'. May I know which is correct?[55]
5. **Flight into Karachi. Page D.** Your suggestion No. 3. May I observe the deletion as you suggest, and not add the suggested substitute as I do not quite understand that it means?[56]

The following are my general comments on the changes you have made:-

In some of the deletions (for instance, Page E of Flight into Karachi, where I quote Jinnah's remark about the 'King of England') you are asking me to meddle with fact. This also applies to the factual account of Jinnah's flight into Karachi.[57]

Deletions – such as the reference to Queen Victoria on Page 55 — are removing my personality from the book.[58]

I would be unhappy if future deletions removed my personality so far as to make the book unacceptable to English readers, and to my publishers. The deletions are so obviously planned to appease Pakistanis rather than to attract English and American readers, that I am apprehensive.

I beg you to realize that deletions—such as the enchanting story of Colonel Birnie and the hats—which is <u>true</u> are removing the human quality in Jinnah, which is what will sell the book, here and in America.

My publishers are very distressed over such cuts as this, and say that the book will be 'dull' without such lively episodes which only add to Jinnah's bigness—since little eccentricities are part of the stature of a really great man.

I would point out, in confidence, that Qazi Isa, Begum Liaquat, and Khurshid, have all read the book and have been enthusiastic in saying that I have 'caught the character and humanity' of Jinnah. I hate seeing this removed.

I enclose, in duplicate, the following additional chapters of the book—bringing the total of words sent to you to 66,000 words:-

1921–1928	pages	124–134
The 'parting of the ways'	pages	135–139
Exile: 1930–1934	pages	140–144
Jinnah reads a book	pages	145–152

With best wishes,

Yours sincerely,

Hector Bolitho.

PRESS INFORMATION DEPARTMENT
Government of Pakistan
Karachi, July 7, 1953

My dear Hector,

Please refer to your letter of June 29.

I write to ask for clarification on a small point.

Dealing with page 62 you say 'I attach the correction, for your approval'. The attached note reads as follows:

> 'The mosques were defiled, the houses burnt, the women outraged and the Muslims slaughtered ... the whole country was ravaged. Mosques and tombs were razed to the ground ...... they slaughtered the inhabitants indiscriminately without regard to age or sex. They butchered, bayoneted, strangled, hanged, shot down, hacked to pieces, and burnt alive, every Mohammedan in the place. Nor was this all. The dead, too, were made to contribute their share towards gratifying the rage of these voracious vampires. The corpse of Wazir Khan was hanged on a tree, and left to the tender mercies of the crows and vultures...'

I presume that this refers to page 53(A) and not page 62. What then is the correction made on page 62 of the script?

I hope to be able to send chapters (1) 'In the Garden' and 'Last Days', (2) 'Jinnah's Right hand' and (3) 'A gentleman of Recognised Position' to you within the next few days. You will be glad to know that there are very few changes in the chapters.

Yours sincerely,
(Majeed Malik)

The Athenaeum,
Pall Mall,
London, S.W.I.

8th July, 1953.

Dear Majeed,

I enclose four more chapters of the book—almost the end of my task. They are:-

Return to India: 1935–1937	pages	153–160
1937–1939	pages	161–169
1940—'Pakistan'	pages	169A–174
The Birthday Present	pages	175–179

Also, addition to chapter, 'Interlude with the Doctors'
And, additions to chapter, 'In the Garden'.

The new chapters bring the total sent to you up to about 72,000 words.

The delays, and constant broken promises in regard to the return of manuscript, are making my work impossible. I have 12 more days in which to finish the book. You hold chapters that were sent to you as long ago as April 25th. This does not conform with Para. 9 of our agreement which states that the manuscript will be returned to me 'without undue delay'. You have had some of the manuscript almost 3 months. How can I possibly give shape to a book, or gauge its length, in these circumstances?

In regard to the cuts you are making, I would remind you, again, that this book is primarily for American and English readers, few of whom know of Quaid-i-Azam. If the little human touches—such as the presentation of the hats to Colonel Brinie are removed, Jinnah will emerge as dull and unwarm, and uninteresting.

I would also remind you again that Mr Ikram promised that you, personally, would make the necessary deletions; that you would be the 'said officer' referred to in the contract. I have received a letter from the Editor of the 'Pakistan Quarterly', saying that you told him that 'it would take a considerable time for the Department to go through' the manuscript. I consider this is a breach of our arrangement.

I do not even know which chapters you have received safely. For all I know, parts of the manuscript may have gone astray. My letters are ignored, and the special 'advice of reception' cards sent through the post office with each batch of manuscript are returned to me unsigned and undated.

May I ask if you can tell me what happened to the mosque (see page 155 of my manuscript—marked xx). I would like to enlarge on this—to be able to state what actually has happened.

With best wishes,

Yours sincerely

Hector Bolitho

>The Athenaeum,
>Pall Mall,
>London, S.W.I.
>
>18th July 1953

My dear Majeed,

Thank you for your letter of 7th July. You are right: the correction refers to page 53A. The correction on page 62 of the script is only your suggestion—'When Hindu leaders of Benares started a movement for replacing Urdu by Hindi.'[59]

I am sorry for this slip and hope the corrections are now quite clear.

>Best wishes,
>
>Yours sincerely,
>
>Hector Bolitho.

The Athenaeum,
Pall Mall,
London, S.W.I.

18th July 1953

My dear Majeed,

In accordance with our agreement, I am sending you the last 'section of the said book' which, together with the Chapters already sent to you, forms the 'completed manuscript' — that is, more than enough to fill a book of '200–250 pages'.

In accordance with Mr Ikram's cable to me, dated May 25, the final date for delivery was extended to July 20th.

In am sending this last section of the book by a passenger — a Mr Burgett — on B.O.A.C., Flight No. 768, due in Karachi on July 20th at 0320 hours.

I have today sent you a cable asking you to be so kind as to have the manuscript collected from Mr Burgett, from the airport. I have asked him to obtain a receipt for the manuscript from your representative. But I would also be grateful if you would send me a cable assuring me that the manuscript has arrived.

With my best wishes,

Yours sincerely,

Hector Bolitho.

PRESS INFORMATION DEPARTMENT
Government of Pakistan
Karachi, July 23, 1953

My dear Hector,

Herewith another chunk of your manuscript. I am sorry I am returning it after a bit of time but so many things are happening here that this was inevitable. I hope to be able to send the next chunk within a fortnight.

Yours sincerely,

(Majeed Malik)

COMMENTS ON THE SCRIPT
[Attached to Majeed Malik's Letter Dated 23 July 1953]

Chapter – 'A gentleman of recognised position'

Page 89-A   Please delete the words 'who sometimes resorted to being a conversational bully'.[60]

Page 89-B   Please delete the sentence in parenthesis—'He did not add any comment......was an end itself.'[61]

Chapter – 'The Lucknow Pact'

Page 94-A   Please delete the words 'for whom biography is an alien form of writing'.[62]

Page 94-B   Please delete the words 'in these only was his mind little'.[63]

Page 96-A   Please delete the words 'of whom Jinnah said to a member of his staff, in later years, "That cunning old fox! When he enters my house the blood congeals in my veins. I never know how he will interpret what I say".'[64]

Chapter – 'Gandhi, Annie Besant, and Samuel Edwin Montagu'

Page 100-A   Would you reconsider the words 'aloof from charity'? After all Mr Jinnah willed away about half a million pounds worth of estate for charitable purposes. He gave it to three educational institutions—one of which is in India.[65]

PRESS INFORMATION DEPARTMENT
Government of Pakistan
Karachi, September 26, 1953

My dear Hector,

Herewith the script together with the changes suggested therein. I am hurrying to catch the mail, more in my next letter.

Yours sincerely,

(Majeed Malik)

COMMENTS ON THE SCRIPT
[Attached to Majeed Malik's Letter Dated 26 September 1953]

Chapter – Jinnah's Marriage

Page 105-A	Delete the word 'Spartan' in the third line of the second paragraph.[66]
Page 105-B	Delete from 'Jinnah had already made a fortune...' to the end of the third paragraph'...Jinnah was a cold fish—much too formal ever to be a good lover'.[67]
Page 107-A	Delete the word 'spartan'.[68]
Page 107-B	Delete the clause, 'it is said also that he greeted her proposal as "a very interesting proposition"'.[69]
Page 108-A	Delete the word 'sombre'.[70]
Page 108-B	In the sentence:- 'The deadly silence and bareness of the advocate's home gave way...' delete the word 'deadly' and the words 'and bareness' so that the sentence reads 'The silence of the advocate's home gave way...'[71]
Page 108-C	Delete the word 'musty'.[72]
Page 108-D	Delete 'It was one or the roots of their difference... in order to save his tram fare'.[73]
Page 109-A	Delete the paragraph 'the wound went deep ...... of his career'.[74]

Chapter – The years of disillusionment

Page 114-A	Delete the words 'and the fervour'.[75]
Page 118-A	Delete the paragraph 'Jinnah's mind...... broadening of his vision'.[76]

Pages 120-A and 121-A	Delete the paragraph beginning 'The last incident, which.........' and ending on page 121-A '......coming to this country'.[77]
Pages 121-B and 122-A	Delete the paragraph beginning 'Dewan Chaman Lal answered ... and ... on his face.'[78]

Chapter – Jinnah and Youth

Page A-1	Delete 'He would bite.........to relax and forgive.'[79]
Page B-1	Delete the sentence 'Khurshid smiled...... newspapers again'.[80]
Pages B, F & G	Delete the whole interview with Mr S.M. Yousuf.[81]

Chapter – Interlude with the doctors

N.B. (This chapter has been incorporated in two other chapters. Amendments have been marked here as well as in corresponding chapters).

Page A-1	To be deleted.[82]
Page B	The whole page to be deleted.[83]
Page C-1	To be deleted.[84]
Page E-1	Delete the words 'your arrogance'.[85]

Chapter – 1921–1923

Page 124-A	In the first sentence of the second paragraph delete the words 'written by Muslims' and the words 'that influences much of their thinking'.[86]
Pages 124-B and 125-A	To be deleted.[87]
Page 126-A	Delete the clause 'rather than be educated at the expense of British funds'. (This is factually incorrect. The funds were Indian, not British).
Page 126-B	For the words 'paid for by the British' substitute 'run on the British educational pattern'.
Page 128-A	Delete the words 'Hindus and Muslims once more turned on each other, and'. This is factually incorrect. The sentence to begin as 'As a measure against ......'[88]
Page 130-A	Delete the words 'and that unless he changed his manner, I would bring no more witnesses before him' substitute 'and had a right to be treated with courtesy and consideration'.[89] An officer of the rank of a Captain could hardly have declined to

	bring witnesses before a Committee which, if I remember a right, was appointed by Royal Chapter.
Page 130-B	For the sentence 'once he was challenged, he became reasonable, and he would never bear malice afterwards' substitute 'He was reasonable, and he never bore malice afterwards even when he was challenged'.[90]
Pages 131-A, 132 and 133-A	Delete beginning with 'whether from dispute...' on page 131 to... was apparently wrecked' on page 133.[91]
Page 133-B	Delete the word 'comic'.

Chapter – The 'parting of the ways'

Pages 138-B and 139-A	Delete the paragraph beginning with the words 'Throughout the years that followed...' and ending with the words '...The fault was mine'.[92]
Page 139-B	To be deleted.[93]

Chapter – Exile: 1930–1934

Pages 142-A & 145-A	Please delete the paragraph beginning with the words 'As one reads his story...' and ending with the words '... the cautious diet.'
Page 143-B	Delete 'and Iqbal talking ......with his own indignations'.[94]
Page 143-C	Delete the parenthetical clause 'his thoughts like eagles, beyond Jinnah's reach'.[95]
Page 146-A	Delete 'He could read of Mustafa Kemal......... had little meaning for him'.[96]
Page 147-A	Delete the paragraph beginning with the words 'Had Jinnah been a man of great imagination,' and ending with the words '...Jinnah was living.'[97]
Page 148-A	Delete the whole paragraph from 'We can but guess....' to '...his religion for himself'.[98]
Page 150-A	Delete the word 'already'.[99]

Chapter – Return to India: 1935–1937

Page 155-A	For the word 'appease' substitute 'protect'.[100]
Page 156-A	Delete the words 'on similar lines to Congress'.[101]
Page 156-B	Delete the words 'to inspire, and direct'.[102]
Page 157-A	Delete the words 'as this was his only language'.[103]

Chapter – 1937–1939: No change in the Chapter.

Chapter – A birthday present

134   IN QUEST OF JINNAH

Page 176-A Delete the words 'perhaps the house was no longer grand enough for Quaid-i-Azam'.[104]

Chapter – 1940–1942: No change in this chapter.

Chapter – 1942–44: Jinnah, Gandhi, and the Doctors

Pages 193-A and 194-A Delete the paragraph beginning with 'All Jinnah's infinite care...' to the end of second paragraph on page 194 ending '...years of poverty, here in Bombay'. As a consequential change delete the footnote on page 193.[105]

Page 195-A Please delete 'Even after partition ...... regarding his investments'.[106]

Chapter – 1945–1947

Page 202-A Delete the words 'And Liaquat Ali Khan'. Consequential change for 'their' substitute 'his'.[107]

Chapter – Partition: 1947

Page 220-A Add the figure '1947' after 15th August.[108]
Page 227-A Delete the words 'a former Chief Justice of India'. He was not.

Chapter – 'Jinnah's Right hand'

The following changes are suggested:-

Page D-1 'Assistant District Commissioner' may be substituted by 'Deputy Commissioner'.
Page G-1 Kindly delete the sentence 'In the short time...'
Page G-2 Will you very kindly delete this paragraph?
Page H-1 Would you consider saying in a footnote that Liaquat Ali Khan's faith in his people was justified and that adequate arrangements were made for her and the children. (As you are aware, she has been given a house and a life pension of over £200 a month. The children will receive £50 a month so long as they are being educated).[109]

Pages I & J Please delete (-(1), J-(1) and J-(2).
Page K-1 For 'He did not speak the language of the people of Pakistan— he spoke to them in English. They did not understand a word, but they listened, bewitched' please substitute 'He spoke to them in English. Not all understood what he said but they listened bewitched'.[110]

Chapter – 'In the Garden': No change.

Chapter – 'Morning in Karachi'

Please delete paragraph 'A-(1)-B(1)'. I am afraid the picture is inaccurate or, at the very least, flagrantly overdrawn. May I respectfully point out that noontime one does not see any people sleeping on pavements or on traffic islands in Karachi or elsewhere. Quite apart from other things, our bright sun and midday heat would make it physically impossible.

When you were here, you must have noticed that working hours in Government and private offices were from 9 a.m. to 4.30 p.m. Only a few shops close for the lunch hour—the biggest ones. There are no midday siesta hours for factory workers nor for other skilled and unsullied labour.

The people of West Pakistan are known for their hardihood. That was the opinion of the British Administration, expressed over and over again by Viceroys and Commanders-in-Chief and District Officers. Every official Gazetteer brings out that fact.

Practically every foreign correspondent who has come here since partition—British and American—has paid a tribute to the zeal and zest with which the people of Pakistan have built their country and made Pakistan into 'a miracle of achievement'. They have praised the people for their determination, guts and stamina. The peasantry of Pakistan—and they constitute 85 to 90% of the population—is known to be amongst the hardiest in the world.

That being the case, I feel, and I hope you will wholeheartedly agree, that no book sponsored by the Pakistan Government should give the impression that the people of this country are incapable—for climatic or other reasons—of building the country at least as well as people of so many other countries. I earnestly request you to delete this paragraph or rewrite it in a more suitable way.[111]

Chapter – 'Ziarat': No change suggested.

Chapter – 'The last task'

Page A-1   Please delete the words 'proved that his experience as an actor'.[112]

Page B-1   Please delete the words 'with more idealism than knowledge of economics'.[113]

Chapter – 'The Last days'

Page F-1   'in a land where efficiency of the western kind is rare'.[114]
Page G-1   Please delete 'and actor's pleasure'.[115]
Page M-1   Please delete the words 'to whom Jinnah was second only to the Prophet, for both sanctity and brilliance'.[116]

NOTES

1. Ref. newspaper cutting and day-to-day notes by M.A. Jinnah. HB, pp. 24, 25.
2. Ref. M.A. Jinnah's indifference to art objects. HB, p. 25.
3. Ref. vultures.
4. Jute not added, but reference confined to West Wing. HB, p. 26.
5. Ref. Karachi climate. HB, omitted from p. 26.
6. Ref. Lahore scene. HB, p. 27.
7. Ref. The past seemed to have no allure for him. HB, p. 27.
8. HB, p. 191.
9. Ref. Anarkali.
10. Ref. Kim's gun. HB, p. 28.
11. HB, p. 27.
12. HB, p. 28.
13. HB, p. 29.
14. Ref. Statue of Queen Victoria. HB, p. 29.
15. HB, p. 34.
16. HB, p. 35.
17. HB, p. 35.
18. HB, p. 36.
19. Ref. to M.A. Jinnah's narrowness of intellectual interests. HB, p. 39.
20. Ref. to students flattering M.A. Jinnah's vanity. HB, p. 43.
21. HB, p. 39.
22. HB, p. 41.
23. HB, p. 41.
24. HB, p. 43.
25. HB, p. 43.
26. HB, p. 45.
27. HB, p. 47.
28. HB, p. 47.
29. HB, p. 50.
30. HB, p. 172.
31. Ref. to Admiral Ahsan's emotions. HB, p. 172.
32. Ref. to M.A. Jinnah's usual reluctance to shake hands. HB, p. 173.
33. Ref. to M.A. Jinnah's dislike of the airplane service. HB, p. 173.
34. HB, p. 174.
35. Ref. again to M.A. Jinnah's reluctance to shake hands. HB, p. 174.
36. HB, p. 174.
37. HB, p. 174.
38. Ref. to M.A. Jinnah's inability to recognize Nanji Jafar in the welcoming crowd. HB, p. 174.
39. Then he permitted himself a little of the intoxication of victory.
40. Sentence completely omitted. HB, p. 176.

41. Not omitted. HB, p. 174.
42. Ref. says Pakistan naturally averse to order. HB, p. 175.
43. HB, p. 175.
44. HB, p. 176.
45. Ref. to 11 August 1947 speech. HB, p. 176.
46. Ref. to Liaquat Ali Khan. HB, p. 176.
47. Ref. to Col. E.J. Birnie. HB, p. 182.
48. Ref. crowd perturbed over communal riots. HB, p. 183.
49. Ref. riots. HB, p. 183.
50. Ref. to Comptroller Major S. McCoy. HB, p. 187.
51. Ref. M.A. Jinnah offers Col. Birnie some hats. HB, p. 187.
52. Retention allowed. HB, p. 30.
53. Ref. to Alexander Shakespeare. HB, p. 35.
54. Author's version retained. HB, p. 39.
55. Only initials used. HB, p. 39.
56. Suggestion not in text. HB, p. 175.
57. King of England' retained. HB, p. 174.
58. Quite true, but the author's personality is not the selling point here. HB, p. 30.
59. HB, p. 35.
60. Deleted. HB, p. 55.
61. HB, p. 58.
62. HB, p. 58.
63. HB, p. 59.
64. HB, p. 60.
65. HB, p. 67.
66. Deleted. HB, p. 68.
67. Deleted. HB, p. 68.
68. Deleted. HB, p. 68.
69. Deleted. HB, p. 68.
70. Deleted. HB, p. 69.
71. Deleted. HB, p. 69.
72. Deleted. HB, p. 69.
73. Deleted. HB, p. 69.
74. SPF.
75. Deleted. HB, p. 74.
76. SPF.
77. SPF.
78. SPF.
79. SPF..
80. SPF.
81. SPF.
82. Ref. to M.A. Jinnah's psychological reason to dress well.
83. SPF.

84. Dr Mehta on M.A. Jinnah. SPF.
85. Deleted. HB, p. 145.
86. Deleted. HB, p. 80.
87. Criticizes Muslim traits.
88. HB, p. 82.
89. HB, p. 83.
90. HB, p. 84.
91. Ref. to M.A. Jinnah's marriage failure. SPF.
92. Ref. to M.A. Jinnah's married life. SPF.
93. Ibid.
94. SFS. HB, p. 93.
95. Ibid.
96. SPF. HB, p. 96.
97. SPF. HB, p. 97.
98. SPF. HB, p. 97.
99. Ref. to oratory of Liaquat Ali Khan. HB, p. 98.
100. Ref. to RTC on minorities. HB, p. 102.
101. Ref. to reorganisation of Muslim League. HB, p. 103.
102. Ref. to Liaquat Ali Khan's contribution. HB, p. 103.
103. Ref. to M.A. Jinnah's sartorial preferences. HB, p. 104.
104. Deleted. HB, p. 121.
105. Ref. to M.A. Jinnah's keeping people at a distance. Deleted.
106. Ref. M.A. Jinnah phones Bombay broker after Partition. HB, p. 136.
107. HB, p. 143.
108. Ref. Lord Mountbatten fixes date of independence. HB, p. 162.
109. Page not found in the MS.
110. Ref. M.A. Jinnah's oratory. HB, p. 141.
111. HB, p. 195.
112. Deleted.
113. HB, p. 196.
114. Deleted. HB, p. 192.
115. Deleted. HB, p. 192.
116. Deleted as blasphemous.

PART THREE

Hector Bolitho: Miscellaneous Correspondence

1081, Fifth Avenue
New York city

24 June [1953]

Dear Mr. Bolitho,

   Your draft and letter has finally caught up with us. I left Bombay 15th May.

   I am sorry, that I am unable to send you letters or 'get' Kanji to help you, as I am not going back to India till November. I shall be in London on 15th July for ten days—the same address.

   I would love to see you apart from the book—Thank you so much for sending the draft to me, it was very considerate of you— there is much one can add, but nothing to delete. I believe Montagu wrote some amusing things about Mother.

Yours sincerely

Dina Wadia.

c/o British Embassy,
Belgrade, Yugoslavia.

10 July 1953

Dear Mr. Bolitho

I shall certainly do all I can to help you in your work of writing a book on Jinnah and Pakistan. Jinnah impressed me more, I think, that any one else whom I have ever met and I was very fond of him.

Unfortunately I do not know when I will next be in the U.K. but I may quite likely be in London for a week or so, some time before the end of the year. If I am, perhaps we could meet at the Athenaeum and have a talk. In the mean time if there is any particular point on which you would like information, I will do my best to give it to you. Letters addressed to me c/o The Foreign Office, Whitehall, S.W.I. and marked 'Belgrade' on the top left hand corner of the envelope come by bag and are quite safe.

Yours sincerely

Francis Mudie

c/o British Embassy,
Belgrade, Yugoslavia.

30 August 1953

Dear Mr. Bolitho

Many thanks for your letter of 20 August. It is difficult to say why I was fond of Jinnah. He was, as you say, cold—at least that was the impression he gave, but I never found him harsh. He was, of course, hard. He never, if he could help it, compromised. Most of the time he knew that would be fatal. His great hold on the Muslims of India was due to his reputation for absolute strength and integrity and any compromise might have been interpreted as a sign of weakness. It might even have been suggested that he had been bought.

I probably knew Jinnah better than any other British officer in India. I was certainly the only British civilian who knew him at all well. I met him first in 1936 when we were both members of the old Legislative Assembly and we started with a most heated controversy, when Jinnah refused to allow a certain clause in a Bill to be re-drafted, though the draft was obviously very bad. He showed himself in his most difficult mood. I knew him later again when I was Home Member of the Government of India, though by that time he had given up attending the Assembly and the Muslim League Party was led by Liaquat. It was then that I got to understand the case for Pakistan, though like most practical administrators in India, I had always preferred the Muslim to the Hindu. I knew him again in 1947, when he was living in Karachi.

My general impression of him, when he became Governor General of Pakistan was that he was vain, arrogant and cold, though I always found him very pleasant socially. Our relations became much closer after August 1947. I then discovered his virtues and learnt to overlook his less attractive qualities. Officially, until near the end when Jinnah was obviously very ill, I found him open to reason or at least to argument. I drafted a number of capers for him when he came up to Lahore shortly after independence and could generally get him to accept a point though, as before in Delhi, he often would not budge on a bad draft! In the end I got to know that I could trust him absolutely. He was thoroughly loyal to those who had supported him in the past. That was the real reason why he did not dismiss Mamdot, the Punjab

Premier. Mamdot had been his main supporters in the early days of the League in the Punjab. Of course he was rude officially, when we differed, as we fairly often did but if you were doing the honest thing and were not playing up to any sort of gallery, you knew that though he differed, Jinnah would bear no ill will and that in no circumstances would he go behind your back.

About this time too, I discovered his charm. And it was not put on if he liked you—and I think that he liked me—he was naturally charming. I stayed with him in Karachi a few days before he made what turned out be his last journey to Ziarat. He was very ill at the time, spending most of his time in bed. We had had rather a violent difference of opinion about the Punjab Ministry and yet within two hours, he got up from what was really his deathbed to say goodbye to me at three in the afternoon and could not have been nicer. There was no hint of our difference and not even a reference to the difficulties that I would obviously encounter in carrying out his policy. We might have been the oldest friends.

And he was not really cold. I remember one very revealing occasion when he was staying with me in September 1947. Everything in Lahore and the Punjab was chaos. Refugees were arriving daily by tens of thousands and Sikhs and Hindus going out. My niece and Jinnah and I were sitting having a drink before dinner, when he suddenly said 'This is very tragic—but very thrilling' and his eyes flashed with excitement. It was tragic, but it was thrilling, like a battle. And particularly thrilling to Jinnah. Here was his Pakistan at last in being. Here was the exchange of population, which he had been ridiculed for suggesting, actually taking place. Possibly what he said was the wrong thing to say. The cold hard lawyer would never have said it. But it revealed the great emotional strain under which he had been living under the cold exterior and we sympathized.

In judging Jinnah, we must remember what he was up against. He had against him, not only the wealth and brains of the Hindus, but also of nearly the whole of British officialdom and most of the Home politicians, who made the great mistake of refusing to take Pakistan seriously. Never was his position really examined. There was no examination of the questions of what the Muslims were afraid of and of whether there was any way to remove their fears, other than the partition. Instead there was nothing but politics and what looked very [much] like attempts to trap Jinnah into some difficult position or other. And when Jinnah did not fall into the trap, when in response to the question 'what will Jinnah do now?' Jinnah just did nothing; he was of course 'cold and intransigent'. When he did respond, as he did when the Cabinet Mission came to India, he was rebuffed and drew himself more into his shell. No man who had not the iron control of himself that Jinnah had could have done what he did. But it does not follow that he was really cold. In fact no one who did not feel as Jinnah did, could have done what he did.

I was very interested to hear that he knew that he was a dying man when Mountbatten came to India. He was in bed in my home, in Lahore for three weeks in late 1947 and never, even by sign, indicated that he would not shortly be all right again.

I am afraid that what I have written will be of little use to you, but I hope that I have shown that there was another side to Jinnah's character than that generally presented to the public and to those who, he felt, were not in sympathy with him.

Yours sincerely

Francis Mudie

Quaid-i-Millat House
Karachi
Pakistan

10 April 1954

Dear Mr Bolitho

It was good to get news of you again after such a long time, and to know that the book is progressing well. I shall certainly look forward to reading it.

I am sorry there is absolutely no available information I can give you on the point you asked for. I, myself, was not in Delhi at that particular time, and no one seems to remember anything he may have said then.

Liaquat never dramatized his own life and actions, especially at that period when his entire energies were bent upon building up Mr. Jinnah's strength and popularity and creating unity, rather than disrupting it by the introduction of his own personality and importance. His memory will for ever go by default on this account. Nor was he the type who frequently and expansively committed his thoughts, ideas or feelings to desultory or impulsive expression, on the pages of a diary. And as regards Mr. Jinnah, he both consciously and unconsciously effaced himself, for with Liaquat also there was never even a trace of vanity, divided loyalty or personal ambition.

I feel very distracted and forlorn at times—but I must keep with God as Liaquat did.

Yours sincerely,

(Raana Liaquat Ali Khan)

29 April 1954

Dear Mr. Bolitho

Thank you for your letter—I will be back in London next month at my club and will then look through some of my husband's papers and see what I can find to help you—as I am afraid my memory is not good enough to be relied on, on this point.

I only came here for a few weeks so have not got many papers with me—and can only hope the delay will not matter to you. I send you my thanks for sympathy on my son's death—I feel quite stunned by misery.

Yours sincerely

Eugenie Wavell

Red House
Thorpeness
Leiston
Suffolk

24 Georgian Ct.
Sunday

My dear Friend,

Before I leave the shores of this beautiful Country I want to thank you most sincerely for your kindness and regard you have shown. I shall always cherish the moments we had together and with your friend and colleague Derek. I know now that there is a corner 'for ever Pakistan'.

If at any time you happen to pass through or have a chance of going to Pakistan do let me know so that I can welcome you as a friend for myself and my people.

With best of wishes and deepest regards to Derek and yourself, I remain for ever

Yours sincerely

Khurshid

P.S. Do remember me to Mr. [?]

23 June 1954

Private & Confidential

Dear Mr. Bolitho

You may think I have forgotten your request re Mr. Jinnah.

Actually I have been reading many volumes of my husband's diaries and recollections in an endeavour to find what [illegible]. So far with no success.

I fear my husband did not much like the subject of your biography. He thought that his judgement was often marred by personal vanity — that his intransigence and nerves prevented his approaching large problems in a large way.

On the other hand Lord Wavell had great sympathy for the Muslims and their fear of being in a minority and he had immense admiration for their troops — as indeed all the Indian Army.

He was as you know determined to see fair play for all as long as he was Viceroy.

I am still searching, and will report any happy find. I do believe that my husband felt Jinnah was honestly trying to do the best he could for the cause he had so much at heart. I was sorry for him — he looked so ill and overstrained.

My Field Marshal admired Liaquat and found him tolerant and sensible and calm — the latter a quality he found congenial having possessed of it himself.

Sincerely yours

Eugenie Wavell

Clare Cottage
Vinkfield
Windsor

Nostell Priory,
Wakefield.

26 June 1954

Dear Mr. Bolitho

By all means—if you wish—say that I said Mr. Jinnah was one of the handsomest of men—he combined the clear cut, almost Grecian, features of the West with Oriental grace of movement.

I am still searching for what you wish.

Here in this wonderful house decorated by Robert Adam, where Chippendale worked for so long, making the furniture one seems delightfully far from political animosities past or present—I sometimes wonder if Statesmen could spend their time in trains and aeroplanes and squabbling at conferences and none in the beauty of the Countryside, if the world mightn't become more secure again.

Yours sincerely
Eugenie Wavell

PS. My host—Rowland Winn—says he met you in a Spanish train in 1934 near Algeciras and you told him to 'make words his friends' as he intended to be a writer. His next book comes out in August.

28 July 1954

Dear Hector

I have read and re-read your completed book with interest and pleasure. I am impressed by the manner in which from first to last the dramatic interest is maintained. There are no blank spaces or dull intervals. Jinnah is your theme. Now in your pages he lives again. That is the purpose of biography, and I could give your book no higher praise. Could Jinnah read what you have written I have no doubt he would agree that in your story of his life he finds a true picture of himself.

I feel however that you have had a particularly difficult task in that part of the narrative which concerns Jinnah's marriage, but there are many signs that you have wished to treat this as delicate ground on which to tread gently for fear of giving hurt. I hope you will not take it amiss that in order still further to remove the impression of sitting in judgment of relations between husband and wife I have mentioned one or two possible verbal changes to Derek.

I have also mentioned to him two small constitutional points which he has noted. In the political problems in which Jinnah played so notable a part there were three components the British, the Hindus and the Muslims. Each might well place the emphasis differently in describing the situation at any given time, but I think all could agree that in your book you give a fair presentation of the facts as the setting for the lead which Jinnah gave to his fellow Muslims.

You are more than kind in mentioning me in your introduction and I value the compliment, but feel I have done little to merit it. I return the copy of your book. You have spared yourself no pains in writing it and I am sure of its success.

Derek tells me you are laid up with a cold. I hope you will soon be well. That signature being for you only.

Yours ever Hawthorne Lewis

Joint Services Staff College, Latimer
Chesham Bucks
90, Lexham Gardens
London W. 8
6 August 1954

My Dear Hector,

I do hope most sincerely that you have recovered fully and are applying your active mind once again to give 'Jinnah' the finishing touches. I read a few paragraphs of the book to the Officers of H.M.P.S. Taimur, and they are anxiously looking forward to seeing it in the bookshops in Pakistan. When I returned from Plymouth, my boy was laid up with flu, but has recovered quite quickly by God's grace.

I have re-read the book a few times and cannot praise it too highly. You have written a great book about a great man. Few readers will ever know the nature and diversity of your difficulties to obtain authentic information. From your book, Quaid emerges as a man who most intelligent people in Pakistan knew him to be, but for reasons all too well known, could not describe.

In time you will hear much praise and some criticism no doubt, but before this great work becomes public, I must record my own insignificant opinion. There are many people who remember what the Quaid said on this and that occasion; I believe I could remember his words and silences better, what he might be thinking on those occasions and what he might say. If he were alive, he would not have wished for another biographer. I believe no living person would have been able to make the West understand Jinnah better than you have done, and for this Pakistan and Pakistanis owe you a very great debt.

I am personally most grateful to you and to Derek for listening to me so patiently and for so readily amending the words which I thought might be misconstrued and given a meaning different to what was intended to be conveyed. I sincerely hope Mr [Majeed] Malik receives the approval from his superiors about Quaid's opinion of Lord Mountbatten. I am writing to Lord Louis now and will tell him that no one in your position could have been fairer to him and to Mr Jinnah at the same time.

I sincerely hope Hector that you and Derek would re-visit Pakistan in not too distant future as I believe you will be received with greater friendship and hospitality than was offered to you the last time.

My very fond regards to you both.

Yours very sincerely,

Syed Ahsan

7 November 1954

My dear Hector

How much nicer to receive this copy of your book on Jinnah from your own hands than by post. I feel that, little though I have done to deserve it, I have been personally honoured, particularly as you told me that this is the first copy to be given. Every time the book is in my hands, I shall remember the special precedence of my copy.

You can be sure of the book's success. You know from much that I have already said how much I admire the skill with which you have drawn a true picture of this very unusual man and made him live again.

Thank you, my friend, and for the kind words you have written in giving me your book.

Ever yours

Hawthorne Lewis

8 November 1954

My Dear Hector,

I am writing for us both to thank you for sending us a copy of 'Jinnah'. I have been neglecting my chores shamefully to day to dip into it at odd moments and I am looking forward to starting to read it properly this evening. How clever of you to have found a smiling photograph of him for the front of the jacket.

Even with the very cursory glance I have had at the book, the imagination boggles at the amount of research you have had to do.

I imagine that the poor Quaid must be turning in his grave a good bit these days. The political aspect is like that of a madhouse at the moment and although the new cabinet may straighten things out, it can hardly be called democracy. I have seen a lot of my chaps lately—scholars amongst them—and they all say that the political cleavage between East and West is now so deep and wide that they almost despair of it ever being healed.

For myself I see the red light in the Army C in C coming in as Minister of Defence—the first step in all Muslim countries down the slippery slope which leads to some form of Military Government—or Dictatorship—or both. Ayub Khan is fortunately not dictator minded, but there is no doubt that the new regime is there with the backing of the Army—and the other two services as well, of course—and that is a bad thing for any country.

A minor but more personal cause for alarm on my part, is the first—which I expect you saw in the 'Times'—that someone was able to walk into the C in C Navy's own office and steal a safe full of 'Top Secret' documents!!

Dorothy had just asked me to send her love and her warm thanks for the book.

We shall probably be passing through Salisbury later this month, and will look you up.

Incidentally the 'Spy' is producing a little 'Secret Agent' in February—we are very pleased.

Au revoir and again many thanks.

Joc[1]

18 Grosvenor Place
London, SWI
Sloane 5297-8
24 November 1954

Dear Mr Bolitho

I have just read your book on my old friend, Jinnah, and would like to congratulate you on a remarkable achievement.

I knew him and his family for many years and realize what a difficult task you must have had in writing his life. He was not a popular figure in the ordinary sense of the word, and was a bad correspondent. Therefore few ordinary official and personal records, which are often clues to a man's life, could have been available to you. Inspite of that, I feel that you have achieved a remarkably accurate portrayal of his character and personality.

I hope this book sells as well as it deserves to.

Yours sincerely

Sir Frederick James
Tata Limited

The Royal Empire Society
Northumberland Avenue
London, WC 2

7 December 1954

Dear Sir,

The publishers of Everybody's have just sent me a copy of the issue containing your article on the Khyber Pass. I am very glad to have this and to put it in the library, particularly as it is very well illustrated. But may I take this opportunity of congratulating you on your book on Jinnah which has just come through my hands. I must say frankly that I have little knowledge of Indian affairs, but from many points of view I thought this an especially valuable biography. Not only was the subject interesting in himself, but the point, to me, was that you had made him so real to western eyes, in a way that no Indian could have done. My own impression is that no Indian could hope to write about a politician, least of all Jinnah, with impartiality or objectivity, but even if he could, he would highlight those aspects of his character which are least comprehensible in western eyes. I do congratulate you on this piece of work, not only as a biography but as an interpretation of East to West.

Yours faithfully

James Pachman
Librarian

1, St. Nicholas Road
Brighton, Sussex
Brighton 27964
17 October 1960

Dear Mr Ames,[2]

You might add this to your collection. It is the sort of small object that is so easily missed. They are strange people. They[3] have invited me to go out there again, but I cannot travel there now without being drawn too closely into arguments over Jinnah. They still attack my biography on one side, and praise it on the other, and go on buying it. It goes into its fourth edition [reprint] next week. I hope Mrs Ames is well—you also.

With best wishes

Yours very sincerely
Hector Bolitho

24 April 1963

Dear Mr Stephens

I am reading your new book[4] with great interest and appreciation; but I am selfishly concerned with your suggestion that I was wrong regarding Jinnah's knowledge of his illness. I also searched out his doctors—and I based by first deductions on what was told me by Dr. Jal Patel. But perhaps I was wrong.

There is a suggestion that my book should be published in a paperback edition—for sale in Pakistan. If this happens, I should correct, or re-write the references to Jinnah's disease of the lungs.

When I was writing my book, I drew up a chart with the dates of his doctors' reports, related to the dates of his actions and state of mind. (I have since parted with this and other papers to the Library of South Asia, in St. Paul, Minnesota.) If I re-write these references to his medical history, would you be so kind as to read them?

I remember your kind review of my biography, and respect your good opinion so much that I wish to nurse it.

Hector Bolitho

NOTES

1. Admiral J.W. Jefford, Commander-in-Chief, Pakistan Navy.
2. Charles Leslie Ames (d. c.1969) was the St. Paul businessman to whom Hector Bolitho sold his collection about M.A. Jinnah. The 'Diary and Notes' was priced at US$300.
3. Pakistanis.
4. Ian Melville Stephens, *Pakistan: Old Country, New Nation*, Harmondsworth: Penguin Books.

PART FOUR

Contemporary Reviews

These clippings of the reviews of Bolitho's *Jinnah: Creator of Pakistan* were retrieved from his collection. Some of them were signed, while others not, but all of them were published in prestigious and influential newspapers and journals. They have been included here since they provide an index to how *Jinnah* was received when it was first published. And it serves as a fitting end to an extremely interesting story of a biographer and his biography.

– Editor

MOHAMMED ALI JINNAH
By T.W. Hutton

India's independence and partition are still too near for a definitive biography of Jinnah to be possible. Hector Bolitho, a conscientious and practised writer, has produced instead a completely satisfying interim report on a very great man. He is not wholly unbiased; to the personal liking for his subject which must always actuate any biographer worth his salt he adds sympathy with Pakistani aspirations. His honesty, though, always stands watch-dog over his partiality, and both are dominated by his conscience as student.

He took two years to write this book, visiting both Pakistan and India; published works apart, he read innumerable diaries and letters; more important, he talked frequently with people who themselves had talked with Jinnah. Repeatedly some quotation from somebody who knew Jinnah is footnoted: "In conversation with the author." In sum, a good book, admirably written, fair on the political side and revealing on the personal side, well-seasoned with anecdotes at once apt and entertaining.

Historians, doubtless, will turn first to the political side. Here two points of first-rate importance emerge—that Jinnah became a Moslem League man and an advocate of partition both tardily and with reluctance; and that as constitutionalist and lawyer, he was slower than any of his fellow-countrymen, to agitate for self-government.

It is significant on the first point that the most important friendship of Jinnah's early years was with Gokhale, greatest of Hindu statesmen. Only with Gokhale dead and Gandhi dominating Congress did Jinnah give up hope of a united India. Even in 1940, he was writing of "two nations who must both share the governance of their common motherland."

On the other point, Jinnah recognised, publicly and early, the value to India of the British connection. Hence doubtless his happy relations, after the transfer of power, with soldiers and civilians who stayed on—or came back at his request—to serve Pakistan.

Unlike historians, biographers must put the personal side first. Mr. Bolitho succeeds in the task, by no means easy, of making attractive in retrospect a Jinnah many of his contemporaries, even his intimates, found easier to admire than to love. Nor is it done merely by the poignant account of Jinnah's gracious spirit in his last, long illness. On the contrary, one begins to like him early. Maybe the key sentence, albeit used in a political connection, is this: "He believed that to stir the masses by way of their emotions was a sin."

This fear of emotion dominated Jinnah personally; made him "hard, though never harsh." Only very late in life did he allow himself to be kind. A constitutionalist, he feared sentiment; a realist, he was very sure of himself, not always of others. He lacked all personal ambition, went into politics as a servant of his fellow-men only when his own fortunes were secure, and returned from England's ease, against his inclinations, only when his friends convinced him India needed a revived Moslem League.

In negotiation he was rigid: bargaining, he gave and expected supreme honesty; denied it, he became resentful, suspicious, difficult. This, in the discussions that preceded and followed transfer of power, handicapped him alongside such men as Nehru and Gandhi.

Yet in the end his character secured, if not victory, substantial success. It won for this Karachi-born Moslem, who made most of his speeches in English, such affection, despite himself, as the East reserves for few of her sons. As time passes, Jinnah's figure will bulk greater; the affection that came to him tardily will endure.

Birmingham Post
23 November 1954

FIRST PAKISTANI

In his 'JINNAH' Hector Bolitho has written his best book for many years—a direct, unpretentious biography of the man whose single and unswerving determination primarily created Pakistan and who—rarity in the East—accepted the sacrifices entailed without demur.

The tall, slight, arrogant figure, speaking in English and ironically requiring an interpreter to announce to his own followers the fulfilment of his, and their, dream, is memorably drawn. There is no visible whitewash on the image of Quaid-i-Azam, whose flagrant rudeness is ruthlessly recorded. But a reader's sympathy is not alienated from the central character—Mr. Bolitho has made Jinnah's supercilious sarcasm almost endearing.

Islam is so much more apprehensible to the West than the involution of Hindu mysticism that there is no wonder that Mr. Bolitho for all his lack of obvious bias, seems to be Moslem rather than Hindu-minded. He makes coherent and inevitable Jinnah's shift from Swaraj to Partition. When the last Viceroy had to share out available assets, Pakistan found herself shorter than its neighbour of everything from airships to typewriters.

Daily Telegraph
Friday, 26 November 1954

THE FANATIC WITH A MONOCLE
By Austin Hatton

Mr. Jinnah once rebuked a guest by saying: "Don't decry fanatics. If I hadn't been a fanatic there would never have been Pakistan."

Looking back, it is not easy to remember Mr. Jinnah as a fanatic. Certainly he had the lean and hungry look, which so becomes the visionary zealot. He was tall—two inches taller than Mr. Nehru—and agonisingly thin. (He weighed less than six stones when he died).

But he seemed too elegant, too fastidious, too proud and distant; too cold, in fact, to be the leader beloved of the millions establishing a new and powerful State.

Inflexible Will

He was so dry, so self-contained, so dehydrate that he seemed to lack any personal appeal. He had many foibles and little affectations. At times he could be very deliberately rude.

He would never hurry, not even though dilatoriness meant endangering something for which he had worked hard. And his stubborn adherence to his own ideas in defiance of reasonable negotiation could at times only be excused as a "singleness and sincerity of purpose."

To the end his will was inflexible. In a fruitless effort to prolong his life it was decided that he should be moved from the perilous heights of Ziarat to Quetta. Though dying, he refused to undertake the trip unless he was allowed to dress as he chose.

"I will not travel in my pyjamas," he said. A new coat was brought—one that he had ordered in Karachi, but never worn. Then his pump shoes; then his monocle on its grey silk cord. (It was the last of many monocles, the first of which he had bought when a law student at an optician's shop in Kensington fifty years before.)

A fresh handkerchief was brought and unfolded: he held it between almost transparent fingers. And only then did he agree to travel.

He survived a gruelling journey by air and road with the same fortitude that he had shown in hiding through years...

[The clipping ends here, but the reviewer seems to be referring to Jinnah's illness. – Ed.]

Yorkshire Evening Press
2 December 1954

A MODERN MOSES

By the test of sheer achievement, Mahomed Ali Jinnah must be reckoned as one of the most dynamic and successful political leaders thrown up by the present century. It has fallen to Mr. Bolitho to write the first full-scale biography of this remarkable man, and he has done it very successfully. And yet, for all the fascination of the subject and of the stirring chapter of history which Jinnah helped to make, it must have been a difficult biography to write, for there seems to have been little of the ordinary raw material of biography, the detritus of a great man's life, available for sorting and selection by the historian.

Apart from the brief story of his unhappy marriage, Jinnah could be said to be as nearly without any private life as it is possible for a man to be. There seem to have been very few letters to quote from and nothing at all in the way of self-revealing diaries or other personal documents; nor had Jinnah any intimate friends to whom he would have bared his heart. Aloof, austere, seemingly devoid of human interests, shunning emotional contacts, he was not the man to provide his biographer with any "human touches."

But if this is not, and could not be, an intimate biography, the very facts of the story, as they unfold, create an absorbing picture of a modern Moses who led the Muslims of India, against all odds, into their promised land; who, though already a dying man when the crisis of partition was reached, saw his dream come true. The story has, moreover, some paradoxical features. It was a curious phenomenon that the creator of the largest Islamic state in the world was himself not a good Muslim, so far as religious observance went, took a strictly secular view of the state, was completely modernised and westernised in thought and habit, and was anything but a demagogue. He could sway huge crowds, but did not even bother to speak to them in their own language, and was far too fastidious to be a popularity-seeker; "public relations" had no place in his scheme of things, and at his press conferences reporters were not even regaled with tea and cigarettes. If he was fanatical in anything, it was only in his uncompromising honesty, both moral and intellectual. It was, of course, this quality which won Pakistan for the Muslim League. A lesser man would have compromised not once but a dozen times along the way, but Jinnah was not to be bamboozled: neither the sentimentalism of Gandhi, nor the subtlety of Nehru, nor the charm of Mountbatten could prevail against his icy defences; there were no chinks in the armour of his mind, which reacted against any kind of humbug as instantaneously as an automatic machine rejecting false coins.

The Congress leaders had, of course, made the mistake of underestimating him for years, just as they refused until the eleventh hour to take the idea of Pakistan seriously. All through the critical period of the thirties they had, in Jinnah, if only they had realised it, a unique instrument for holding India together. Not only was he free from bigotry and racial prejudice, but his friendships (such as they were) lay at least as much among the Hindus and the Parsees as among the Muslims, and he was actively disposed to be a champion of Hindu-Muslim unity. This aspect of his earlier life is well brought out in Mr. Bolitho's book, which also clearly outlines the stages by which he was gradually forced, by the short-sighted attitude of the Congress leaders, to draw back from this position and nail the colours of Pakistan to his masthead, where they stayed for the rest of his life. It was logic, not sentiment that drove him to this position.

The Economist
4 January 1955

JINNAH
By Ian Stephens

The man who brought Pakistan into being, an independent country of more than 80 million people, certainly needed a biographer. It is six years since Quaid-i-Azam Jinnah died; and although some in Britain may remember him as just one of India's many contending politicians, he ranks, on what he achieved in 1946-8, among the international figures of this century; a nation-builder; someone whom historians may have to mention with Bismarck or Cavour.

The State which he created has experienced crises; but it exists, in prohibitive facts of geography and economics and of initial disbelief in its feasibility by Hindus and most British. "Few take it seriously," Mr. Nehru felt able to say, well on into the 1940s, "except for a small handful of persons." How wrong events proved him! A main reason for this was Jinnah's character—but not the sole reason. That Pakistan has survived, in spite of loss of her creator soon after her birth and of his chief helper. Mr. Liaquat Ali Khan, in 1951, and in spite of a continuing cold war with India and scepticism of ignorance about her prospects elsewhere, shows that she was not the "dream-child" of a contemptuously termed "handful." Jinnah was the greater realist.

Mr. Bolitho's biography, therefore, from its subject, is necessarily important. It can scarcely be accounted final, however. Like much else connected with Pakistan, it was done amidst strange difficulties. The preface does not mention these; there is a gentlemanly omission only. But students of Pakistani affairs will be aware that contrary to expectations, he got no help whatever from Miss Jinnah, the possessor of the private political papers, and the only person qualified to tell much about her brother's early, obscurer years. As result, the book is uneven.

It may well be, however, as he suggests (p. 122), that Jinnah was temperamentally indisposed to write or speak self-revealingly, and that a biographer enjoying generous "access to sources" would be faced with numerous gaps.

Making allowances for these perhaps double limitations the book depicts Jinnah for us with surprising, sometimes brilliant clarity; aloof, as in life, but by no means inhuman; a hard, impressive actuality; immaculately clad, fastidious, lonely; having immense self-confidence, and integrity. First the early phase of self-made success as an advocate in Bombay; the marriage; tragically unsuccessful; politics—for years as a supporter of Hindu-Moslem unity; then disillusion, as a result of the Congress leaders' conduct at the All Parties' Conference in 1928; withdrawal to England; return, and the sustained campaign for Moslem separateness which culminated in the tremendous events of 1947— during which he overworked himself into his fatal illness. It is an enthralling story, and Mr. Bolitho tells it with practised skill. Great care has evidently been taken to seek accurate data from everyone who had Jinnah's acquaintanceship.

Perhaps the outstanding impression is of the tragic folly of those Congress leaders who by failure to respond to the Moslems' honest misgivings about their future caused a person of such pre-eminent talents as Jinnah to quit their company and seek his own courses. But for that profound failure in tactics and psychology, partition of the subcontinent might never have been called for.

Manchester Guardian
4 January 1955

SEVEN YEARS TO PAKISTAN
By Louis Fischer

The partition of India and the creation of the cleft state of Pakistan in 1947 was Jinnah's doing. The British Labour Government did not want it. Mahatma Gandhi considered it "blasphemy," but Mohammed Ali Jinnah insisted on a Moslem nation and he won.

For many years Jinnah had strenuously fostered Hindu-Moslem unity. Then he withdrew to England and made a long and brilliant career practicing law. Returning to India in the mid-Thirties, he became convinced that the Congress party policy of Jawaharlal Nehru would provoke "class bitterness" and "communal war" and that the Congress would not accept the Moslems as "equal partners." To that time Pakistan was an idea in the head of a poet, Iqbal. The Moslem League of India first adopted it as policy, under Jinnah's guidance, in 1940. Many Moslems opposed it, but Jinnah surmounted every obstacle and in seven years reached his goal. It is one of the remarkable feats in modern history.

Hector Bolitho who, according to his publishers, wrote this book "with the active support of the Pakistan Government," does not explain how Jinnah did it. Having proclaimed all his life that "the constitutional way is the right way," Jinnah abandoned the right way. Unconstitutional violence followed in mounting crescendo. Clement R. Attlee's Labour Cabinet had neither the heart, force nor patience to cope with this phenomenon. It wanted to quit India. The Congress party, with the exception of Gandhi, was tired and eager to get an independent state. Thus Jinnah won.

Moslems called the Present Pakistan—thirty-three million people in West Pakistan, then a thousand miles of India, then forty-three million in East Pakistan—"impracticable." Jinnah, according to Mr. Bolitho, called it "a moth-eaten Pakistan." But he took it because it was better "than no Pakistan." Having unleashed the movement, Jinnah could not draw back when the only possible solution of his "two-nation" theory was today's bifurcated Islamic dominion.

Jinnah, who died in 1948, was a very unusual person. Most Moslems are warm, friendly, temperamental, somewhat poetic and attractive. Mr. Bolitho etches a cold, repelling, fascinating, tragic figure. "Up to 1913, when he was 36 years old," Mr. Bolitho writes, "he had never attached himself to any human being, in love or friendship...he liked laying down the law to the young...he discouraged intimacy and was still a celibate introvert, timid of human relationships." His vocabulary was "cold" and he had "an Englishness of manner and behaviour that endured to his death."

Jinnah, says the author, did not like Lord Chelmsford, who became Viceroy in 1916. "He thought him 'cold'—a fault he could scarcely damn in anyone. This dislike influenced his conduct and his speeches." Jinnah disliked Mahatma Gandhi and Jawaharlal Nehru with a cold passion. That influenced Jinnah's politics. When he achieved some success against them, according to Mr. Bolitho, it "was a day of private retribution." Jinnah gave "the impression of a man deeply aggrieved."

By strange coincidence, an Indian doctor treated Gandhi and Jinnah at the same time. Gandhi, the physician reported, "was scrupulously clean in all his physical habits, yet he would perform dirty work and soil his hands in doing some kindness for the poor. Jinnah was not like that: his cleanliness was a personal mania. He would wash his hands and change his underclothes several times a day. But he did not wish to touch people; it was as if he wished to be immaculate and alone." Begum Liaquat Ali Khan, widow of the Pakistan Prime Minister who succeeded Jinnah, told Mr. Bolitho that Jinnah's "physical aloofness was shown in the way he would sometimes avoid shaking hands with people."

"My God, he was cold," Lord Mountbatten, the Viceroy, exclaimed after a talk with Jinnah. "It took most of the interview to unfreeze him." A member of Mountbatten's staff called Jinnah "the rudest man east of Suez." When this story was told to Mrs. Neville Wadia, Jinnah's only daughter, Mr. Bolitho writes, she remarked, "My father was arrogant, but never rude." Those who worked near Jinnah after the birth of Pakistan, according to the author, "were devoted, but intimated."

Once Mountbatten asked Nehru for his opinion of Jinnah, and Nehru came very near the truth when he replied, "The secret of his success— and it has been tremendous, if only for its emotional intensity—was in his capacity to take up a permanently negative attitude."

Jinnah and Nehru had a cordial dislike of one another. Of Nehru, Jinnah said, "He will never learn anything or unlearn anything." Writing "In Memory of Jinnah" in *The London Economist* of September 17 1949, a correspondent, who knew Jinnah well, declared that while Jinnah was practicing law in London someone "repeated to him that Nehru, whom he despised and hated, had imprudently said at a private dinner party that 'Jinnah was finished.' Outraged, Jinnah packed up and sailed back to India at once just to 'show Nehru'. To Cleopatra's nose as a factor in history one should perhaps add Jinnah's pride."

The New York Times
17 July 1955

[Mr Fischer is the author of *The Life of Mahatma Gandhi*.–Ed.]

JINNAH—CREATOR OF PAKISTAN
BY HECTOR BOLITHO

To few men is given the chance to see a dream beginning to come true, even when the attempt to bring a dream into existence becomes their life's work.

Mohammad Ali Jinnah is one of the few, though even he was given but a glimpse of the realisation of his dream—from the inauguration of Pakistan and his own inauguration as Governor General of the new state in August 1947, till his death from tuberculosis of the lungs brought on by overwork little more than twelve months later.

Hard, even harsh; sparing of others almost as little as he spared himself; arrogant, but incorruptible, and compassionate towards the sufferings of the masses of India, he was a man Carlyle would have been happy to number among his Heroes. And if his passionate devotion to the making of Pakistan split a sub-continent, it is fair to be reminded that it was the intolerance of the Hindu leaders of Congress, never able to forget their Hindu majority, who forced Jinnah to abandon hope of a Hindu-Moslem partnership in India, and work for Muslim self-government.

Mr. Bolitho does justice to the great subject of his biography—difficult though it be to assess the full greatness of the "Quaid-i-Azam" only five or six years after his death.

He has taken the greatest care to check his facts, and to take the opinions at first hand of Jinnah's contemporaries. The result is a fascinating biography packed with incident and anecdote, which does not forget the magnitude and the growth of Jinnah—a biography that is eminently readable.

If criticism there must be, it is a criticism that would lie with any other European biographer of Jinnah. Mr. Bolitho does not assess, because of the extreme difficulty of doing so the effect of the creed of Islam and of the Koran on the young Jinnah from adolescence to manhood.

We are told that when, as a youth, Jinnah came to London to study law (and the authority is Jinnah's own) he joined Lincoln's Inn because, at the entrance, the name of the Prophet Mahomet was included in a list of the world's great lawgivers. That may have been nostalgia in a youth in voluntary exile. But Jinnah's honesty was complete—with himself, as with his colleagues and opponents.

"Failure is a word unknown to me," Jinnah once said. That, fittingly, could be his epitaph.

Nottingham Journal
1 February 1956

SEPARATE NATION
By A.L. Potex

This is no Monypenny and Buckle biography, but Mr. Bolitho has written a most readable and vivid sketch, in his familiar style, of the character and career of the creator of Pakistan. He has collected anecdotes and assessments from a large number of Mr. Jinnah's colleagues and acquaintances, and he has strung them together very skilfully upon an outline of the domestic events of Mr. Jinnah's life and of the great political events in which he played so dominant a part. Particularly if read in conjunction with Mr. Louis Fischer's excellent life of Mr. Gandhi, this book will go a long way towards explaining the conflicts of personality which underlay Indian politics during the final generation of the British raj.

It is a fascinating field. Mr. Jinnah's public life falls into two entirely diverse parts. In the first, which ended in Hampstead in 1931, he worked with Congress for Hindu-Muslim collaboration. When he returned to India in 1934 at the behest of Mr. Liaquat Ali Khan he worked with unremitting zeal for partition. In 1931 he had seemed to despair of finding any solution to the Indian problem; after his return he despaired merely of Congress. In his intensely penetrating lawyer's mind the conviction was formed that partition was the only possible alternative to Congress and Hindu domination of the sub-continent. He never looked back or doubted; Mr. R.G. Casey suggested that "it does not ever occur to him that he might be wrong." That he achieved Pakistan does not prove that he was right, for after the British Government's declaration of February 1947, the mere fact that he refused to countenance any other solution made partition inevitable. It may be that he was wrong to despair of Congress. Even as late as 1937 (from which the final break may be dated) it may be that collaboration between Congress and the Muslim League might have led to a just and bloodless solution. But in 1937, tragically, Mr. Gandhi and Mr. Jinnah had ceased to speak the same language.

Mr. Bolitho's book does not, and could not, tell us whether Mr. Jinnah was right or wrong: his history is necessarily too superficial, and in any case we are too near the events for an answer to be possible. But he performs for the historian of the future the essential task of liming a convincing portrait of a man cold, rational, arrogant, utterly single-minded, utterly honest; the astonishing courage and perseverance in the face of opposition, discouragement, ill-health; the tragic private life and its effects; the rare glimpses of humanity and humour. Mrs. Sarojini Naidu is here quoted as saying: "Not his the gracious gifts of mellow scholarship, or rich adventure or radiant conversation; not his the burning passion of philanthropy or religious reform.... Outside the twin spheres of law and politics he has few resources and few accomplishments." It is the great strength of this book that such a man is brought to life in its pages. Pakistan was created at a dreadful price in human suffering and her nationhood is still precarious; the historian must judge whether the price was too high, but the reader of this book can scarcely doubt the stature of her creator.

Convincing as this portrait is, there is one aspect the omission of which is startling until one remembers that this is a semi-official biography. Like that of the Jewish community in Palestine the separate nationhood of the Muslim community in the Indian sub-continent is, first and last, a religious conception. Mr. Bolitho mentions that Mr. Jinnah could communicate with his followers only in English and he refers to his repudiation of the religious title of Maulana; but he nowhere emphasizes the extraordinary fact that Mr. Jinnah's leadership of an essentially religious movement appears to have been wholly unreligious and unspiritual in character. The contrast in this respect between him and Mr. Gandhi, to which Mr. Bolitho hardly refers, is inescapable and could well have been a central theme of his book. The Mahatma, however exasperating, was undoubtedly saintly; the Quaid-i-Azam, with all his great qualities and all his integrity, was a politician still.

Tablet
5 February 1955

A DEDICATED LIFE

Mohammed Ali Jinnah was in many respects a puzzle to his contemporaries. His generation in India can boast many patriots, both Hindu and Muslim; but somehow he stands apart from them all, somehow he stands apart from them all, as it were, in a kind of isolation. This of itself was curious in a country like India, where individualism is at a discount and group life is everything. But there was something even more unusual about Jinnah. In many ways he was not typically Indian at all—in habits of life, in mental processes, in his relations with his fellow-beings.

At a time when politics was the most promising career for a man of ability, a high road to fortune as well as to fame, Jinnah stuck to his professional work at the Bar until he had earned the competence which gave him independence. Even when he finally entered political life, he did so with plain reluctance; nothing save the desperate plight of the Muslim community sufficed to drag him from the seclusion which he loved into those personal contacts, inevitable for a political leader, which to the end of his career he disliked and rather despised. If we can imagine a tough, literal-minded, patriotic Englishman, impatient of compromise, inclined to look upon politicians as a set of self-seeking scoundrels, but impelled by love of his people to immolate himself upon the altar of their freedom, we shall have some notion, however inadequate, of Jinnah's general outlook.

No Compromise

In a land where courtesy is so highly valued that it ranks almost with sincerity among the virtues of a leader, Jinnah's bearing was arrogant to the verge of rudeness—except that mere rudeness is a term which fails to convey an idea of the devastating iciness of his bearing. In a land where compromise, at least as a method of gaining one's end, is the breath of life, he never made the least concession to friends or to foes. His directness was astonishing; the subtle reservation, the half-truth, the tortuous manoeuvre—in fact, the entire armoury of political leaders, not merely in his own country but almost everywhere in the world—was abhorrent to his mind. That, no doubt, was why Englishmen and Hindus alike talked of him as "impossible to deal with," as "the rudest man in Asia," as an "arrogant poseur without political instinct." In fact, he saw further ahead than those with whom he dealt. At first a firm supporter of Hindu-Muslim unity, he was at length convinced by sad experience that the Indian nationalism of his day was not only Hindu in inspiration but would remain Hindu in outlook. From that moment he worked, single-mindedly and with courage, unmoved by good report or ill, to one end; a homeland for Indian Muslims. Lonely always, often ill, his determination never wavered. His story is very moving, and Mr. Bolitho's skill makes the most of it. This is an excellent book which brings to life a very great man.

The Times
17 November 1954

IN COMMEMORATION OF MR JINNAH

L.C.C. PLAQUE UNVEILED

The High Commissioner for Pakistan, Mr. M. Ikramullah, unveiled yesterday a plaque erected by the London County Council on the wall of 35, Russell Road, Kensington, which records that "Quaid-i-Azam Mohammed Ali Jinnah, 1876-1948, founder of Pakistan, stayed here in 1895."

The brief ceremony, enlivened by spirited music from the Pakistan Police pipe band now taking part in the Royal Tournament, was attended by many Pakistanis and their friends and by the diplomatic representatives of several Islamic states.

Mr Jinnah, the future Quaid-i-Azam (Great Leader) and first Governor-General of Pakistan, spent four years in London from 1892 studying for his call to the bar by Lincoln's Inn. His biographer. Mr. Hector Bolitho notes the scantiness of material for writing of this period. The letters kept at Lincoln's Inn were given for salvage during the late war and Mr. Jinnah's bankers in England lost their records in an air raid. Only his reader's ticket for the British Museum, dated 1895, is available and gives the Russell Road address.

The High Commissioner expressed his warm thanks to the L.C.C. and the people of the United Kingdom for this gesture of goodwill towards Pakistan, its founder and father.

The Times
23 June 1955

ARCHITECT OF A NEW NATION

Mohammed Ali Jinnah was such a puzzle to his contemporaries that many books have been written about him by Englishmen and Hindus, as well as by members of his own Muslim community. Inevitably his life and work have been discussed from many angles; myths and legends have grown round his name. Standing as he did on a peak of eminence, some of the isolation which marked his life was the concomitant of the position which he held; but even so he was singularly devoid of the human contacts that surrounded the other leaders of his generation. From first to last he was a lonely individual, with few human weaknesses and without camaraderie, who called out from his followers and adherents fearful admiration rather than affection or emulation. He scorned the facile emotionalism of the mob; reason and logic were his only guides in public life. It is his greatest achievement that with no aid but these weapons and his iron courage he more than held his own against men whose mastery over the arts of popular appeal made them the idols of the moment. By his own single hand he shattered the image of India which had been presented to the world so carefully by Indian Nationalists through many years—the image of a people united, in spite of all differences in caste and creed, to throw off an alien yoke and to become a single nation.

Mr. Bolitho has built up from many sources a convincing picture of this strange but very great man. He has traced his career from early days to its climax as Governor-General of a new Dominion, the greatest Muslim State of our time. He has shown how Jinnah, patriotic as men of his generation inevitably were, at first took his full share in the Indian National Congress and in its struggle for self-government. He has traced the stages by which an Indian Nationalist who happened to be a Muslim became convinced that the future of the Muslims in a free India would be insecure. There can hardly be a more damaging indictment on the shortsight of the leaders of the Hindu wing of the Congress—including even the Mahatma himself—than the fact that they should have allowed such disillusion to transform the man who from his earliest entry into political life had been the most convinced and forceful champion of the cause of Hindu-Muslim unity. Utterly devoid of personal ambition, Jinnah's first reaction to the shock was to retire altogether from political life. He only returned to the arena, and to the public contacts with all and sundry which made politics so distasteful to his fastidious soul, when he became aware that world opinion, in adopting the cause of Indian nationalism, was accepting the claim of Hindu leaders to step without reservation into the shoes of the British.

This would not have mattered if they had been empowered to treat Muslims in all respects like fellow Hindus. But however liberal the ideas of Mahatma Gandhi and Mr. Nehru might be, the ordinary Hindu man in the street did not share them. To him the Muslim was "outside the brotherhood" of the prevailing social structure; a fellow-citizen perhaps, in the wider sense, but one excluded from intimacy and subject to certain jealousies and reservations in the sharing out of power. In an atmosphere such as this, as Jinnah quickly saw, the introduction of western democratic institutions under a system of responsible government would convert the Muslims into a perpetual minority. He was shocked and startled to find that the Hindu leaders were so unrealistic as to reject this view in favour of the idealistic conception of the secular State in which all men can equally share. To Jinnah this was either madness or self-deceit; Hindu-Muslim equality in a free India might come in the course of generations; but he was concerned with the here and now. But it was when the Congress completely monopolized political power for Hindus under the 1935 Constitution in the years immediately preceding the last war that Jinnah came to realise how well founded his own apprehensions had become. He saw that Iqbal was right; that if the Indian Muslims were to be free to live the life of Islam as equals in all respects with the adherents of other creeds, they could do so only in a part of India which they could call their own.

It was from this point that Jinnah made the cause of the "Two nation theory" his own, and forced it in turn, by sheer single-minded courage and determination, down the throats of the British, of the Hindus and of the world. It is surely among the ironies of history that Jinnah, who of all Indian leaders of his time was perhaps most disliked by the British for his savage irony, uncompromising arrogance, and deliberate flouting of high officialdom, should be accused, not only in his lifetime but even today, of being a "tool of the British". Not only was he composed of far more intractable material than any out of which "tools" can be forged; but, in addition, his policy was an active embarrassment to the successive British Governments which desired nothing more than to devolve all responsibility upon "Indian" leaders. Scheme after scheme broke upon the rock of his determination that Muslims should not be handed over to a Hindu majority, until finally in sheer desperation his opponents and his critics, with a weary sigh, yielded to his insistence.

Mr. Bolitho's story is that of a lonely, hardly lovable, but magnificent leader of men, who fought hard and ruthlessly, without thought of self, to win freedom for a new nation. In some ways this story is curiously touching. There was almost wholly lacking in Jinnah the "common touch"; he knew this, but could not help it. His reliance was entirely placed upon God and upon himself; he had few acquaintances and fewer friends. His sister counted for something with him; she was perhaps the only individual human being who did so after his tragic marriage came to an end. He was a dedicated soul compelled by his genius and his destiny to walk alone.

Times Literary Supplement
10 December 1954

'JINNAH, THE CREATOR OF PAKISTAN'
By Percival Spear

There are books whose importance is made by their subject and subjects whose importance is made by books. I think that this book can fairly claim to come into both categories. Any book on Jinnah must be of interest because hitherto only a political study by Mr. M.H. Saiyid and brief appreciation by Mrs. Naidu (written in 1917) have appeared. And any light thrown on the enigma of Jinnah's personality is also light thrown on the genesis of Pakistan. For Jinnah stands alone among the nation-builders of Pakistan in a way that no Indian, not even Mahatma Gandhi, stands among Indian patriots. Of him it can be said with some truth, that "alone he did it". The more this is realized, the more puzzling does the question become of how one so aloof and alone, so haughty, so reserved and so self-contained, so disdainful of most of his fellow-creatures, could fire the imagination of millions of peasants, and, a rationalist to his fingertips, arouse the religious passions of millions.

The book is written with the author's accustomed grace and ease. Indeed the touch is sometimes almost too light for the rather sombre nature of the subject, like a water colour on a granite monolith, while patches of thin biographical ice are traversed so deftly that we hardly realize the depths that are being evaded. One of the author's major difficulties has clearly been lack of first-hand material. In particular he has been denied the co-operation of Miss Fatima Jinnah and presumably access to the material in her possession. Letter writing is not an art which has taken root in India; almost the only contribution from that quarter has been the letters of Iqbal. Mr. Bolitho has done his best to fill the gaps by means of personal recollections and has skilfully tried to divert attention from what cannot be covered in this way. We are therefore left with official writings, published speeches, and a number of anecdotes. It is not perhaps surprising that omissions are visible to any serious student.

There are mysteries which abide and there are political omissions. One of the first is the circumstances of Jinnah's birth and upbringing. The author does something to clear up the former but he raises nearly as many questions as he answers. What of the circumstances of the Jinnah family and Jinnah relatives in general? How did it come about that money was available for maintaining Jinnah for four years in London while none of his six brothers and sisters (except Fatima, who took training in Bombay later) even went to College? What happened to them all, and do we know nothing of their fate? There is no suggestion that Jinnah took any interest in any of them except Fatima when rising to affluence and fame in Bombay. A second mystery is Jinnah's relations with his daughter, which after her childhood days in Hampstead, are dismissed in a sentence. Mr. Bolitho writes with restraint and judgement about his marriage, and it is a pity that he can reveal so little about this other personal relationship, which, in a life so lonely and emotionally austere, must have been of great importance. The repressions and puzzles of Jinnah's mature personality suggest some deep-seated stresses in early life. The clue to these, and perhaps the essential clue to the whole personality, is to be sought in this direction, but Mr. Bolitho has not yet succeeded in finding it. Jinnah's independence amounting at times to arrogance, his frozen formalism, his occasional parsimony, even his almost extravagant rectitude may all become more intelligible in the light of fuller knowledge of this period.

On the political side there are certain omissions which make the picture less than complete. The importance of Jinnah's role in the twenties is, I think, underestimated, and his part not brought out as clearly as it might have been. During the two Legislative Assemblies which sat between 1924 to 1930 he was leader of the Independent party or group which often held the balance of political power. It was a mixed body it is true, without an organization in the country, but it was predominantly Muslim and may be said to have represented Indian Muslims on the national stage as distinct from the pan-Islamic daydreaming or parochial communalism alternately favoured by the Ali brothers. In these years, when Congress was making its parliamentary experiment in the guise of the Swaraj party, his was the only Muslim voice that was also modern. And it was a voice, which was listened to with respect and increasing attention. It was the events following the appointment of the Simon Commission which led to Jinnah's eclipse, because they favoured the popular as distinct from the parliamentary politician. Jinnah lost ground as a nationalist because he pleaded for understanding when most men were inciting to passion. His pleas at the All-parties discussions were thrust aside because he had no popular following. The Independent party is not mentioned in this book, and Jinnah's part in those years confined to describing his efforts to promote Hindu-Muslim understanding.

A second, and perhaps more important omission, occurs in tracing the growth of the League's power from 1936 onwards. At the same time it is a point far easier for anyone not fully acquainted with the intricacies of Indian politics to miss. It is Jinnah's difficulties with the Muslim majority provinces, specially Bengal and the Panjab. It is a fact that where the Muslims were strongest they were most reluctant to support the Muslim League. Their ardour was in inverse proportion to their strength in the different provinces. The Panjab was perhaps the key to the whole situation, for there could be no Western Pakistan without the Panjab and no Eastern without Western Pakistan. Yet the Panjab maintained a non-League majority-Muslim ministry until 1946 and a non-League minority-Muslim one for some months longer. Some analysis of the situation and explanation of the non-League forces within Indian Islam would have been very valuable, because it would have helped to explain the reservations which both Congress and the British made to the power of the League right up to mid-1946. The Congress was guilty of bad judgement when it failed to give proper weight to the League success in the provincial elections of early 1946, but until that time it could fairly claim that the League was only partially representative of Muslim opinion. These facts help to explain both the underestimation of the League's power and the excessive stiffness of Jinnah's own attitude to both British and Congress leaders.

Enough has been said to show that this book is neither complete nor authoritative as a political record, nor wholly satisfying as a personal story. It is as a political and personal interpretation that it will retain its place in the literature of Pakistan. For behind an omission noted here or a misunderstanding there arises the profile of a man clear-cut, finely-proportioned and dominating. If Mr. Bolitho has not written a full life he has certainly sketched a vivid portrait. What was the secret of Jinnah's personality? The secret of its make-up, I believe, is to be found in his early life, if and when this can be fully revealed. But whatever the factors may be which compounded his character, the main ingredients stand out clearly enough. Behind the stiffness, the irritability, the calculated rudeness, the hauteur, all symptoms of some deep-seated malaise or psychic hurt, certain qualities stand forth which gave him his power. The first was his massive and at times meticulous integrity. Jinnah was not only incorruptible in a world of easy standards, but also single-minded. Sacrifice of principle was no more in his nature than compromise with money. This was a secret of his power and the failure to perceive this quality a major cause of his underestimation. Financial honesty was readily conceded, but it was generally supposed that personal ambition and love of power was the next most important constituent. It was widely thought that his championship of Pakistan was induced by resentment at the Congress rejection of his overtures at the time of the 1937 elections and exclusion of League nominees from their provincial ministries. I think Mr. Bolitho has shown that he risked and apparently wrecked his career in the twenties in the interests of communal unity, that his return to India in 1934 was in the nature of a forlorn hope, and that he resisted Iqbal's persuasive separatism until the Congress made it clear that there could be no political co-operation with it but only subordination or absorption. What finally made Jinnah a communalist was Congress totalitarianism. Congress *hubris* rather than Jinnah's wounded vanity precipitated the great change-over.

To personal integrity and devotion to principle must be added courage and the absence of petty feelings or motives. Whether holding the balance between Swaraj and government forces in the Assemblies of the mid-twenties, or facing Hindu contumely in the All-parties discussions, or pursuing a lonely course against the prestige of a Gandhi or the determination of a government immersed in a world war, or standing firm against the pressures of the post-war negotiations his courage never faltered. The elegant man of fashion was no wooden figure painted to look like iron, but made of finely tempered steel. His single-mindedness created respect and drew men to him when other programmes and leaders had failed, his clarity of vision provided a beacon for their hopes, and his courage sustained them in their efforts. He was not a man who fitted into a situation, but one to whom a situation must be fitted. In other times he might have been nothing more than an eminent lawyer or polished parliamentary politician. Jinnah's greatness lay in his inherent qualities; they did not develop as the result of a crisis, but were revealed by the particular crisis which occurred. If one searches for a parallel character in the Valhalla of great men one will need to go far before finding one comparable for combined taciturnity and aloofness and power of leadership. No recent of figure in British politics will serve and we return to the Victorian age before there emerges the figure of Charlès Stuart Parnell. The Irish leader and Jinnah had many points of resemblance. Both stood somewhat apart from their own people, the one as a Protestant leader of Catholics and landlord leader of tenants, the other as an unorthodox Muslim, the westernised leader of an Islamic revival, the professional director of a mass movement who could not speak his people's language. Both had the knack of leadership by repulsion; the more they withdrew from or disdained their followers, the more they were run after. Both lacked eloquence or charm in the ordinary sense; they attracted attention by their single-mindedness and sheer force of character. The power of both seemed to feed on intransigence. Both enshrouded their private lives in mystery. Parnell's whole life has been dragged in the public light and dissected in great detail; Jinnah's remains largely obscure. May we not hope that further reflection on the known facts of Parnell's life may furnish fresh clues to the secrets of Jinnah's personality?

The Twentieth Century, 'Book Notes',
April 1955, pp. 384–88

PART FIVE

Expunged Passages from *Jinnah: Creator of Pakistan*

EDITOR'S NOTE

This first draft of the manuscript was not submitted in historical sequence. The death of Jinnah comes before his marriage in the published version the sequence was corrected.

AUTHOR'S NOTE

My contract to write the biography was made at the suggestion of Liaquat Ali Khan, who promised to help me and work with me. Between my signing the agreement and my arrival in Pakistan, he was assassinated. I was therefore obliged to deal with many politicians and officials, instead of one, helpful, intelligent man.

This first draft was submitted to the government, and the hundreds of enforced amendments and deletions were such that I had to write the book again, from beginning to end.

This first draft, with the deletions and corrections clearly marked, would be helpful to anyone writing of Jinnah or Pakistan in the future.

I must stipulate that none of the deleted material is used for ten years—that is, until 1964.

Hector Bolitho.

– Approach by Sea –

Soon after we left the Suez Canal, I sat on the deck with a map of the west coast of India, studying the outline of the Kathiawar peninsula. This land, which lies between the gulfs of Cutch and Cambay, is shaped like a challenging fist, with thumb raised, and is thrust out into the Arabian Sea. The challenging fist suits the spirit of my story: this was the native land of the parents of Mohammed Ali Jinnah—the creator of Pakistan.

On the ship were two lieutenants of the Royal Pakistan Navy— Abdul Wali and Mazhar Ahmad—who had been on a course in England. They were refreshing company. Wali came from the North West Frontier, and he had all the solid qualities of the Pathan. He was silent, wise when he did talk, married and kind. Mazhar, who was Jinnah's naval ADC during the last months of his life, was ebullient; a writer of romantic verses which he read aloud. Though Wali was of the earth, and Mazhar of the clouds, they met on common ground in their eagerness to make me love Pakistan.

When we first spoke of Mohammed Ali Jinnah, Mazhar said, "His great quality was his honesty. Never once, in the time I was with him—living in the house and working at his side—did this honesty weaken. His truthfulness was almost frightening—and his lack of humbug." Mazhar said that Jinnah's correctness of behaviour never relaxed, even when they were alone. One day, when they were working at the same desk, Jinnah remarked, "I think we should have a window open." Mazhar said, "He would not permit me to open the window, but rang the bell and summoned a servant. He was quite willing to hold up our work for this little formality."

Wali told me of the day when Jinnah visited H.M.P.S. *Dilawar*. After the inspection, he talked to the younger officers in the wardroom. One of the lieutenants became excited over the plight of Kashmir and he spoke passionately against India. Jinnah interrupted, "My boy, be patient."

Then Wali said, "When he signed the visitor's book he placed his monocle in his right eye with a gesture so exquisite, so beautiful."

I liked the choice of words, *exquisite* and *beautiful*. (First draft, pp. 1–2)

– Beginning of a Task –

I arrived in Karachi on a January morning; in the capital that Jinnah chose, on the edge of the Sind Desert. The long, golden city seemed to rise from the sea in a haze of light. In 1881, Karachi was a shipping port, with only 75,000 people. At the time of the partition of India, in 1947, the population numbered 350,000. Today, it is the busy, throbbing headquarters of the biggest Muslim state in the world; in five years, refugees, officials and businessmen have swelled the numbers to a million and a quarter.

I liked the scene; clean, sunny and alive. The bunder-boats passed by, their huge sails bowing amiably over the smooth blue water; then tiny craft, frail as cigar-boxes, and the big ships from the ports of the world. Two grey destroyers crossed our path, tossing the foam from their bows. I was in a mood to enjoy everything about the new country that was opening before me—and to enjoy my task.

Some of my pleasure, I believe, arose from the prospect of writing about a man who was so fiercely honest. A biographer is naturally influenced by the man he is writing about; sometimes he is caught up in a metaphysical experience in which there is a curious mingling of himself with his subject. I expected some inward refreshment while working on a story in which, it seemed, there was nothing to hide. (First draft, p. 3)

* * * *

Reference: Fatima Bai said M.A. Jinnah never played games
This was not quite true. As Fatima Bai finished her little speech, an old man appeared at the door; a merry warrior, with snow-white hair, tousled like the hair of a boy at play. He came in and sat—bravely, I thought—in the big rocking-chair. His name was Nanji Jafar, and he described himself as "in my eighties". (First draft, p. 6)

– The Birthplace –

One afternoon I went to the house in Newnham Road where Jinnah was born. The building was enlarged and remodelled some years ago, but I believe that the first floor, where the family lived, is much the same—except for the addition of an iron balcony. I stood in the street a long time—with the untidy procession of rickshaws and camel-carts threatening my safety—and looked up at the window of the room in which the incredible boy with the fierce will power was born.

– A Student in London –

Reference: M.A. Jinnah's choice of Lincoln's Inn
One chooses Verse 90, Chapter XVI of the Quran as a text for this part of the story. We read, "Verily God commands justice and doing good and charity to the kindred, and he forbids indecencies and evil and revolt." Or Verse 2, Chapter V, which reads, "And do not help one another in sin and aggression." They fit well into the pattern of a man who created a nation, without the support of an army, [one] who reprimanded the angry young naval officer with the advice, "my boy, be patient." (First draft, pp. 14–15)

* * * *

We would like to talk to his tailor—the first of many servitors who dressed the slim, elegant figure: and we would also like to find the optician from whom he bought his first monocle. Was it the example of Joseph Chamberlain that excited this experiment in fashion—this first of the attractive vanities that make great men human to us. It must have been an important moment in the development of his courage, and his personality, when Jinnah went into the optician's shop and bought the first of the many monocles, which he wore during the next fifty years—even at the end when he was being carried into his capital on a stretcher: dying warrior holding the circle of glass between his almost transparent fingers. (First draft, pp. 15–16)

– The Young Advocate –

In case these stories of Jinnah as the arrogant young advocate still leave an over-harsh impression, we might soften the picture, with a woman's judgement of his talents, and manner, about this time. Mrs Sarojini Naidu, who had her own share of brilliance, and who was devoted to Jinnah, wrote of him:

"Never was there a nature whose outer qualities provided so complete an antithesis of its inner worth. Tall and stately, but thin to the point of emaciating, languid and luxurious of habit, Mohammed Ali Jinnah's attenuated form is the deceptive sheath of a spirit of exceptional vitality and endurance. Somewhat formal and fastidious, and a little aloof and imperious of manner, the calm hauteur of his naive and eager humanity, an intuition quick and tender as eminently rational and practical, discreet and dispassionate in his estimate and acceptance of life, the obvious sanity and serenity of his worldly wisdom effectually disguise a shy and splendid idealism which is the very essence of the man."

Mrs Naidu was obviously a spendthrift with words. (First draft, pp. 33–34)

* * * *

Jinnah was still a silent member of the Congress—a watcher, learning his trade. It was about this time that he said his ambition was to become the "Muslim Gokhale". (First draft, p. 38)

– The Virtuous Young Man –

One evening in May 1952, I sat in a big, elegant room in a house on Malabar Hill, enjoying the view of the Arabian Sea through the scarlet tracery of a flame tree, and listening to a very old lady, in a white sari, searching back more than forty years into her memory. (First draft, p. 41)

– Passion for Newspapers –

I have since learned that these books of cuttings still exist, with the day-by-day notes that would be such a valuable record of what was happening in Jinnah's mind. But I have not been allowed to see them. (First draft, p. 42)

– Talk of Alexander –

It is a pity that Jinnah did not bother with the voices of history. (First draft, p. 45)

– Shalimar Gardens –

While I was in Lahore I made a habit of rising at five o'clock each morning and driving to the edge of the city, to the Shalimar Gardens. In the first light of morning they were as entrancing as the fountains of Dresden; or Sans Souci, at dawn, when the marble statues seem to emerge, milk-white, naked, from sleep between the trees. Many of the exciting places I have known and remember most warmly seem to belong to the washed light of the new day: Greenwich Palace, seen across the Thames from Poplar, floating on the river edge, with shreds of night mist still dawdling in the morning light. Windsor Castle, seen at dawn as only the foresters and the deer see it, from the high level in the Great Park. Then it is not of grey stone, as Wyatt rebuilt it, but of gilt and ivory. Shalimar Gardens gave me similar pleasure: the white marble walls and fountains and pagodas, spaced by their Moghul builders with such sublime correctness over the surface of grass, catching the first splashes of brazen gold light that the Punjab enjoys.

You enter the gardens beneath a broad, deep arch, so that the full splendour is spread before you suddenly: the magnolia-petal turrets, the outer walls of red sandstone and creamy, confectionery marble; and the high, massive trees. Some of the trees are very old: they have seen, since they were little trees, the passing of Moghuls, Sikhs and Britons. Immemorial, sullen trees, surviving the follies of all the people who have struck attitudes, dreamed, or picnicked in their shade.

Beneath the great trees, at dawn, are the only other men in the gardens, sweeping up the dead leaves: old men and coffee-brown boys, their panther thighs showing between the folds of their sparse clothes. I imagined that these little sweeping men perhaps lived in nests in the trees; that they were as old as the trees; a race of different animals, who slide down the trunks at dawn to sweep up leaves, all day, until, with the night, they climbed back into their nests to sleep. Servitors of the ancient trees, slithering down, snake-like, to sweep up the offending scales that fall from their masters, when summer goes. Theirs was the only sound—the taffeta silk whisper of their leaves, being brushed through the grass.

In the luxurious days when the Moghuls strutted here, the lawns were of clover. The grass lawns, mown and correct, were an English—Victorian—innovation. The Moghul kings must have looked very sumptuous and aloof, moving over the close-cropped clover—velvet of deeper green than grass. On hot days, the kings could order the four hundred and fifty fountains to be turned on; not only for beauty's sake, but because of much artificial rain, leaping up from the white marble basins, cooled the air and made the torture of the heat more tolerable.

As I moved from the shelter of the trees, and the company of the leaf sweepers, I came to the immense beds of canna lilies—each bed a battalion of red or yellow flags, with horizontal morning light shining through them so that the big petals were like flags of ruby or yellow glass. I cannot tell you how splendid they were; so immense and extravagant and fiery. Then came another sound, after the leaf sweepers—a hundred bright green parakeets, setting up such a fuss; a jubilee of little emerald birds, above the red and yellow flowers. Then another movement; the blossoms falling from the gold mohur trees; a rain of sealing-was red blossoms, falling among the cannas. When the birds had fled, I could hear the blossoms making faint bumps as they hit the lawn.

Beyond this exotic sight was another long bed of flowers, where hollyhocks and mayflowers grew, prim as in an English Vicarage garden. Then, as I came to believe my eyes, the Englishness was made more authentic by a cuckoo, with its silly noise. But, as I walked by the marble platform on which the Moghul kings no doubt sat, while the houris danced and the refreshing fountains played, the cannas and the green parakeets came into view again, and I believed that the Emperor Shah Jehan really walked here, sometimes bending down to touch the red roses, brought across the mountains, from Persia. (First draft, pp. 47–49)

– Names on the Land –

There is one change in the monuments of Lahore that saddens the heart of the Englishman as he passes by. Queen Victoria's statue had been removed from under its ornate stone canopy near the Punjab Assembly, and it is now in a corner of the museum. Muslims are taught by the Koran to abandon all effigies and graven images, so there was a convenient argument against allowing the sitting bronze figure to remain beneath her canopy any longer. But someday, when tempers are quiet and life again permits the value of gesture, I hope that the Queen will be brought from her dark store; and that some Punjabi boy, who has studied his history, might carve on the base of the bronze the remark Queen Victoria made when the draft of the Indian Proclamation was placed before her, in 1858. She thought that the phrasing was entirely wrong in spirit; that as a "female sovereign" was speaking to "a hundred million Eastern people on assuming the direct government over them", the proclamation should "breathe feelings of generosity, benevolence and religious toleration." (First draft, p. 55)

– BACKGROUND FOR PAKISTAN –

... the lack of which [university education] was to show in his speeches and in the narrowness of his intellectual interests. (First draft, p. 65)

– 1906–1910 –

It is our object—without the help of letters, of which he wrote so few—to trace the growth of Jinnah's sympathies with the Muslim people, as opposed to the principles he avowed as a staunch member of the Indian National Congress. We must therefore examine the meaning of the 'purely secular interest' through which he achieved his first appointment. The Muslims of Bombay, who chose him as their representative, were mostly Ismailis, the followers of the Aga Khan; the most astute and least bemused of all the Muslim sects in India. Although Jinnah had become more of a realist than an unquestioning follower it was recognised that he had been born into the Ismaili sect. It was natural therefore that the Ismailis should choose one of their own to represent them on the Council—especially as Jinnah was a brilliant advocate and a 'personality' in Bombay. If we then seek for the reason why he accepted this secular role, we must remember that, at the age of merely thirty-three, it was not likely that he would be nominated to join such an august assembly. He was already ambitious for political experience and it was sensible that he should have taken advantage of this first opportunity of joining the highest legislative body in the land.

In accepting the support of the Ismailis, Jinnah was in no way obliged to abandon his broader dream of an independent, united India. If he thought at all of the serious differences between the Hindus and Muslims, we might take notice of a trifling episode about this time, when he sat one evening in his house with a friend; after two of his servants one a Hindu and the other a Muslim—had gone from the room. Jinnah said, 'You see, there is our problem: those servants receive the same wages. The Hindus educating his children and they are well-dressed. The Muslim is not educating his children and they are not well-dressed; we have to teach our people the value of money.' (First draft, pp. 71–72)

* * * *

...being February, he [Lord Mountbatten] was probably whacking a hockey ball through the mud of Surrey.

– 1910–1913 –

[In a speech] that had neither style nor originality of thought—only facts, (First draft, p. 77)

* * * *

Although the [Education] Bill failed, it is important for us to consider Jinnah's speech. (First draft, p. 78)

– A Gentleman of Recognised Position –

The pert advocate, and the politician who sometimes resorted to being a conversational bully, merged into a man of authority after the session of Congress in Karachi, in December 1913. (First draft, p. 89)

* * * *

... as one of the 'gentlemen of recognized position in the public life of India.' (First draft, p. 89)

* * * *

(He did not add any comment on the anomaly that he was to fight for the freedom of a hot-blooded people for whom illogical conflict was an end in itself.) He revealed the truth of his self-estimate when he arrived in London, in May 1914, leading the delegation of five, with the purpose of laying before the Secretary of State the views of the Indian National Congress on the 'Council of India Bill', which was to have its first reading in the House of Lords on 25 May. (First draft, p. 89)

* * * *

One must resist the temptation to ramble on, among these bills and arguments: they are recorded, for those who seek them—with a whimsical disregard for dates, authorities and indexes—by Indian political historians of the time. (First draft, p. 91)

– THE LUCKNOW PACT –

[Muslim authors] for whom biography is an alien form of writing. (First draft, p. 94)

* * * *

in these [parsimony and sharpness of Tongue] only was his mind little. (First draft, p. 94)

* * * *

As our purpose is to study the human beings in this drama of India, rather than the political argument, one is tempted to dwell on the scene of this meeting between the man of "cold-blooded logic", and Gandhi, of whom Jinnah said to a member of his staff, in later years, "That cunning old fox: When he enters my house the blood congeals in my veins. I never know how he will interpret what I say." (First draft, p. 96)

* * * *

Mrs Naidu's estimate of her hero was perhaps too grand with words. (First draft, p. 96)

* * * *

At Lucknow, in December 1916, Jinnah justified Gokhale's prophecy: his 'freedom from all sectarian prejudice' had made him 'the best ambassador of Hindu-Muslim unity'. The 'irreducible minimum' of reforms, first discussed by the joint committee in April, were announced by both Congress and the League, and the news and terms of this agreement were passed on to the Government of India. The main domestic problem of separate electorates had also been overcome: Congress had heeded Jinnah's appeal; they had the 'confidence and trust of the Muslims' by agreeing that in 'certain provinces' in which the Muslims were in a minority, they should be 'guaranteed a proportion of seats in the future Legislative Councils in excess of the number they could otherwise hope to win'. (First draft, p. 98)

– Gandhi, Annie Besant and E.S. Montagu –

Jinnah, on the contrary, was *aloof from charity*. (First draft, p. 100)

* * * *

There was another force that was to confuse him. At the beginning of 1916, Mrs Besant had begun her 'Home Rule League'. (First draft, p. 101)

* * * *

... a man of remarkable sympathies and force came into the story— Edwin Samuel Montagu, a member of one of the great Jewish families that had made no sacrifice of principle and spirit in becoming English patriots. (First draft, p. 101)

– Flight into Karachi –

For the naval ADC, Commander Ahsan, the emotions during the flight were perhaps different. He had been naval ADC to Lord Mountbatten: he was a man of exceptional intelligence and ethics, and he had been a watcher at many of the scenes of conflict during the arguments before Partition.

Only a small group of people—mostly stenographers and servants from the Viceroy's house—had gathered at the airport to see the Quaid-i-Azam depart. But Jinnah was all amiability, and, contrary to his habit, he went up to the little group and shook hands.

Jinnah sat next to his sister; the ADC's occupied a seat in the rear. One of them noticed a blemish, most unusual, in his master's dress: on his sunglasses was a small manufacturer's label that had not been removed in the haste of leaving. Once or twice they saw him shaking his emphatic finger at Miss Jinnah as he talked to her. Then lunch was served, from baskets provided by the Viceroy's kitchens. Jinnah was displeased: the food, the crockery, the cutlery were, he considered, of inferior quality, and this he resented.

Even in this hour—flying, as near as matters, over the land that Alexander the Great had conquered—Quaid-i-Azam did not forget his curious habit of pouncing on little details of error. He might have enjoyed more lordly emotions, soaring in an aircraft over earth that had been torn by battle and anger for hundreds of years—flying in to take possession of a country which he had fought for, and defined, all on paper. (First draft, p. B= p. 107)

* * * *

It had been his habit, through the years, to refuse to shake hands with people unless they were formed in a line: he disliked undisciplined amiability: but this time, he relaxed. (First draft, p. C= p. 108)

* * * *

... but they were poor and humble.... He was of them, and he had sat at table with them in the house in Newnham Road, but he had become their ruler and they had to watch his advent from afar. (First draft, p. D= p. 109)

* * * *

Then he permitted himself a little of the intoxication of victory. (First draft, p. D= p. 109)

* * * *

For a people naturally averse to order, the task was doubly terrible. (First draft, p. E= p. 110)

* * * *

With this speech, we have come to the truth in research of Jinnah. He had reached his full stature. (First draft, p. F= p. 111)

* * * *

Nor, in this hour, need Jinnah have blushed in any comparison with Lincoln, who said at Gettysburg, '...these dead shall not have died in vain...this nation under God shall have a new birth of freedom... government of the people, by the people, for the people, shall not perish from the earth.' (First draft, p. G= p. 112)

* * * *

Liaquat Ali Khan, Jinnah's trusted friend and his first Prime Minister his equal in integrity, in a continent where integrity is so easily sullied. (First draft, p. G= p. 112)

– 27 October –

I had to see me yesterday a very nice looking young Muslim of 20 years of age, sent here by Douglas Cuerre. His elder brother was killed in Delhi, and when his father, who was chief treasurer at the Viceroy's House, came down from Simla to attend the funeral, with his wife, both were dragged out of their train and murdered. (First draft, p. D= p. 116)

– 30 November 1947 –

Comptroller was Major S. McCoy, who stayed only a few weeks. It is incredible to read of the finicky maters that Jinnah allowed to trouble him during these first months when a nation was being made; incredible, until we insist again on remembering that the illness that killed him had already begun. Jinnah would summon Major McCoy and address his as 'Mr Coy'—a habit that would exasperate the most humble of majors, especially if he bore so proud a name. One morning the Quaid said to him, 'I understand, Mr Coy, that an armchair has been moved from bedroom 9 and put in bedroom 15. On whose orders was this done?'

'On my orders', said Major McCoy. 'When the Commander-in-Chief came to stay, there was no comfortable chair in his room, so I took the one from bedroom 9.'

The Governor-General answered, 'No furniture will be moved in this house except by my orders.'

We judge such incidents in relation to the state of Jinnah's health (First draft, p. E= p. 117)

– 18 December 1947 –

Then he recalled the last incident of farewell, when he stood beside Quaid-i-Azam's desk. A servant walked into the room bearing three hats, on a cushion—a black top-hat, a grey top-hat and an opera hat. The Quaid explained that he had bought them when he was last in England—'but there was Labour government in power at that time, so I could not wear them.' Colonel Birnie wrote, 'Unfortunately they are all just too small for me. Perhaps I can swap them for others. However, we thought it a nice gesture as a possible substitute for a "bowler-hat". (First draft, p. H= p. 120)

– In the Garden –

It must have been written many times, that a man reveals all his life in the way he dies. This was true of Mohammed Ali Jinnah, although his slim body—which came to weigh no more than seventy pounds—moved so vitally, and his eyes kept their fire so that only those near him saw that his will, not his physical strength, was deciding the time of his death. A palmist said that the lines on Jinnah's hands prophesied an earlier end; that only his inward forces kept him alive. (First draft, p. A= p. 121)

* * * *

Perhaps Jinnah's 'limitations' were synonymous with his 'singleness and sincerity of purpose'—without which he could never have made a nation out of a scattered and forlorn people. It is only when one has lived in Karachi, near the multitude of refugees who were part of the greatest migration of human beings ever made in the world, that one can imagine the extent of Jinnah's daring. 'Yes. He was a great man', is the phrase that comes to end these conjectures. Then comes argument: 'But what does greatness mean?' I recall a remark made to me by the Aga Khan—'Jinnah was greater than Garibaldi, or Cavour, or even George Washington for that matter, because he achieved what he did with nothing behind him—no army, but his own will.'

It is my view that he was remarkable because, except for his marriage—which opened and then closed forever the doors of his private emotions—Jinnah lived entirely for causes outside himself. His talents were not a galaxy of stars: they were a lonely rocket that would brook no interruption. (First draft, p. E= p. 125)

* * * *

As an old man, perilously near death, sitting in the garden of Government House, Jinnah admitted that he was 'tired'. Perhaps, among the crowds that gathered to acclaim him, whenever he drove along the streets, were the boys he had ordered to abandon the dirty game of marbles, more than half a century before. He never went back to the house in which he had been born, nor did he ever make much effort to retrace his way over any remembered ground. He was not to live long enough to be corrupted by power, even if that were possible. 'All power tends to corrupt. Absolute power corrupts absolutely', wrote Acton. Jinnah was to die before this temptation came. Somewhere else I have read, 'Power is in itself expansive, egotistical and self-indulgent, and those who wield power cannot themselves be otherwise, unless they are prepared to be dethroned.' Jinnah never came to these frightening crossroads: he died before be was tempted by subterfuge and compromise; before his worshippers could be exhausted by their ideals and turn to political criticism as a relaxation: before this ancient folly could spoil the shape of what he had created. (First draft, p. F= p. 126)

– MORNING IN KARACHI –

The long burning days in Karachi seem to liquefy one's bones so that all effort is drudgery; and tempers are sharpened by the heat of the sun. But there are sublime hours, at dawn and sunset, when a soft silence advances over sea and earth. These hours sometimes have all the tropical fierceness drained out of them: their lights and colours are cool, as in East Anglia, in spring.

If one rises early to catch the dawn, there is plenty of reward. To watch the light coming to the mile-wide stretches of mud is a lesson in colour values. The first, timid rays are cold silver, and they pick out unsuspected colour in what seems to be only repulsive grey slush. As the light increases, the mud banks are spread with sheets of purple and amber, which suddenly become edged with crimson when the actual sun rises. The challenging nip goes out of the air and the heat begins: it penetrates every cupboard, and one's morning shower is so warm that it is no refreshment. The petals of the zinnias in the vase shrivel as if you had burned them with a lighted match.

I do not know how people work at all in this enervating temperature, year after year. By noon, the lazy ones succumb in hundreds, and they sleep where they fall, on pavements and even on the traffic islands in the middle of the road. In the afternoon comes siesta, when those who cannot fall on their beds, or doze on the pavements, take a nap at their desks. As one watches this dangerous stage of slumber—dangerous in a young country which should not miss an opportunity, which should not dissipate one urgent hour—one cannot understand the ruthless drive of Jinnah. He was no longer strong: the slim, emaciated figure was already touched by the dread finger of tuberculosis. Yet he laboured in the same climate as these sleepy people, working on and on, thrashing others into unnatural pace, impatient with delay and indecision. The doctors cannot explain this passionate urgency: there is no explanation, unless the stars truly achieved a fabulous pattern on the day that Jinnah was born. (First draft, p. A-B= pp. 127–128)

– Ziarat –

Mazhar Ahmad told me, 'When I went to be interviewed, I found Mr Jinnah sitting on a sofa at the far end of a big room. I knew that he was assessing me as I walked towards him; but he stood up, shook my hand, and was very kind. I had been told that he was harsh and forbidding on such occasions, but I found none of this in his manner. I was appointed, and, at the beginning of June, we moved from Karachi to the bungalow at Ziarat, seventy miles or so from Quetta. The bungalow is high in the rocky hills, with a tennis court, fruit trees, and the smell of Juniper and wild lavender. (First draft, p. A= p. 129)

* * * *

I remember one day when I was working beside him, at his desk: the room was stuffy and he suggested that we might have a window opened. I made to move, but he restrained me and rang a bell. A servant appeared and Mr Jinnah told him to open the window. We paused until we could feel the cool drought of air—until the servant left us—then we went on with our work. (First draft, p. A= p. 129)

* * * *

'Yes', said Mazhar Ahmad, 'Quaid-i-Azam was in love with discipline but I think he was a little lonely also. As much as his nature would allow, he liked to unbend with his ADCs. One day at Ziarat, when we were playing tennis, he paused on the edge of the lawn and said, 'Oh, I wish I had some tennis shoes. I would play too.' But he walked on, and we could only guess that perhaps our great leader, who was to die so soon, was thinking of the days when he was young. (First draft, p. B= p. 130)

* * * *

Mazhar Ahmad, who was at Jinnah's beck and call every day during these last months, said, 'I believe that Quaid-i-Azam had two important thoughts at this time—that he was soon to die, but also that nothing must prevent his returning to Karachi to open the State Bank. This was to be the absolute proof that he was right in insisting that Pakistan should have its own national bank, its own currency, and economic freedom. Everyone from Nehru down had said that Pakistan was bound to fail, economically. The opening of the State Bank was to refute this. (First draft, p. B–C= p. 130–131)

* * * *

'On June..., we left the bungalow at Ziarat, for Quetta. For some days I had watched Quaid-i-Azam working on his speech—little knowing that it was to be his last. From Quetta we flew the journey to the Capital and to Government House. My last picture of him that day is of his head bent over his desk and the pages of his speech. Beyond the quiet garden, the people were waiting, already, for their leader to appear. I can remember him pausing, as he turned over the pages, to raise his hand and dismiss me—and his voice, very tired, saying, "Good-night, Mazhar." (First draft, p. C= p. 131)

– THE LAST TASK –

Quaid-i-Azam's phrases were mostly out of the universal store of public speeches: he spoke of 'destiny' 'equality' 'peace', with more idealism than knowledge of economics. Within six years of his death, after a long spell of good fortune, Pakistan was to endure hunger and economic crisis—a world disease which the young nation could not escape. But the speech showed that, with barely enough physical strength to walk to the platform, the old warrior had not lost his valour.

In front of the platform from which the Quaid spoke sat Liaquat Ali Khan, who had shared with him the long years of political vicissitude. Once, during the speech, Liaquat Ali Khan thought that Quaid-i-Azam was about to fall; and those near saw that Jinnah's old friend started forward, as if to help him. But it was not necessary: Jinnah rallied his strength and went on. (First draft, p. B= p. 133)

– The Last Days –

For the story of Quaid-i-Azam's last illness and death, I have been helped by Lieutenant Mazhar Ahmad, his naval ADC, Colonel Geoffrey Knowles, his Military Secretary, Sister Phyllis Dunham, his English nurse and Lt.-Col. Dr Ilahi Bakhsh, the doctor who was with Jinnah continuously, to the end. In addition to Dr Bakhsh's diary, I also had two long conversations with him, at his home and at the King Edward VII Hospital, in Lahore, of which he is medical superintendent. I walked into the hospital, past a severe white marble bust of King Edward VII; past masses of waiting patients, some in terrible pain, with piteous faces, gaunt limbs and dirty garments; and babies that seemed to multiply before my eyes, all huddling as if they had been swept into the corners by a great broom.

Dr Bakhsh sat in a cool office, aloof from the miseries. He was a well-built, healthy, friendly man. He told me proudly that he was trained at Guy's Hospital in London, and added, 'While I was in England I played cricket for Leicestershire.' Then he said, 'So you have come to talk to me about the great man.'

I asked him, 'Having been so close to Quaid-i-Azam, tell me why you think that he was a great man—apart from the fact that he created Pakistan.'

The doctor paused, then answered, 'Because of his sense of justice, and his fearlessness. Everything was clean about him, inside and outside.' (First draft, p. A= p. 135)

* * * *

These plans [for shifting Jinnah to Ziarat] are interesting: they show how, in a land where efficiency of the western kind is rare. (First draft, p. F= p. 140)

* * * *

So the master made his last gesture in sartorial pride; his last bow as the immaculate public figure for whom perfection was a duty to himself and to those who might see him on the way. (First draft, p. G= p. 141)

* * * *

During the first week or so after Quaid-i-Azam had moved to Quetta there were hopes of recovery. (First draft, p. H= p. 142)

* * * *

Reference: M.A. Jinnah lifted his hand to return people's salute
It was the last gesture he was to make to any of his people. (First draft, p. J= p. 144)

* * * *

Near the aircraft stood Colonel Geoffrey Knowles, Jinnah's Military Secretary, not knowing whether his master was already dead. (First draft, p. K= p. 145)

– JINNAH'S MARRIAGE –

Jinnah had already made a fortune at the Bar, and he guarded his rupees carefully, Some years later, when a secretary saw him adding, up his accounts—so much for fish, so much for a chicken, so many gallons of petrol used in the car—he asked, 'But, Sir, how do you find time for all this?' Jinnah clenched his fist and answered, 'This is hard-earned money.'

He spent little within the house, with its lovely views of the sea; there was chill emptiness. His evenings were devoted to briefs and politics: he still had little talent for pleasure. When someone asked him, 'Do you dance, Mr Jinnah?' he answered, 'No, I don't like it, because you have to ask a favour of a lady.' A contemporary who knew him well told me, 'Jinnah was a cold fish—much too formal ever to be a good lover.' (First draft, p. 105= p. 148)

* * * *

No wonder Jinnah fell in love with her. She was lively, witty, full of ideas, jokes and laughter. The staid bachelor, sitting on a verandah in Poona, watched Sir Dinshaw's only daughter running in and out of the house. He put his briefs and his political reports aside: his heart had been awakened, for the first and only time. It is said that Ruttenbai proposed to him; that the precocious girl of seventeen lost her heart first: it is said also that he greeted her proposal as 'a very interesting proposition'. (First draft, p. 107= p. 150)

* * * *

Then he led his wife from the dining-room; and, from that time, refused to go to Government House again. [Lady Willingdon denied this incident to Hector Bolitho] (First draft, p. 109= p. 152)

* * * *

The wound went deep: Jinnah developed his first prolonged enmity against a human being [Lord Willingdon], which led him to commit the first unconstitutional public act of his career. (First draft, p. 109= p. 152)

– The Years of Disillusionment –

Jinnah's mind had always worked nervously towards any new realization: he was a lawyer, approaching the next grain of truth with a hen's superstitious step. For the first time, he had made a speech in which he compared India's aims with those of Russia and Ireland. It proved, perhaps, that he had read too many newspapers; but also, the speech revealed a broadening of his vision. (First draft, p. 118= p. 161)

* * * *

The last, which digs into the roots of Jinnah's feeling, belongs to the months after Partition. Gandhi had sent a letter to the Pakistan Government, asking if he could visit the country. Many members of the Government thought it was most important that he should be received. Jinnah replied that, as Governor-General, he would veto the decision of the entire Cabinet, if necessary. He stood up at the meeting and said, 'Look at the seal! If you decide to invite Gandhi to Pakistan, I wish you God-speed. But if you do, you may lift me up and throw me into the sea, rather than that I should witness his coming to this country.' (First draft, pp. 120–121= pp. 163–164)

* * * *

Reference: Author's interview with Dewan Chaman Lal
I interrupted, 'I have been told all this—only the word unsophisticated is new: that is a fresh aspect.'

Dewan Chaman Lal answered, 'I remember one day in 1924, when we were dealing with the Obscene Publications Bill. Jinnah was for it curious puritan that he was—and I was against it. To force my argument, I stood up and said, 'This bill will exclude some very important works of literature from our lives.' Then, turning to Jinnah, I said, 'Have you read Catullus? Have you read Rousseau's *Confessions*?

'From a distant corner, Ranga Iyer, the author of *Father India*, piped up, 'Quite right; Jinnah never reads anything.' Poor Jinnah sat down, in silence, with a look—I would certainly call it an unsophisticated look—on his face.' (First draft, pp. 121–122= pp. 164–165)

– JINNAH AND YOUTH –

In an earlier chapter I wrote of Mohammed Ali Jinnah and his relationship with the students at Aligarh. In the last years of his life he came to a state of patience with the young that was surprising: when he found intelligence, and devotion, in a young man, he would—as one friend said—'take him up like a puppy'. He would bite the head off an older person, for the slightest offence. One evening, at a reception in Karachi, when a minister arrived in a lounge suit, having just returned from a long journey, Jinnah said to him, 'This is the last time you shall come here improperly dressed.' But with the young, he learned to relax, and forgive. (First draft, p. A= p. 167)

* * * *

Reference: M.A. Jinnah bought books
Khurshid smiled when he ended the story, and added, 'Dear Quaid did not read them himself; he left me to them and turned to his newspapers again.' (First draft, p. B= p. 168)

* * * *

Among the young men who served Quaid-i-Azam after Partition was a secretary, S.M. Yousuf, whom I went to see when I was in Karachi. I found him, beyond a guard of hushed servants and clerks, in a big, cool office, sitting at the sort of big desk assumed by men of power. On the desk were at least six green glass paper-weights. Yousuf was a good-looking young man, with the right mixture of warm charm and cold judgment. A sense of humour, no bureaucratic pretension—most refreshing. And perfect English, spoken without the Welsh sing-song up-and-down drawl which is the habit in Karachi.

He was working with Liaquat Ali Khan in the August after partition, when Quaid-i-Azam was without a secretary. Yousuf went to Jinnah because Liaquat Ali Khan said, simply, 'Take mine'.

While we talked, Yousuf played with one of the glass paper-weights a green bubble which he turned over and over in his hand. He said, 'You must remember that Quaid-i-Azam was very old and tired when I went to him. All my feelings were subdued into awe of him. And the awe never relaxed or faded, all the time I was with him. We all felt this; there was something in the steady gaze of his steel grey eye— enlarged through his monocle—that made even ambassadors tremble. I once saw a senior diplomat come to Jinnah, to present his credentials. He began to read his speech, in a steady voice, but each time he looked up at Quaid-i-Azam, with his piercing eyes, the poor man became nervous; so much so that his voice was husky and the sheets of paper shook in his hands. At the end, he pressed the paper hard against his side and finished in a splutter.'

I asked Yousuf if he did not think that this habit of intimidating people sometimes antagonized them, but he went on turning the glass paper-weight in his hands and did not answer. Then he said, 'Jinnah's energies were dwindling when I went to him, and he frequently said, 'I am tired. I am tired.' His seriousness was contagious; there was little lightness or humour in our work. He was also unpredictable. When

Bills arrived, to be signed, he would go through them, sentence by sentence. 'Clumsy and badly worded,' he would complain. His legal training made him examine each clause, minutely. I had to prepare myself beforehand, for a cross-examination of the Bill, as if I had been the minister who drafted it. He would make alarming suggestions— 'Split it up into more clauses:' 'This should go back and be rewritten:' One had to plead, tactfully, 'You will be holding up a useful piece of Legislation.' Then he would relent, But his vigilance did not weaken to the end. 'They can't hustle me: I won't do it:' he would protest, and, the scrutiny of every word would go on'.

I interrupted Yousuf and said, Jinnah was still impatient with everyone else's point of view', but he protested, 'Oh, not always. I remember a foreign newspaper correspondent who sought an interview with him. They talked about the fate of Kashmir, and Jinnah spoke his mind. At that time, the Kashmir dispute had not been referred to the Security Council—Jinnah and Nehru were to meet in a few days, to discuss the question. When the newspaper man's version of the talk was handed to Jinnah for correction, I suggested that it was perhaps not the moment for expressing opinions on Kashmir, in print, the master immediately cut the paragraph out. Oh, no, I think that when he was approached in the right way, he was willing to listen to the other man's point of view.'

At the end of our talk I asked Yousuf if he became fond of Jinnah while working with him, and he answered, 'I never broke past that wall of formality with him: I knew him no better at the end than at the beginning.'

I repeated my question, 'But did you become fond of him?' Yousuf played with the glass paper-weight for what seemed a long time before he answered me. Then he looked into the glass, as if into a crystal, for his answer. 'There were many endearing qualities. Sometimes he would be sharp-tempered—you must remember that he was old, and ill—and he would wave me away when I spoke to him. After a few minutes he would ring and I would go to him. Then came kindness. 'I am old and weak and sometimes I am impatient. I hope you will forgive my bad manners.'

Yousuf looked into the green crystal again, for one more truth. Then he said, 'I think one can become fond of a man who makes gestures like that.' (First draft, pp. E-G= pp. 171–173)

– INTERLUDE WITH THE DOCTORS –

All Jinnah's infinite care about his dress was his way of perfecting his defences. (First draft, p. A= p. 174)

* * * *

Jinnah was always over-conscious of himself. Gandhi was an instrument of power: Jinnah was a cold rationalist in politics; a man with a one-track mind, but with great force behind it. That was the fundamental difference between them.'

Dr Mehta said he thought that Jinnah was 'potentially kind', but that he had been 'deeply hurt' in his life, 'by the years of poverty in Bombay and by the failure of his marriage'. 'All this', said the doctor, 'made Jinnah guard himself from his potential kindness, as against a weakness. It also made him put up defences against close human relationships.' (First draft, p. B= p. 175)

* * * *

Dr Mehta then dared the full depths of psychiatry and gave me the following analysis of Jinnah. 'I treated Quaid-i-Azam for the first time about the middle of September 1944. One of my prescriptions for him is dated 15 September. He was one of the most remarkable characters with whom I ever came in contact. Analysing it psychologically, I came to the conclusion that he was an introverted thinker around a "positive" centre in his consciousness in his private life, and a "negative" one in politics. Because of his dynamic qualities, backed up by clarity of thinking, directed into politics—which were his principal purpose in life—he was able to achieve the "positive" result of creating Pakistan, even though he was actuated by "negatives" in his consciousness.' (First draft, p. C= p. 176)

* * * *

From this time, Dr Patel attended Jinnah constantly. He told me, 'You must emphasise the weakness of Jinnah's body at that time—it makes his achievement all the more remarkable. When he went to the second Simla Conference, in May 1946, he fell ill again. Miss Jinnah telephoned me and asked me to be ready to see her brother as soon as he arrived in Bombay. Some fifty thousand of his followers had prepared to greet him as he stepped from the train, so I arranged for him to be taken off at Dada, ... miles before Bombay. I saw that he was exhausted, so I induced the station-master to allow him to leave by a gate, to save climbing the stairs. Again it was bronchitis. It was always bronchitis. He had a temperature for ten days and his lungs were very weak. It is possible that he always had lung fever.

'When he was a little better, I asked him what had happened at Simla, and he said, "Gandhi was sitting on the right side of Lord Wavell. You know Lord Wavell is deaf in his right ear, so he could not hear what Gandhi said. I sat on the left side. As you know, Lord Wavell is blind in that eye, so he could not see eye to eye with me."

I then told Dr Patel of my idea, that a biographer should place a man's medical history beside the record of his acts and relate them carefully.' (First draft, p. D= p. 177)

– 1921–1928 –

I have a notion—perhaps extravagant—that all this is deep-rooted and to be blamed on an aspect of the Muslim religion; on the banning of all effigies, likenesses and monuments. The warm and lively conception of human nature, and character, given to English history by diarists like Pepys, Evelyn, Boswell and Fanny Burney, and by painters like Holbein, Hilliard, Van Dyck, Gainsborough and Winterhalter, does not exist for the writer who enquires into the story of the great figures of recent Muslim history. The personal element had been sublimated for so long in their records that they are unaware of history in terms of human conduct. As I have already observed, they resort to fantasy and extremes of ideology in their writing, because they lack the discipline of documents and references. (First draft, pp. 124–125= pp. 179–180)

* * * *

General Sir Douglas Gracey then described 'one more incident' that revealed Jinnah's 'scrupulous honesty'. He said, 'Jinnah bought Flagstaff House, in Karachi, which was let at the time, by the Parsee owner, to the British army. I occupied the house, as Commander of the First Corps, in Karachi. When Jinnah bought it, I had to move out. I had spent some six hundred rupees on electric light in the servants' quarters, and, directly I advised Jinnah of this, he sent me a cheque for the full amount. You will hear stories of his being parsimonious, but you will never hear one of him avoiding a just debt.' (First draft, pp. 130–131= pp. 185–186)

* * * *

... whether from disgust over the confusion of his political affairs, or for private reasons, we do not know. We know only that, at this time, his married life was wrecked; that Jinnah and his wife could endure each other no longer. (First draft, p. 131= p. 186)

* * * *

The capriciousness in Ruttenbai Jinnah, which was part of her enchantment, offended Jinnah's correct ideas: she went so far as to offend his genteel proprieties in public. One evening, in Simla, when they were driving to dine with the Governor, she stopped the carriage and bought a roasted corn-cob from a man beside the road. She began to eat it as they came near Government House. Jinnah accepted the foolish hurt in silence. Some years later he recalled the story, to a woman he trusted, and said, 'It was not level-headed: would you do a thing like that?'

There had been a similar episode in London, almost at the entrance of the Savoy Hotel, when Mrs Jinnah bought a banana from a barrow and ate it as they walked along the street. She was all spontaneity: there was none in him.

'It is my fault: I married the child.' The Parsee went to Mrs Jinnah and pleaded, 'It will hurt his political career if you stay apart.' She said she would return if she could be sure that she would be welcome. The friend hurried from the hotel, to Jinnah's house, and said, 'I have something personal I wish to discuss with you.'

Jinnah was immediately on the defensive: he answered, 'Personal about you or about me?'

'About you,' said the friend.

But Jinnah would not even allow him to begin: he said, 'I have nothing to discuss. The chapter is closed.'

His boast was untrue: his wife sailed for England, with her parents, and Jinnah followed. His griefs were doubly heavy: his political life was in dark confusion, and his family life—his one experiment in happiness—was apparently wrecked. (First draft, pp. 132–133= pp. 187–188)

– THE PARTING OF THE WAYS –

Mahatma Gandhi began to spin. He was at his spinning wheel for three hours. I know this. (First draft, p. 137= p. 192)

* * * *

Throughout the years that followed, when none of his friends dared speak to Jinnah of his dead wife, he formed his own views on marriage. Seventeen years later, when two of his friends—man and wife—decided to part, someone asked Jinnah to intervene. He refused and answered, 'What passes between a man and his wife, no third person can understand.' Later he relented so far as to say, to the wife of his friend, 'What does it matter if you are divorced! Only you, yourselves, can understand the differences between you. No one could ever understand what happened between Ruttie and me. We never got on: she got on my nerves—she drove me mad. She was a child and I should never have married her. The fault was mine.'

Jinnah began his years of widowhood at the age of fifty-two. He was a man of few inward resources: we know that neither history nor literature had any real hold on his imagination, and music passed him by. Now and then he would read a little Dickens, or Trollope, which satisfied the English tendencies in his mind. But briefs and newspapers occupied him most. He ordered more newspapers, from New York and London, and he marked and cut them. The selected articles were pasted into books, with his comments written beside them. His friendships with men were limited, because he liked people only for what was tangible, practical and proper about them: he never learned to like someone for his faults, and his virtues, as a whole. (First draft, pp. 138–139= pp. 193–194)

– EXILE 1930–1934 –

It is interesting, as an aside, to read Mr Winston Churchill's gloomy opinion of these efforts on behalf of India. In a speech made some four months before the Conference opened, he said:

"No responsible person supposes for a moment that the forthcoming Round Table Conference can produce Dominion Status for India or that Dominion Status is likely to be obtained for India within the lifetime of anyone now living." (First draft, p. 141= p. 196)

* * * *

[Reference to Iqbal]
... savours his poetry, one is drawn away from Jinnah's respectable history: the temptations to lose oneself in the richness of Iqbal's talents and forget one's purpose; to enjoy the banquet and neglect the cautious diet.

When he came as a delegate to the second Round Table Conference, in 1931, Sir Muhammad Iqbal was fifty-eight years old. Jinnah was then almost fifty-five. I like to think of them walking together across Hampstead Heath, 'among the alien corn', and Iqbal talking to Jinnah with a spaciousness of thought Jinnah could not comprehend; Iqbal, who already knew that 'to think is to be full of sorrow', and Jinnah, still in love with his own indignations. Iqbal—his thoughts like eagles, before Jinnah's reach. (First draft, p. 143= p. 199)

* * * *

In the cool English air of Hampstead, the argument must have lost some of its power: almost a decade was to pass before Jinnah—back in India (First draft, p. 143= p. 199)

– JINNAH READS A BOOK –

When his hour came, Jinnah was to feel so weary within himself that the prestige, the pinnacle and the greatness had little meaning for him.

The setting in which Jinnah read *Grey Wolf* adds colour to the picture. He was not in Bombay, with the hot, ancient angers of his inheritance pressing in upon him: he was in Hampstead, where there were no ancestral voices to disturb a middle-aged Muslim advocate, who fitted in amiable into the precise, ordained habits of English life. Had Jinnah been a man of great imagination, we might think of him walking across Hampstead Heath, to Jack Straw's Castle—the inn before which Karl Marx had died in London: his grave was at Highgate Cemetery, only an after-breakfast walk from where Jinnah was living. (First draft, pp. B–C= pp. 202–203)

AFTERWORD

My "Pakistan Day" Complaint
By Hector Bolitho

When I look back to the days I spent in Pakistan, while I was writing my biography of Mohammad Ali Jinnah, there is one episode that still makes me unhappy. It was in Lahore where I saw the statue of Queen Victoria relegated to a cellar in the Museum, and the elegant canopy in the street, under which the statue once sat—empty. I thought then of London, where the house in which Jinnah lived when he was a student here, is marked with a memorial plaque, to remind the Londoners of his talents, as they pass by.

I turn then to December 1857 when Lord Canning, the Governor-General of India, wrote to Lord Granville,

"As long as I have breath in my body, I will pursue no other policy than that I have been following: I will not govern in anger. Justice, and that as stern and inflexible as law and might can make it, I will deal out. But I will never allow an angry or undiscriminate act or word to proceed from the Government of India, as long as I am responsible for it."

Proclamation

Then, to a day in 1858 when Queen Victoria and the Prince Consort were in Germany and the draft for the Indian Proclamation arrived in a red leather box from Whitehall. They both read the draft and decided that it "was entirely wrong in spirit". It mentioned too much about Britain's power over India, instead of her munificence. The Queen wrote to her Prime Minister that the proclamation should "breathe feelings of generosity, benevolence and religious toleration". So she sat down with the Prince and they re-wrote it. Then they sent the wise and gentle draft back to the Prime Minister in London. It was in this form that the Proclamation was made.

Queen Victoria set an example that her descendants followed. When her son, Edward, Prince of Wales, wished to go to India, we read in a private report that the idea "emanated entirely" from him and that it was not a duty thrust upon by either his parents or the Government. His wife, Princess Alexandra, was not allowed to join the all-male party and she was bitterly disappointed. She wrote in a private letter, "The one wish of my life was to see that wonderful, beautiful country."

The Prince landed in Bombay. Certain passages from his private letters reveal his true reactions to India. He was furious when some officers referred to the "colour" difference between the Indians and themselves: he wrote, "Because a man has a coloured face and a different religion from our own, there is no reason why he should be treated as a brute."

He remained fond of India for the rest of his life, and he trained his son to feel the same. King George V was still Prince of Wales when he visited India with his wife, during the winter of 1905-06. The man chosen to look after them was Sir Walter Lawrence who was privately described as having "deep sympathy for the Indian people".

The Prince of Wales began his journey; when he came to almost the end, he talked with Gopal Gokhale, at that time President of the Indian Congress Party. The Prince said to him, 'I have now been travelling some months in India, seeing vast crowds of Indians in many parts of the continent, and I have never seen a happier-looking people, and I understand the look in their eyes.'

Later, he wrote in some notes that are still kept in archives at Windsor Castle and which I have been allowed to see, "I could not help noticing that the general bearing of the Europeans towards the Indians was to say the least unsympathetic."

* * * *

This was only half true, for there is still another theme that I wish to trace—the story of those Britons who came to love the sub-continent— the India that then included what is now Pakistan. But first, allow me to say that Queen Victoria had begun a theme of understanding and manners in the relationship between the monarchy and what are now the separate countries of India and Pakistan. It has continued in the minds of the royal family ever since.

The other theme is this. It is not easy for Britons visiting Pakistan to comprehend the entire differences in thought between us. It will not be bridged unless we both try. The effort must not only come from those like myself, who abhor nationalism and who have tried desperately to like and be liked, by Pakistani's, especially when I was there.

Many years have passed since then and my life and my work as a writer have taken me around the world three times. My mental interests have therefore drifted to other lands. But I still recall days of acute despair when I was in Karachi, especially of the day when I read a vast headline in a Karachi newspaper, "Send the foreign Hireling home."

I have seldom been so hurt within myself as I was that day. I wasn't a "hireling", but that does not matter. I was an unhappy man and sometimes, at my desk in the hotel, I felt so frustrated that I would look at the photograph of the Quaid, which was always on my desk, and almost pray to him for inward quiet, and the courage to go on.

ENDURING FRIENDSHIPS

I made two enduring friendships out of the experience of writing the Quaid's biography; with Mr. Majeed Malik, and Mr S.M. Haq, now your Press attache in London. Without them, and the encouragement of Derek Peel who helped me with the research, I could never have finished the book. Derek Peel was fourth generation born in India. His comprehension was deeper and more patient than mine. It is some satisfaction to me now that no other biography of the Quaid has been written, and that my book has been published in America and translated into Urdu.

Another satisfaction is coming, after all the years. A deeper satisfaction, from the fact that young Pakistanis whom I have never met write to me and thank me for what I wrote about the "Father" of their country. And I was so delighted a few weeks ago when both the Pakistan Youth Federation and the Pakistan Students Association in London asked me to speak to them.

There is a purpose in this article. I wish to believe in the younger generation of Pakistanis. To believe that they are not merely romantic about the Quaid. He was a realist. It is not enough to worship him. He must be comprehended in the quiet of each young Pakistani mind.

Manners

Now to my final purpose. We have in London that plaque on the house in which Jinnah lived. Imagine how you would feel if you were here and one day, suddenly, you saw the plaque torn from the wall of the house. Then imagine how I, and other Britons feel, when we walk through the streets of Lahore and see that empty canopy; then go to the museum and see Queen Victoria discarded.

Manners perish when they are all on one side. I wish I could read that the young Pakistanis in Lahore decided to restore the Queen to her canopy. Then Britons would not have to curl up within themselves and become silent, as they see the empty space. She was the first monarch to accept the image of your great land. She pleaded for generosity, benevolence and religious toleration'. Set her back in her place and prove not only her greatness and generosity of mind, but also your own.

– Morning News (Karachi)
Pakistan Day Supplement
23 March 1966

Index

A

Abdul Qadir, Sheikh, 18
Abdul Wahid, 38, 39
Abdul Wali, 7, 31, 188
Afghanistan, 55
Aga Khan, 20, 45, 78, 86, 200
Ahmad, Lt. Col. H.I., 42
Ahmad, Mazhar, 7, 8, 9, 10, 11, 14, 21, 31, 38, 39, 43, 50, 18, 202, 203, 204
Ahmed, Nasim, 82-83
Ahsan, S.M., 41, 59-61, 62, 67, 197
Ali, Salman, 5, 79
All India Muslim League, 42
All Parties National Convention, 35
Allana, Ghulam Ali, 16, 32, 33
Amin, Farrukh, 44
Amir of Bahawalpur, 60
Ashir, M., 19, 26, 66
Atiya Begum, 63
Attlee, Clement R., 169

B

Bakhsh, Lt.-Col. (Dr) Ilahi, 21, 204
Baluchistan Muslim League, 42
Baluchistan, 8
Baqar, S.N., 12, 13
Batley, Claude, 76, 77
Bengal, 27, 36
Besant, Annie, 36, 76, 197
Birnie, Colonel, 80, 200
Bombay, 13, 15, 20, 26, 27, 30, 35, 47
Brelvi, Professor Mahmud, 16, 23, 57, 61, 70

C

Chaman Lal, Dewan, 207
Chelmsford, Lord, 170
Churchill, Winston, 213
Creagh-Coen, Terence, 69

Crocker, Col., 42

D

Desai, Morarji, 73
Dunham, Phyllis, 10, 88, 89, 90, 204
Dwarkadas, Kanji, 35, 73, 75, 76

F

Fatima Bai, 14, 189

G

Galitzine, George, 18
Gandhi, Mohandas Karamchand, 5, 7, 10, 12, 22, 23, 27, 29, 35, 36, 71, 77, 84, 90, 161, 162, 165, 169, 170, 174, 175, 179, 180, 182, 185, 196, 197, 207, 210, 211, 213
Gokhale, Gopal Krishna, 51, 86, 161, 196, 216
Gracey, General Sir Douglas, 85, 211

H

Habibullah, A.B. 'Sonny', 27, 28, 46, 47, 65
Habibullah, Ibrahim, 27, 28
Hack, Robert, 44
Haji, Major, 83, 84
Hardy, James, 51-52
Hashmi, Prof. B.A., 43
Hidayatullah, Ghulam Hussain, 33
Hissamud Din Khan, Brigadier Sir, 53, 54
Hoover, Mr, 90
Hussain, Mohammed, 31

I

Indian National Congress, 15, 35, 47, 49, 55, 174, 179, 180, 184, 185, 194, 195, 196

INDEX

Iqbal, Muhammad, 61, 214
Irwin, Maj.-Gen. S.F., 42
Isa, Qazi M., 42, 43
Ispahani, 27, 81

J

Jafar, Nanji, 22, 189
Jaffer, Ahmed E.H., 17
Jefford, Admiral, 34, 67, 79, 80
Jehangir, Sir Cowasjee, 72, 73, 83, 86, 104
Jinnah, Fatima, 6, 9, 10, 16, 18, 24, 25, 26, 27, 29, 41, 42, 44, 57, 58, 60, 63, 65, 66, 76, 81, 87, 88, 89, 90, 96, 182, 197, 210
Joshi, C.N., 73, 74

K

Karachi, 47, 9, 10, 11, 18, 20, 21, 25, 29
Kashmir, 20, 48, 51, 60, 84, 188, 209
Khaliquzzaman, Chaudhri, 7
Khan, Begum Raa'na Liaquat Ali, 21, 25, 29, 57, 58, 65, 69, 85, 88, 90, 170
Khan, Ismail, 46
Khan, Khan Abdul Qayyum, 54
Khan, Liaquat Ali, 10, 17, 24, 26, 38, 41, 45, 46, 51-52, 61, 67, 87, 84, 88, 167, 174, 187, 199, 204, 208
Khan, Sadik [Siddique] Ali, 52
Khan, Sir Zafrullah, 61
Khurshid, K.H., 79, 85, 86, 90, 208
Khyber Pass, 23, 55
Knowles, Colonel Geoffrey, 80-81, 204, 205

L

Laithwaite, Gilbert, 6
Linlithgow, Lord, 75
Lucknow Pact, 196

M

Mahmudabad, Raja of, 15, 46, 47
Malik, Majeed, 13, 14, 22, 61, 69, 217
Mamdot, Khan of, 38
Mauripur, 10, 41, 60
McCoy, Lt.-Gen. Sir Ross, 52

McCoy, Major S., 199
Mehta, Dr D.K., 77, 210
Mehta, Sir Pherozeshah, 51
Messervy, General Sir Frank, 84, 85
Mir of Hunza, 32, 33
Mohammed, Din, 63
Mohammed, Ghulam, 34
Montagu, Edwin Samuel, 197
Mountbatten, Lord Louis, 5, 26, 48, 60-61, 68, 84, 87, 89, 165, 170, 195, 197
Mudie, Sir Francis, 33, 34
Muslim League, 17, 35, 46, 47, 48, 49, 55, 82, 174, 196

N

Naidu, Sarojini, 28, 63, 80, 96, 175, 182, 190, 191, 196
Naoroji, Dadabhai, 29
Nazimuddin, Khwaja, 13, 67, 68, 80, 89
Nehru, Jawaharlal, 22, 35, 47, 55, 68, 84, 162, 165, 167, 169, 170, 180, 209
Nehru, Pandit Motilal, 51
Noman, Mohammad, 5, 17, 61, 26, 27, 28, 29, 30
Noon, Feroze Khan, 82
Nooruddin, Fakir Syed, 45
North West Frontier Province, 54, 188
Nusserwanjee, Jamshed, 35, 73

O

Owain-Jones, 48

P

Pagaro, Pir of, 63, 64
Patel, Dr, 210, 211
Peel, Derek, 6, 39, 56, 66, 98, 217
Peel-Yates, D., 48
Pethick-Lawrence, 13, 25
Petit, Lady, 73, 74
Petit, Ruttenbai, 26, 30, 40, 43, 47, 50, 63, 89, 206, 212, 213
Petit, Sir Dinshaw, 50, 206
Punjab Muslim Students' Federation, 49

Q

Qureshi, Dr, 31, 32

R

Rabbani, Ata, 25, 40, 59
Radcliffe Award, 36, 48
Rahimtoola, Habib Ibrahim, 6
Rashidi, Pir Ali Mohammad, 64
Raza, Sajjad, 33

S

Setalvad, Motilal, 73
Shah Nawaz, Begum Jahan Ara, 40
Shah Nawaz, Sir, 67
Simla Conference, 210
Singh, Raja Sir Maharaj, 73, 86, 87
Soldinger, Dr L., 21
Suleri, 11, 56

T

Tajuddin, Peer, 50, 51
Thar, Shantilal L., 77-78

V

Victoria, Queen, 37, 45, 49-50, 53, 66, 193, 215, 216, 218

W

Wadia, Dina, 50, 63, 88-89, 170
Wadia, Neville, 50, 73
Wavell, Lady, 90
Wavell, Lord, 211
Willingdon, Lady, 47, 206
Willingdon, Lord, 47

Y

Yousuf, S.M., 208, 209

Z

Ziarat, 9, 11, 203, 205